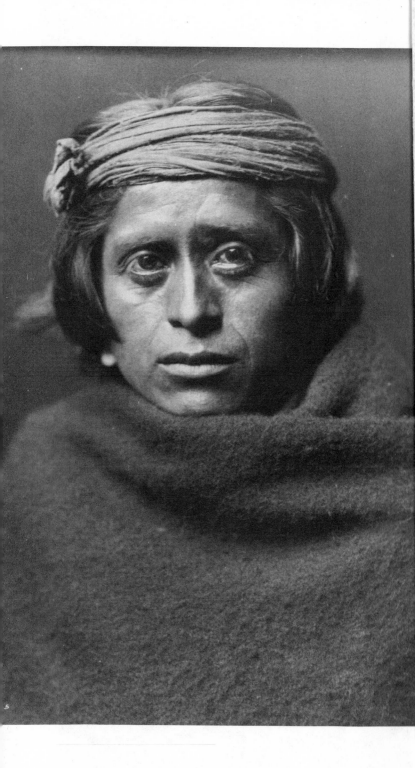

Pueblos, Spaniards, and the Kingdom of New Mexico

JOHN L. KESSELL

University of Oklahoma Press : Norman

OTHER BOOKS BY JOHN L. KESSELL

Mission of Sorrows: Jesuit Guevavi and the Pimas, 1691–1767 (Tucson, 1970)

Friars, Soldiers, and Reformers: Hispanic Arizona and the Sonora Mission Frontier, 1767–1856 (Tucson, 1976)

Kiva, Cross, and Crown: The Pecos Indians and New Mexico, 1540–1840 (Washington, D.C., 1979; Albuquerque, 1987)

The Missions of New Mexico, Since 1776 (Albuquerque, 1980)

(with Rick Hendricks, et al.) *The Journals of don Diego de Vargas, New Mexico, 1691–1704* 6 vols. (Albuquerque, 1989–2002)

Spain in the Southwest: A Narrative History of Colonial New Mexico, Arizona, Texas, and California (Norman, 2002)

Frontispiece: A Zuni man, by Edward S. Curtis, 1903. Courtesy Palace of the Governors (MNM/DCA), no. 143712.

LIBRARY OF CONGRESS CATALOGING-IN-PUBLICATION DATA

Kessell, John L.
    Pueblos, Spaniards, and the kingdom of New Mexico / John L. Kessell.
       p.   cm.
    Includes bibliographical references and index.
    ISBN 978-0-8061-3969-2 (hardcover : alk. paper)
    1. New Mexico—History—To 1848. 2. Spaniards—New Mexico—History—17th century. 3. Pueblo Indians—New Mexico—History—17th century. 4. New Mexico—Race relations—History—17th century. 5. New Mexico—History—To 1848—Biography. I. Title.
    F799.K378   2008
    978.9'02—dc22   2008013234

The paper in this book meets the guidelines for permanence and durability of the Committee on Production Guidelines for Book Longevity of the Council on Library Resources. ∞

Copyright © 2008 by the University of Oklahoma Press, Norman, Publishing Division of the University. Manufactured in the U.S.A.

1　2　3　4　5　6　7　8　9　10

For my loving parents and teachers

John S. and Dorothy L. Kessell
Francis A. and Betty Wiley

CONTENTS

List of Illustrations ix

Preface xi

Introduction: Conflict and Coexistence 3

1. The Pueblo World 7

2. Spaniards Come to Stay: Founding the
   Colony, 1598–1610 25

3. A Franciscan City of God on the
   Rio Grande, 1610s–1640s 51

4. A Colony of Cousins, 1630s–1660s 73

5. Troublous Times, 1660s–1670s 97

6. The Pueblos' Holy War, 1680s 119

7. Resettlement, 1690s 149

   Epilogue: A Lifetime Later, 1760 177

   Postscript 183

   Notes 189

   Bibliography 201

   Index 209

ILLUSTRATIONS

FIGURES

A Zuni man, by Edward S. Curtis, 1903 — *Frontispiece*

Jemez kachina masks — 13

Turquoise kiva, Cochiti, by Adam Vroman, 1900 — 14

Spanish horseman and dog — 21

Taos Pueblo, north houseblock, by John K. Hillers, 1879 — 23

Captain Gaspar Pérez de Villagrá — 27

Acoma — 39

A Franciscan friar — 55

Fray Andrés Juárez's grand Pecos church — 62

Drawing of a buffalo, from the Oñate documents — 75

Plains Apaches, from a painting on hide — 80

Seal of the Mexican Inquisition — 90

María de Jesús de Ágreda preaching — 100

Mounted Pueblo auxiliaries fighting unidentified Apaches — 110

Cliofi Arquero, Keresan Pueblo Indian — 132

Diego de Vargas as a young man — 144

A ceremonial dance at Zuni Pueblo — 147

Restored kiva — 151

The Hopi pueblo of Walpi — 168

The Bishop's visit — 180

Pecos burlesque of the Bishop's visit — 181

John Sherrill Houser's equestrian statue of Juan de Oñate — 185

Cliff Fragua's statue of Po'pay — 187

MAP

Native Groups in and around
   Seventeenth-Century New Mexico   10

PREFACE

Seventeenth-century New Mexico was like no place else. Home to long-centered Pueblo Indians and to recently arrived, peripheral Spaniards, this new but poverty-bound kingdom forced an awkward confluence. Invading Spaniards meant to dominate. Whether they called it conquest or pacification, the project did not go as planned. To understand the messiness of colonial New Mexico—the unrhythmic pulsation of conflict and coexistence—it behooves us to set aside cherished stereotypes of Native American Edens, the Black Legend of singular Spanish cruelty, and even the self-congratulatory condemnation of European colonial expansion and overzealous Christian evangelism.

Between the colony's founder Juan de Oñate (gov. 1598–1609) and refounder Diego de Vargas (gov. 1691–97, 1703–1704), lesser-known but equally intriguing characters emerge. Among the Pueblo Indians, these include agonized strategist Esteban Clemente, steadfast Bartolomé de Ojeda, and the fiercely partisan Felipe Chistoe (whose lives reveal a great deal more about the Pueblo–Spanish encounter than what little we know of the shadowy Popé, leader of the 1680 Pueblo Revolt). Living alongside them were Spaniards fray Andrés Juárez and Francisco Gómez, who oversaw the Spanish colony's grandest construction project; plains trader and Inquisition prisoner Diego Romero; and the ill-starred Francisco de Anaya Almazán, who lost his entire family in 1680. Not one of these fits a ready stereotype. The community of Pecos, eastern gateway to the Pueblo world, also figures prominently.

Far from an inclusive history of Pueblos and Spaniards during the seventeenth century, the pages that follow offer a series of linked stories. While there are many ways to present history, I prefer narrative, weaving analysis and interpretation into the flow of events, circumstances, and people's lives. While I do not consider myself an ethnohistorian, much less a social theorist, I trust my respect for the work of such scholars shows in my own. I claim no insider's knowledge of either Pueblo or Hispanic culture and wish to respect the esoteric traditions of both. Keeping a focus on people and believing that all humankind acts and reacts in similar ways, I hope to favor neither Pueblos nor Spaniards, despite the latter's overwhelming dominance in the surviving documentary record. Because Spaniards so often indulged in institutional self-criticism and individual faultfinding, thereby preserving the testimony of aggrieved Indians, Pueblo voices can be heard as if on a side wind—but never, unfortunately, in their own languages.

I identify Pueblos and Spaniards in a largely cultural sense, based more on how they lived and died than on blood mixture or color. In Spanish, the word *pueblo* means town or people. Throughout, I employ "Pueblo Indians" or "Pueblos" (uppercase) for these town-dwelling people, and "pueblos" (lowercase) for the communities they inhabited. I use "Spaniards" as the noun and "Spanish" as an adjective. Place-names still current (e.g., Rio Grande) appear without Spanish accent marks.

For a variety of kindnesses and for sharing, I should like to thank heartily James F. Brooks, Colin G. Calloway, Carolyn Carlson, Jim Donovan, Richard and Shirley Cushing Flint, Robert Fullilove, Ellen Garrison, Diana Hadley, Rick Hendricks, Stanley M. Hordes, John Sherrill Houser, James E. Ivey, Douglas Johnson, Marcia Keegan, Vi M. Kessell, Frances Levine, Hartman H. Lomawaima, Charles E. Rankin, Deborah Reade, David Schneider, Jody Schwartz, Julie Shilling, Marc Simmons, Carla Van West, David J. Weber, and Sarah Whalen-Kraft.

Pueblos, Spaniards, and the
Kingdom of New Mexico

INTRODUCTION

Conflict and Coexistence

> *What we are dealing with . . . is a universal and noble human aspiration—namely, the will to survive.*
>
> ALFONSO ORTIZ, PUEBLO INDIAN ANTHROPOLOGIST

For ten thousand years, thin waves of people and ideas shifted across the dry, unforgiving American Southwest, contributing unknowingly to the archaeological record. Some took root. Cultures mixed and diverged. Archaeologists of our day have detected lineal ancestors of the Pueblo Indians as far back as two thousand years. Along with architectural and skeletal remains and implements, such early dwellers left petroglyphs and traces of lifestyles still practiced. Then, less than half a millennium ago, literate Spaniards began the written record. Measured within the context of evolving cultures, these artifacts, analogues, and documents track in reverse how successive generations lived and died in this dry, storied landscape.

During the seventeenth century, as Pueblo Indians and Spaniards contended and compromised in a marginal environment, Spanish colonialism did not produce unrelieved tragedy. Abuses occurred, to be sure, from rapes, murders, and dispossessions to minor swindles, and because Spaniards ruled, they were more likely to go unpunished. Pueblo Indians, for their part, killed Spaniards—among them unarmed missionaries, women, and children—in addition to contriving more subtle ways of obstructing the colonial regime: misinterpreting their missionaries' words, absenteeism, foot-dragging, idols behind altars, or parody of notable Spaniards. Most days, however, the sun rose and set on face-to-face cooperation for economic gain, advantage in war, even marriage or foot races.

No one intended the devastation wrought by alien disease. Yet Spaniards and their livestock, coughing, spitting, and expelling bodily matter, became vectors. Smallpox, measles, typhus, and influenza struck periodically, slashing the Pueblo population by 80 to 90 percent from the late sixteenth to the mid-eighteenth century (from an estimated sixty thousand or more to fewer than ten thousand).[1] Native peoples who had withstood violence, cultural collapse, and regeneration before contact with Europeans, often by moving about in search of favored niches in their arid surroundings, now found themselves pinned down. The essential trade-off was a more reliable and varied food supply. Domestic animals and new crops, along with the Spaniards' suite of metal tools and agricultural techniques, proved for the most part beneficial.

Unfortunately, no one cared to record the ordinary days when Pueblos and Spaniards laughed together, repaired a fallen wall, watered the sheep, or prepared for a buffalo hunt. While such mundane happenings went largely unnoticed, accounts of conflict, crime, and punishment filled the archives. At the same time, some Pueblo Indians, despite reduced numbers and mobility, sought to assimilate Spaniards, as previous generations had done with other wandering peoples who possessed useful tools or knowledge. And more than a few Spanish colonists mixed ungrudgingly with their Pueblo neighbors. Countless times during the century, Spaniards and Pueblos campaigned shoulder-to-shoulder against the common enemies of the kingdom, sharing the risks and spoils of war.

The Pueblos rarely acted in league, in peace or in war—with the notable exception of the 1680 Pueblo Revolt (resulting as much from unprecedented drought as from Spanish oppression)—and Spaniards stood famously at cross-purposes over material and missionary gain. So preoccupied were they with their own internal struggles, Pueblos and Spaniards engaged in violence against each other only in exceptional cases. In contrast to the notoriety of such cases, much of life in the formative seventeenth century moved more quietly toward *convivencia,* coexistence, setting precedents for the well-known accommodations of later centuries.

————•◆•————

Seventeenth-century New Mexico never measured up to Spaniards' expectations. A tiny, peopled rift in the arid vastness fifteen hundred miles north of Mexico City, on the far side of every crossroads or market center, impossibly distant from seaport or navigable river, the colony nevertheless represented Spain's visionary claim to half a continent. While modern maps of the United States contain New Mexico—the fifth-largest state in the Union—within a neat box bisected by the Rio Grande and bordered on the south by Mexico, Spaniards cast their claim westward across mesa and desert as far as the Pacific Ocean, and to the east over the countless, slow-ranging buffalo herds of the Great Plains. To the north, no one knew how far, surely New Mexico extended to the south shore of the fabled Strait of Anián (the Northwest Passage on English charts).

Spaniards broke into the Pueblo world to stay in 1598. Since then, for over four hundred years, Pueblos and Spaniards have coexisted vigorously. They have also, from time to time, tried to exterminate each other and failed. Circumstances largely beyond their control, combined with notable resilience on the part of both, dictated mutual survival. Had the Kingdom and Provinces of New Mexico proven the bonanza of the Spaniards' golden dreams, sheer numbers of Hispanic immigrants might have buried the Pueblo peoples. Instead, the colony's abiding poverty discouraged immigration long enough for the Pueblos' disease-thinned ranks to stabilize and come about. In 1599, Spaniards estimated the Pueblo Indian population at 60,000; the United States Census of 2000 made the number 59,621.[2]

Even while sharing blood and traits, Pueblos and Spaniards have chosen, or been forced, to recognize the cultural identity of the other—living together yet apart. Their intricate dance through time, especially passionate in the seventeenth century, bids us to look closer.

1 The Pueblo World

In the beginning, gods, mortals, and animals lived together in a dark chamber beneath Sandy Place Lake far to the north. In that place, no one died. Yet the mothers of summer and winter—Blue Corn Woman and White Corn Maiden—begged a man to find a way out. Three times he refused. The fourth time, he agreed. Reporting back after he had ventured to the north, to the west, to the south, and to the east, he told the mothers that the world beyond was hazy and unfit. Then go up, they directed.

As the man emerged through an opening, predator animals—mountain lions, wild cats, wolves, coyotes, and foxes—and predator birds—vultures and crows—attacked him, clawing and pecking his body. Suddenly the creatures spoke as friends. The man's wounds vanished. He found himself provided with a bow and arrows, dressed in buckskin, his face painted black, with feathers in his hair. The animals told him that the things they had given him were to better prepare him for the future. Returning as Mountain Lion—or Hunt chief—the man thus became the first Tewa Made person, assuring his people that through him they had been accepted into a wider world.

Presenting each with an ear of white corn, Hunt chief created Summer and Winter chiefs, the second and third Made people, who in turn called upon six pairs of brothers—blue, yellow, red, white, dark, and all-colored— to explore north, west, south, east, above, and below. The *first five pairs, although they saw mountains in each of the cardinal directions and a brilliant star in the sky, informed the people that the earth was still "soft." The sixth pair found that the earth had become harder, and they saw a distant rainbow. It was time to leave their home beneath the lake. Led by Summer and Winter chiefs, the people came forth, while the original corn mothers, other gods, and the predator animals and birds stayed behind.*

As the people migrated southward, many fell sick. Since this was a bad sign, the Summer and Winter chiefs led the people back to their refuge under the lake. There, Hunt chief discovered a corn mother full of pebbles, ashes, and cactus spines, sure omens that witchcraft, evil, and death were afoot. Replacing these with seeds, Hunt chief entrusted the people's health to a medicine man, the fourth Made person, and again they set out. Three more times they were forced to return, since they were still not fully prepared. Clowns, Scalp chief, and the Women's society came into being.

Before he sent them out again, Hunt chief divided the people. The gathering and farming Summer People migrated south through the mountains on the west side of the Rio Grande, halting to build eleven successive villages en route, while the hunting Winter People descended along the mountains on the river's east side, pausing the same number of times. At the twelfth stopping place, near present-day Ojo Caliente, Summer and Winter peoples reunited to form one village where they prospered for a long time. Finally, dislodged by an epidemic, six groups, each containing Summer and Winter and the necessary Made people, came to found the six Tewa pueblos we know today.

PARAPHRASE OF A TEWA PUEBLO INDIAN CREATION STORY

On the eve of their first face-to-face encounter with Spaniards, the town-dwelling native peoples who came to be called Pueblo Indians inhabited a landscape of high desert plateau and basin-and-range country. Situated within present-day north-central New Mexico and the northeastern corner of Arizona, sixty to eighty thousand people lived in a hundred multistoried towns (or *pueblos* to Spanish eyes). Their world was large. Three hundred miles separated the farthest Hopi pueblo of Oraibi in the west from Pecos in the east, and from south to north along the Rio Grande, Senecú nestled two hundred miles downriver from northernmost Taos. Each community, home to a few hundred or as many as two thousand residents, was largely self-governing, although seven or eight geographical groupings or confederations clustered loosely within specific drainage basins and spoke that many distinct languages: Piro–Tompiro, Tiwa, Towa, Tewa–Tano, Keresan, Zuni, and Hopi. The Tano language, spoken by people of the Galisteo Basin south of Santa Fe, is also called Southern Tewa. Tewas and Tanos often acted in league. The eastern or Rio Grande pueblos—where Spaniards had a greater impact—are sometimes distinguished from the western pueblos, namely Acoma, Zuni, and the Hopi towns.

The Pueblo Indian way of life had evolved over millennia. As early as 1500 B.C., seed corn (maize) and squash had taken root along trails of trade reaching up from the agricultural cultures of central Mexico. Beans (with higher protein count) and cotton (eaten for the seed oil as well as woven) followed a few centuries later. The people domesticated dogs and turkeys, yet life and legend always centered on corn. To placate the forces of nature and enhance village living and plant cultivation, powerful images of the plumed serpent and cloud symbols came north from Mexico. Other ceremonial precedents designed to control weather, cure sickness, and assure fertility—along with weaving, basketry, building and irrigation techniques, weapons technology, musical instru-

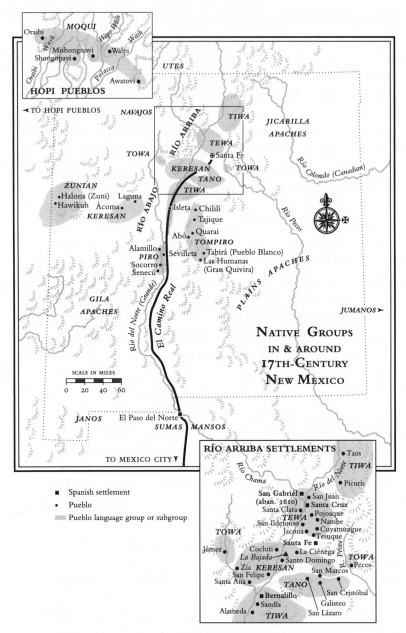

Native Groups in and around Seventeenth-Century New Mexico. Drawn
by Deborah Reade, Santa Fe.

ments, ceramics, copper bells, macaws, and the kachina cult—
had reached the Southwest by the 1300s, transforming the
Pueblos' homeland into a Mesoamerican periphery.[1]

The more recent illusion of Pueblo Indians as peaceable
folk notwithstanding, endemic warfare, more intense in certain areas of the Southwest and at certain times—particularly
during the drier, colder period from about 1250 into the
1500s—shows in the archaeological record: defensive architecture and site location, burned villages, mass graves, skulls
with cut marks from scalping, projectile points embedded
in skeletons, as well as fierce rock and mural art illustrating
shield-bearing warriors in combat. The arsenal with which
they would one day confront Spaniards included spears, bows
and arrows with fire-hardened shafts and knapped flint points,
stone axes and knives, heavy war clubs, and rocks. Cannibalism
occurred in rare instances, for reasons still unknown. It might
have been a form of terrorism inflicted by tyrannical elites or
by invaders from the south, or as the last means to stay alive in
a slowly starving community.[2]

Considerable variety characterized Pueblo social organization, from the grouping of several lineages (each descended
from a common ancestor) into clans—identified by such names
as Coyote, Bear, Ant, Mountain Lion, Pine, Earth, Crow, Corn,
Oak, and Badger—to the larger division of a community into
two halves, or moieties, based on kinship ties—Summer and
Winter people, South and North, Pumpkin and Turquoise.
Clans prevailed in the western pueblos, while moieties were
the rule along the Rio Grande and its tributaries. Although
Pueblo society has been represented as largely egalitarian in
terms of material possessions, specialized religious, political,
and occupational knowledge gave certain individuals and
groups higher status.

Most Pueblo peoples seem to have converted to kachina
religion two hundred to three hundred years before Spaniards
came to watch and condemn. Evidently imposed by native

people from the south, its ragged adoption in the fourteenth and fifteenth centuries had coincided with intense warfare. There must have been holdouts, individual priests of pre-kachina religious societies, some of whom in the sixteenth and seventeenth centuries may have seen in Christianity an appealing alternative. Proselytizing Franciscans, therefore, may not have seemed so severe or so strange to peoples still relatively fresh from previous, pre-Spanish conversions.[3]

Pueblo adherents saw kachinas as ancestor spirits who conveyed the intercessions of mortals to their deities—Sun Father, Earth Mother, the Twin War Gods, Morning Star, Blue Corn Woman, White Corn Maiden, the savior figure Poseyemu, and dozens of others. Kachinas took many forms, from bears to butterflies. They came among the living only during half the year, approximately between the winter and summer solstices, and for the remaining six months they dwelt in the underworld (where, some believed, night and day, winter and summer, were the reverse of their counterparts in the upper world).

Ritual public dramas lay at the heart of kachina religion. Precisely costumed males wearing masks to depict their particular form became emissaries of the deities who enabled rain in season, fertility, and victory in battle. Sacred corn dances featured long rows of women adorned in their best mantas, symbolic rain sashes, high wrapped white moccasins, and terraced headboards (clouds) carrying evergreen branches (life). Children, as perfectly costumed as their parents, followed in descending height, down to five- and four-year-olds. Because letter-perfect performance of such elaborate rituals required the cooperation of everyone in the pueblo—as participants, auxiliaries, or rapt observers—each community developed its own variations on the kachina theme, rendering itself somewhat different from its neighbors.

Architecturally, adoption of kachina religion led to the structuring of large open plazas where the public performances

Jemez kachina masks. From Elsie Clews Parsons, *The Pueblo of Jemez*
(1925).

could be enacted. These coincided with rites conducted in
kivas (a Hopi word)—the distinctive round, partially subterra-
nean Pueblo ceremonial chambers, with a fire pit in the floor
and low benches around the sides. Colorful murals depict-
ing the community's kachina figures commonly adorned kiva
walls. Often freestanding within a plaza, Pueblo kivas were
increasingly placed inside houseblocks after Spaniards began
imposing their militant Christianity.

Correct staging of kachina ceremonials in plazas and kivas,
accompanied by drumbeat and chanted Pueblo stories, con-
trasted with the deviant acts of "sacred clowns" meant to rein-
force proper behavior by acting out its opposite. Such ritual
clowns, whose antics of gluttony, obscenity, sexual-role reversal, and extreme individuality along with their burlesques of

Turquoise kiva, Cochiti Pueblo, by Adam Vroman, 1900. Courtesy Nation
al Anthropological Archives, BAE Neg. no. 2169.

outsiders, reinforced the boundaries of Pueblo culture, wherein
the self was always submerged in the group. Dissenters tended
to leave the community and strike out on their own.

The Pueblos' recurring, religiously exact calendar—based
in part on astronomical observations of the sun's location at its
rising and setting along the horizon—told the seasonal phases
of mother earth and father sun by the extremes of the solstices
and the balance of the equinoxes. The rites of autumn and
winter were believed to induce health, fertility, and success in
war, while those of spring and summer brought the rains.

Each Pueblo community drew inspiration and strength
inward from natural boundaries, from four sacred mountains
or bodies of water in the cardinal directions, each associated
with a different color and deity. The people wrapped sacred

space—on the three cosmic levels of earth, sky, and underworld —ever closer around them to a center place, a *sipapu,* or earth navel, symbolically repeated as a hole in the floor of their kivas. Like germinating plants, human beings had emerged through the sipapu from the world beneath this one and would return to it without judgment after death.[4]

No single item of Pueblo ritual held more significance than feathers, both of brightly plumed macaws traded into the Pueblo world and of eagles taken in carefully orchestrated hunts. Feathers adorned ceremonial costumes and altars and carried the people's prayers in the form of *pahos,* sticks with feathers attached, often placed at shrines. Later, feathers, sacred ears of corn, ritually ground cornmeal scattered during rites or sprinkled in a line across a path to prohibit entry, along with kachina masks, effigies of animals, and all manner of Pueblo ceremonial paraphernalia would draw the ire of Spanish missionaries as "idolatrous" vestiges of "pagan" religion.

The Pueblos' cosmos, as they came to view it, had taken shape over eons. Now, in the sixteenth century, Spaniards pushing north from Mexico meant to subvert the kachinas and put in their place a new religion. The Pueblos reacted in a variety of ways ranging from violent rejection to rote toleration, curiosity, and selective adoption. They had long practiced trial and possession of new traits. Their habitual mobility, which the Spaniards would curtail, had included splinter groups estranged from one community and taken in by another for the new blood or ceremonial powers they possessed. Early in the encounter, before their numbers plummeted, the Pueblos may have envisioned absorbing the invaders and their ways. Later, many Pueblo "Christians" complied outwardly to keep the peace, while inwardly observing traditional ways as circumstances and their hearts dictated.

Even the Spaniards' enticing material goods—especially their domestic animals and new food crops—forced unforeseen adjustments among the Pueblos. Abundant mutton and occasional beef diminished the hunt chief's role, while winter wheat, planted as early as February, threw off the aboriginal cycle of ritual, planting, and harvest.

Still, whether or not they chose to acknowledge it, Pueblos and Spaniards had much in common. The kachina religion and Christianity were both heavily patriarchal. And while Christians looked up to their one creator God and Pueblos looked down to the underworld for their origins, much of the new Christian pageantry was appealing: the music, dressing up, sacred images, and processions. If Christians did appear to the Pueblos unduly obsessed with a proper death, their baptismal and marriage rites seemed harmless enough.

Both Pueblos and Spaniards revered stories, hallowed places, and ritual, sacred and profane. Both embraced visions and believed that the physical and invisible worlds were somehow one. Both had their elders and their clowns. Pueblo coyote and Spanish *pícaro* were brothers, roguish tricksters both. Neither people suffered witches to live. And who among either, save a few priests, claimed the esoteric knowledge to fully comprehend the power and glory of the Pueblo savior god Poseyemu or Jesus Christ, the Corn Mothers or the Blessed Virgin Mary?

For all that, Spanish Catholicism, forged during the eight-century-long, on-again, off-again Reconquista of the Iberian Peninsula from Islam, bristled in comparison with the Pueblos' more accepting and still evolving ways. The Church Militant stiffened even further at mid-sixteenth century. Bracing against Protestants and folk religion in Europe, leaders of the Roman Catholic world had gathered intermittently at the Council of Trent in Italy between 1545 and 1563 to institute reforms, to more closely define doctrine and practice, and to demand strict adherence. Every time a Franciscan priest in New Mexico baptized, married, or buried Pueblos or Spaniards and recorded the fact, he did so according to the dictates of the Council of Trent.

Notably less formal, the persistent folk Catholicism of up-country parishes in Spain, with its roots deep in paganism, bore notable resemblances to Pueblo religion.⁵ During times of drought, the intent was the same whether the procession carried out into dry fields an image of a saint or of a kachina. But because the Order of Friars Minor (the Franciscans), as an agency of the Roman Catholic Church, responded more quickly and uniformly to the reforms of the Council, New Mexico's missionaries were less tolerant of Pueblo ways than were most Spanish colonists. The latter, as neighbors of Indian communities, often got on remarkably well, learning Pueblo languages more readily than the friars, and subsequently serving as interpreters for Spanish governors and officials.

Aside from religion, other basic similarities became evident. While men appeared to rule in the Pueblo world, women were just as essential to their households as Spanish women were to theirs, and their roles were just as invisible to outsiders. Because Franciscans looking through their patriarchal lenses saw only male idolaters, for the most part influential Pueblo women, members of women's ritual organizations, even female kachina dancers and shamans, escaped their gaze. Children in both cultures went through similar rites of passage: from naming —with Pueblo babies held up to the sun four days after birth and Spanish babies receiving baptism in their first days—on through rituals of acceptance by the larger community and lifelong learning by imitation of parents and wise counselors.

Pueblo midwives and mothers consoled their Spanish counterparts. As women, they learned from each other. Recipes, cures and curses, and words in their languages passed back and forth, forming small cultural sutures. As soon as Pueblo boys taught Spanish boys to crack piñon nuts, snare a rabbit, and find the local hot springs, the newcomers lost their unfamiliarity. Sexual relations by consent between natives and colonists rarely left a documentary trail unless a third party objected. As Spaniards buried their babies and their

grandmothers in New Mexico's soil, place became as impor-
tant to them as to the Pueblos.

New Mexico's discouraging poverty, too, rendered them
ever more alike. Except for the dozen or more interrelated
Spanish families of landholders, tribute collectors, and colonial
officials who put on airs, Pueblo and Spanish commoners,
sharing clothing, food ways, and subsistence, soon looked not
so different.

Yet in the beginning—in the Christian year 1540—the initial, face-to-face encounter of Pueblos and Spaniards proved a
profoundly unsettling, two-year-long star-crossed false start.

——————•◆•——————

If only his father could see him now. Even as the older
man's curses rang in his ears, Juan Troyano had no regrets. A
virile youth of fifteen, he had run away from the town of
Medina de Rioseco in north-central Spain, soldiered with
the armies of Carlos V in Italy, then sailed for the Spanish
Indies in the entourage of the first viceroy of New Spain
(Mexico). Shedding his estranged father's surname, he girded
himself with the fighting name Troyano, Spanish for Trojan.
He prided himself in his service record. Between 1540 and
1542, as a veteran artilleryman in the expeditionary force of
Francisco Vázquez de Coronado, Juan Troyano rode with the
first Europeans into the world of the Pueblo Indians.

Troyano was there to witness the first large-scale conflict
between Pueblos and Spaniards when, in July 1540, famished
Spanish men-at-arms and their Indian allies from the Valley of
Mexico fought their way into the Zuni pueblo of Hawikuh
in the midst of sacred summer ceremonials. The Zunis were
no match. The aliens next bivouacked in the Rio Grande valley through two long winters—hundreds of Spaniards, their
servants and trail hands, and a fearsome contingent of twelve
hundred or more Mexican Indian auxiliary troops. During a
vicious war with the Tiguex people, other Pueblos supplied
food to the invaders. Scarcely twenty years had passed since
conquistador Hernán Cortés captured the Aztec (Mexica)

capital of Tenochtitlán, restyling it Mexico City. Now, fifteen hundred miles to the north, Coronado's trespass upset the prevailing balance of power in the Pueblo world.

In the 1992 PBS special *Surviving Columbus,* the late Alfonso Ortiz, a widely known Pueblo Indian anthropologist, termed Coronado's entrada "a destructive rampage through Pueblo country" and its leader "a savage."[6] As a sworn witness, Juan Troyano himself, shifting blame away from Coronado at the general's trial in 1544, nevertheless admitted savagery on the part of certain Spaniards.[7]

Possessed of a curiosity uncharacteristic of his comrades-in-arms, Troyano liked these Pueblo Indians. They appeared to him not so different from Europeans. They crowded around him, teaching him words in their languages. He wanted to live among them, however much he may have viewed them as potential servants or laborers. In Troyano's opinion, this Tierra Nueva, with its farming, town-dwelling Indians and the endless grassy plains to the east, rivaled New Spain.

With Spaniards swaggering among them, Pueblo elders in dozens of communities debated. Must we fight these metal men, should we side with them against our own enemies, or should we flee? At the easternmost pueblo, which the Spaniards first called Cicuique and later Pecos, an impressive Pueblo Indian, "a tall young man, well disposed and with a vigorous expression," volunteered to lead a delegation bearing gifts of cured animal hides, shields, and leather helmets for the Spaniards' leader along with an invitation to visit Cicuique and the buffalo plains beyond. Eagerly Juan Troyano joined the twenty horsemen who accepted this Pueblo overture. They called their guide "Bigotes, because he had long mustaches," uncharacteristic of most Pueblo men.[8]

What eventually befell Bigotes turned Troyano's stomach. His fellow expeditionaries, so desperate to find larger, more sophisticated populations like those to the south—whose tributaries provided Cortés's men with marketable products of precious metals, craft wares, cloth, and foodstuffs—resorted to any means to further their quest. When another Indian claimed that Bigotes guarded among his possessions a gold bracelet from the rumored kingdom of Quivira to the east, the Spaniards took him prisoner and tortured him to learn the details. Dogs of war, the thickset mastiffs or fleet greyhounds that frequently accompanied Spanish New World armies of the sixteenth century, were set on Bigotes. The dogs, according to Troyano's testimony, "bit him on a leg and the arm," yet the bracelet remained a fiction. His captors eventually released Bigotes and returned him to Cicuique. Although no more was heard of him, his strong Pueblo community not surprisingly turned against the invaders.[9]

When a dispirited Coronado, having decided to withdraw, decreed that all Indian captives be freed, Juan Troyano asked for an exemption. Years later, the career soldier and military engineer boasted that he was the only Spaniard to have brought back to Mexico City a native woman from La Tierra Nueva. "God was pleased," Troyano wrote in 1568, "to give me . . . a woman [or wife] from that land," likely a captive Pueblo Indian from the middle Rio Grande province of Tiguex. Whether or not he married her in the eyes of the Roman Catholic Church, Troyano and his Indian companion lived together half a lifetime. Troyano eagerly contributed to proposals during the late 1560s to colonize the far north— today's greater American Southwest—volunteering his services as official protector of Indians. And while authorities regularly denied such petitions to return to the land of the Pueblos, the singular union of Spaniard Juan Troyano and this Pueblo woman foretold a renewed encounter.[10]

Yet because the first Spaniards to break in upon the Pueblo world, bound by the technology and markets of their day, found no exploitable resource to set Bigotes and his people producing, digging, or gathering, they decamped in April 1542. Troyano had recognized how different Pueblo Indians were from the less settled, mostly Apachean (including Navajo)

Spanish horseman and dog. After Lienzo de Tlaxcala, central New Spain, sixteenth century; redrawn by Jerry L. Livingston. From Kessell, *Kiva, Cross, and Crown.*

and Plains peoples who buffered them on all sides. Although Coronado's Spaniards noted cultural similarities among all the Pueblos—primarily their towns, dress, and agriculture—they did not yet refer to them collectively as Pueblo Indians, but instead grouped them in various provinces, such as Tiguex (Tiwa-speakers) or Quirix (Keresan-speakers), according to perceived language boundaries.

Coronado's failure to reward the investors in his venture stunted the Spaniards' advance in the Pueblos' direction, although illusions persisted. The discovery of silver-rich veins of ore late in the 1540s at Zacatecas, 350 miles northwest of Mexico City, not only set Spaniards gazing northward again but also redirected their focus from imagined high cultures to the raw and real sources of precious metals—mines.

New rumors, however, of the Pueblo Indians' settled ways amid so vast and unstable a heathendom led Spaniards in the second half of the sixteenth century to once again presume great wealth and numerous souls to save. The very name, New

Mexico, fanned the old illusions. Employed imprecisely in 1561 by a daring former soldier turned Franciscan lay brother who penetrated the far north two decades after Coronado, the term dimly foresaw another or "new" Mexico as dazzling as Aztec Tenochtitlán. Finally, transient Spaniards in the 1580s and 1590s who "rediscovered" the Pueblo world gave it the name New Mexico. They did not, however, presume to call it a *kingdom*.[11]

Neither had King Felipe II of Spain authorized the term kingdom in 1583 when he decreed pacification of the region by a rich entrepreneur who would spare the royal treasury. Cocksure Juan de Oñate, eventual founder of "the kingdom of New Mexico," simply elevated it on his own authority. Praying April 30, 1598, don Juan bid that God "give to our king, and to me in his royal name, peaceful possession of these kingdoms and provinces for His blessed glory. Amen." Looking to the future, Oñate fancied himself reporting directly to the royal court in Spain, as the equal of the viceroy in Mexico City. Hence, he must rule a kingdom.[12]

One of the Spanish "rediscoverers," in midwinter 1591, had described admiringly the large pueblo that had been home to Bigotes fifty years earlier, Coronado's Cicuique:

> Most noteworthy were sixteen kivas—all underground, thoroughly whitewashed, and very large—constructed for protection against the cold, which in this country is very great. They do not light fires inside but bring from the outside numerous live coals banked with ashes in so neat a manner that I am at a loss to describe it. The door through which they enter is a tight hatchway large enough for only one person at a time. They go down by means of a ladder set through the hatchway for that purpose.
>
> The houses of this pueblo are arranged in the form of houseblocks. . . . And they are built back to back. They are four and five stories high. There are no doors opening on the streets on the floor just above the ground.

Taos Pueblo, north house block, by John K. Hillers, 1879. Courtesy Palace of the Governors (MNM/DCA), no. 16096.

They use light ladders which can be pulled up by hand. Every house has three or four rooms [per floor], so that the whole of each from top to bottom has fifteen or sixteen rooms, very neat and thoroughly whitewashed. For grinding, every house is equipped with three and four grindstones with handstone, each placed in its own little whitewashed bin. Their method of grinding is novel: they pass the flour they are grinding from one to the next, since they do not make tortilla dough. They do make from this flour their bread in many ways, as well as their atole [corn meal gruel] and tamales.

There were five plazas in this pueblo. It had so great a supply of maize that everyone marveled. There were those who believed that there must have been thirty thousand fanegas [a dry measure of between two and three bushels], since every house had two or three rooms full. It is the best maize seen. There was a good supply of beans. Both maize and beans were of many colors. . . . They store abundant herbs, greens, and squash in their houses. They have many things for working their fields.

The dress we saw there was for winter. Most if not all the men wore cotton blankets and on top of these a buffalo hide. Some covered their privy parts with small clothes, very elegant and finely worked. The women wore a blanket tied at the shoulder and open on one side and a sash a span wide around the waist. Over this they put on another blanket, very elegantly worked, or turkey-feather cloaks and many other novel things—all of which for barbarians is remarkable.

They have a great deal of pottery, red, varicolored, and black—plates, bowls, saltcellars, basins, cups—very elegant. Some of the pottery is glazed. They have an abundant supply of firewood as well as timber for building their houses so that, as they explained it to us, whenever anyone wanted to build a house he had the timber right there at hand.

There is plenty of land as well as two water holes at the edges of the pueblo which they use for bathing since they get drinking water from other springs an arquebus shot away. At a quarter league's distance flows the river [the Pecos] along which we had made our way.[13]

When next, in 1598, Spaniards penetrated the Pueblos' homeland, they came as migrant settlers. They hoped at first for an easier life, but they found no mines. Not surprisingly, their active competition with the native peoples quickened the endless reshaping of the Pueblo world. Out of conflict and coexistence, together Pueblos and Spaniards forged seventeenth-century New Mexico.

2 Spaniards Come to Stay
Founding the Colony, 1598–1610

*Here I cannot forbear to commend the patient virtue
of the Spaniards. We seldom or never find any nation
hath endured so many misadventures and miseries as
the Spaniards have done in their Indian discoveries. Yet
persisting in their enterprises, with invincible constancy,
they have annexed to their kingdom so many goodly
provinces, as bury the remembrance of all dangers past.
Tempests and shipwrecks, famine, overthrows, mutinies,
heat and cold, pestilence, and all manner of diseases, both
old and new, together with extream poverty, and want of
all things needful, have been the enemies, wherewith every
one of their most noble discoveries, at one time or other,
hath encountered. . . . Yea, more than one or two have
spent their labor, their wealth, and their lives, in search of
a golden kingdom, without getting further notice of it than
what they had at their first setting forth.*

SIR WALTER RALEIGH, *THE HISTORY OF THE WORLD* (1786)

In January 1599 Captain Gaspar Pérez de Villagrá looked out
on a scene at once hideous and enchanting. Noxious smoke of
burning households, screams of defiance and pain, contorted
shapes in mortal combat, fear-struck Acoma women and

children pressed against rock walls—all this fury atop a confined mesa rising like an altar above the vast winter landscape
of plateau, distant cliffs, and seemingly endless natural beauty.
Fits of exhaustion broke the fighting awkwardly. As darkness
fell, random bonfires lit men's faces leaning in toward the small
warmth. The stars shown wondrously bright. Ecstatic, alive in a
heroic struggle worthy of *The Iliad,* he knew he would never
forget this scene.

A decade later, staring out from the woodcut frontispiece
of his *Historia de la Nueva México* (1610), his head served up
on the stylish ruff of the day, balding, with furrowed brow, sad
eyes, and mouth hidden by drooping moustache and goatee,
Captain Villagrá had definitely not forgotten.[1]

A criollo born about 1555 of Spanish parents in Puebla
de los Ángeles east of Mexico City, Villagrá was shipped off
at a young age to Spain for an education, where he studied
the classics at the University of Salamanca. He resided then in
Madrid for seven years at the court of Felipe II, likely as a lesser
bureaucrat. His father's death may have called him home. Back
across the Atlantic in New Spain, he fell in with the influential
don Juan de Oñate. A wealthy mine developer and native of
Zacatecas, New Spain's silver boomtown north of Mexico
City, Oñate had won a royal contract in 1595 to colonize New
Mexico. The viceroy in Mexico City, the highest-ranking official in New Spain and a personal friend of Oñate, had favored
him in the negotiations, which called for the recruitment of
two hundred soldier-colonists. Seizing the moment, Villagrá
invested in the enterprise. He outfitted half a dozen retainers
and signed on as chief supply officer. Barely forty but already
graying, Villagrá fancied himself a warrior knight. The deeds
of this noble company, he envisioned, would merit more than
mere account books.

When, years later, the manuscript of Villagrá's 11,877-
line epic poem recounting those deeds was reviewed by
the required literary and ecclesiastical censors in Spain, they

Captain Gaspar Pérez de Villagrá. From his *Historia de la Nueva México*
(1610).

agreed that it contained "nothing derogatory to our faith or
contrary to good morals." Although one professor judged it
"lacking in imagination and poetical worth," he allowed that
"the variety of such extraordinary events will please many."

The Dominican friar who read it was kinder: "In pleasing style it relates the deeds of those valiant captains and soldiers who in remote regions serve your highness and their holy church. This book will encourage others to do likewise. It should be printed."[2]

Outright conquest propaganda, the saga was alive with allusions to Greek and Roman classics, reflecting the author's university education. Still, Captain Villagrá was an eyewitness to the events of Oñate's first tumultuous year among the Pueblo Indians of New Mexico. His poetic *Historia* complemented the prosaic archival record, which also attested to his heavy involvement. Colonizer Oñate, contract in hand, had not anticipated two years of bureaucratic entanglement, a change in viceroys, endless inspections, and delays. Initially, more than enough colonists rallied to his banner, but the luster soon wore off. Not a few deserted. Villagrá rode back and forth from Mexico City to the expedition's temporary camps, acting as detail man, agent, and publicist. He endorsed the bond tendered by Oñate's chief financial backer that allowed the column finally to proceed with only 129 qualified colonists (heads of household), 71 short of his promised total.[3]

——◆◆——

At an elevation of six thousand feet, the Tewa-speaking Pueblo Indian community of Ohkay Owingeh (Place of the Strong People) occupied a favored site on the east bank of the Rio Grande near the confluence of the Chama River, twenty-five miles north of today's Santa Fe (and sixteen hundred miles north of Mexico City). Its several hundred residents planted the alluvial floodplain with corn, beans, and squash. They collected wild foods and hunted rabbits and deer in the surrounding hills, holding in sacred wonder the purple mountains rising to the east. Their main houseblock of coursed earth—three, four, and five stories high—presented an almost unbroken wall to the outside. According to Villagrá, four defensible passages gave access to the rectangular central plaza within. Before Spaniards arrived, the plaza pulsed with summer activity: cutting up and drying food, cooking, gossip, wood stacking, children at chores or at play, and the seasonal public ceremonials of their kachina religion (most of which took place in fall and winter).

Ever since Coronado in the early 1540s, invading Europeans had noted the Pueblo Indians' distinctive kivas. These the outsiders termed *estufas,* or hot rooms, likening them to their own chambers for dry or sweat baths. Whatever other functions such rooms may have served, their religious nature did not escape Captain Villagrá, who en route to Ohkay had observed kiva murals.

> A mighty store which they had there
>
> Of haughty demons pictured,
>
> Ferocious and extremely terrible,
>
> Which clearly showed to us they were their gods,
>
> Because the god of water near the water
>
> Was well painted and figured out.
>
> The god of the mountains, too, near the mountains,
>
> And next to fishes, seeds, battles,
>
> Were all the rest that they revere.

Less riveting, there had to have been corn plants and tassels.[4]

A typical individual Pueblo family apartment, several constricted rooms deep and several stories tall, shared common walls with neighbors on both sides. Families could not help knowing each other's joys and sorrows. Rooms were entered not by doors at floor level, but through hatchways in the ceiling just large enough for one adult at a time. Storage compartments occupied the lower floors. Smoke from fire pits below, escaping through the hatchways, signaled living chambers set back one upon the other in receding tiers. The covered terraces were also punctured by hatchways giving access to the flat roofs above, ideal for stringing foods to dry. Other Pueblo communities like Keresan-speaking Acoma, 125 miles south-west of Ohkay by the crow's flight and perched upon a seem-ingly invulnerable mesa, were laid out not around a defensible plaza but instead in several parallel rows of tiered apartments back-to-back.

The most notable feature of Ohkay's plaza, looking like so many wind-tilted saplings leaning randomly against mud walls and poking up through hatchways, were the long ladders that went from the ground to the first terrace, then to successively higher terraces and flat roofs, or descended into the smoky darkness of living quarters. Such ladders could be yanked up in the event of trouble.

Oñate's venturesome corps of Spaniards who eventu-ally broke in upon the Pueblo world in the summer of 1598, counting dependent women, children, servants, and slaves, ran to around six or seven hundred. By way of comparison, two to three times as many intruders had trailed Coronado fifty-eight years earlier. This new invasion came in notable contrast to Coronado's, without a mighty contingent of Mexican Indian warriors. As migrant families, driving eighty-odd wheeled vehicles, they brought with them tools, building materials, household belongings, mining apparatus, root stock, seed, and bawling herds of animals for breeding. Most of the colonists were young, in their twenties, and many had children.[5]

Of those who considered themselves *españoles* (Spaniards), about half had immigrated from the Iberian Peninsula and half, like Captain Villagrá, listed birthplaces in New Spain and the Spanish Indies. Single men and women outnumbered married couples. Whatever they chose to call themselves, they were a racial potpourri: Europeans, Indian servants from the Valley of Mexico, Africans, and sundry mixed-bloods. A few, given the simultaneous persecutions in Mexico City, were likely crypto-Jews (overtly Christian but secretly still practicing Jewish rites) fleeing the Inquisition. Heads of household, male or female, who stayed the course for five years, could look forward to grants of land, Indian tribute, and titles as *primeros pobladores,* or first settlers, and *hidalgos* (literally, children of something; that is, property), the gentry level of Spanish nobility.

Having met Spaniards previously, too often in battle, Pueblo elders could see that this latest incursion of "metal people" meant to make themselves at home. The Pueblos began to understand what that meant for them at Ohkay Owingeh during harvest time that first year. The aliens' choice of Ohkay as their initial base camp sprung from a persistent memory that had become family lore among the Oñates. The major chronicler of Coronado's earlier venture recalled that some of the Spaniards had seen beautifully glazed pottery at two pueblos in Tewa country. "Also," the chronicler went on, "many jars were found full of choice shiny metal, with which the Indians glaze their pottery. This was an indication that in that land there were sources of silver, if they had been looked for."[6]

Precious metals were always uppermost in Oñate's mind. In mid-August 1598 his eager colonists moved right into Ohkay Owingeh. Some occupied vacant apartments or rooms in the existing building, some probably forced Pueblo families to double up, and others erected tents or lean-tos in the central plaza or close by outside. In retrospect, Captain Villagrá assured readers of his epic that the pueblo's residents gladly divided their living quarters with this swarm of guests. Juan de Oñate bestowed on Ohkay the name of his patron saint, San Juan Bautista, which he used invariably on documents executed at the Spaniards' earliest New Mexico headquarters. Subsequently, Villagrá exalted the place as San Juan de los Caballeros (San Juan of the Warrior Knights) in honor of Oñate's captains. Still later, romantics turned the name inside out, making it San Juan of the Gentlemen for the alleged hospitality shown by the native people toward the Europeans. Today, thanks to recent efforts by Pueblo governor Joe García, official highway signs no longer read San Juan Pueblo, but instead Ohkay Owingeh.[7]

Whatever the incentive, work crews of Tewa men, fifteen hundred of them according to Oñate, aided the colonists in digging or deepening an irrigation ditch to enlarge fields for the next year's crops. Until then, the newcomers exacted levies of food, giving in return gifts of little value: glass beads of various colors, hawk bells, religious medals, and the like. Since Pueblo women were accustomed to building walls, Spaniards likely showed them how to make, in uniform wooden molds, the sun-dried mud blocks they called adobes. Whether of adobe or *jacal* construction (upright poles chinked with mud), the kingdom's first recorded Spanish building, the simple Christian church of San Juan Bautista, deserved a fitting dedication. Oñate invited delegations from Pueblo communities far and wide. On the Christians' calendar, it was September 8, 1598, feast day of the Blessed Virgin Mary's birth.

All eyes followed the solemn, multihued procession of Franciscan friars and Spanish officials, vested for the occasion; then, a sung Mass, dedicatory rites, a morality play, and, if Villagrá remembered correctly, the festive Christian baptism of many Indian children. Pouring water on their heads, as on corn plants, surely symbolized growth to the children's parents. Much as such ceremonies held the attention of Pueblo onlookers, they paled in comparison to the Spaniards' magnificent control of their horses. Riders jousted with canes, galloped at the ring with lances, baited bulls, all the while performing intricate feats of horsemanship. Firearms, loaded without ball, roared. Then came the pageant, as purposely staged as the Pueblos' sacred kachina dances, in Oñate's words, "a good sham battle between Moors and Christians, the latter on foot with harquebuses, the former on horseback with lances and shields."[8] In the Moors' ritual defeat lay the lesson.

Already though, certain colonists, depressed by New Mexico's evident lack of mineral wealth, were conspiring to desert, an offense punishable by death. Under cover of the

September festivities, four men stole a number of horses and struck south down the Rio Grande. Furious at this open challenge to his authority, Governor Oñate at once dispatched Villagrá along with Captain Gerónimo Márquez and a posse to overtake and execute them. Fourteen days later, near the mines of Todos Santos in Nueva Vizcaya (the closest settled province south of Oñate's New Mexico), they caught up with two of them and slit their throats. As proof, the posse cut off the victims' right hands to send in brine to the governor. The other two escaped.

Writing to the viceroy from Santa Bárbara in Nueva Vizcaya, Captains Villagrá and Márquez sought to justify their actions, at the same time "praising highly the quality, richness, and fertility of the provinces of New Mexico." Years later, Villagrá, along with Márquez and Oñate himself, was found guilty not only of denying the deserters a fair trial and confession to a priest but also of lying about New Mexico, since "the opposite is true, as it is a sterile and poor land, sparsely populated."[9]

Villagrá's closest call came en route back from pursuit of the deserters. Eager to present his version of the executions directly to the governor, he had ventured off alone from the Rio Grande, veering westward in hopes of overtaking Oñate, who was off on a probe toward the Gulf of California. The captain's dog, likely a big greyhound, loped along beside him. Accosted on the trail by Acoma Indians, the lone Spaniard, wary of their intentions, spurred onward despite his hunger. A storm broke over him, and it began to snow. The lay of the land forced him to urge his horse into a narrows, where the Acomas had dug a trap set with sharpened spikes. In they fell. The horse, pierced, struggled and died. The dazed Villagrá climbed out, and with only the dog as companion, put his boots on backwards to confuse pursuers, a senseless ruse unless he also carried the animal.

Yet he survived. So vivid was his memory of the pitfall that long after, in Spain, he created a coat of arms featuring a knight tumbling from his horse, reminiscent of Saint Paul on the road to Damascus, and placed it beneath his portrait. Especially poignant lines in the *Historia* confessed his deranged decision, wandering lost and starving, to kill and eat his dog, not thinking that he had no way to roast the meat. A party of Oñate's men, searching for horses scattered by the storm, came upon the half-dead knight several days later near the Zuni salt lake and revived him. Villagrá spared no detail in his report to Governor Oñate.[10]

The Acoma Indians inhabited a single, all but impregnable pueblo set atop an awesome mesa. Their hostility toward Villagrá gave Oñate pause. Less than two weeks earlier, late in October 1598, the Spanish governor had parleyed with Acoma representatives, guiding them through the ritual of vassalage to King Felipe II (who had died in Spain the month before). Oñate lectured them through an Indian interpreter named Tomás "that he had come to their country to bring them to the knowledge of God and the king our lord, on which depended the salvation of their souls and their living securely and undisturbed in their nations, maintained in justice and order, safe in their homes, protected from their enemies, and free from all harm."[11]

Henceforth, the people of Acoma Pueblo were subjects of the Spanish crown and, in Oñate's mind, governed by the laws and punishments of Spain, whatever that meant to them. Suspecting no good, the Spanish governor had declined descent into the cool darkness of an Acoma kiva and ridden on with his numerous entourage, reining up seventy-five miles farther west before the Zuni pueblo of Hawikuh. On November 9, as Oñate engaged Zuni leaders in a similar act of obedience, the governor's young son and the resurrected Captain Villagrá stood by to witness the document.

Bundled up against the cold and remounted, the horse-men pressed on to the Hopi pueblos and beyond, when an ambush behind them changed everything. Oñate, ignorant of the terrain and of winter in New Mexico, had foolishly summoned his nephew and second-in-command, Maestre de campo Juan de Zaldívar, with an additional thirty men-at-arms, to join him in an exploration to the Gulf of California.

Zaldívar stopped at Acoma to extract provisions in exchange for iron hatchets and other trade goods. When the Indians delayed bringing down the ground corn, he and a number of his men climbed up the trail to the mesa-top pueblo. They probably strode about arrogantly, demanding too much. Or perhaps the attack, as survivors swore later, had been planned in advance. Whatever the circumstances, the Acomas invited the Spaniards to various homes, dividing them into small groups; then, armed with bows and arrows, clubs, and rocks, they fell upon them in a fury. One Spanish survivor recalled Acomas cursing them in Nahuatl, a distant echo of the Mexican Indians who had deserted the Coronado expedition a lifetime earlier.

Depositions taken later from survivors lend credence to Villagrá's blood-and-guts, secondhand account. Zaldívar, ten other officers and men, and two servants fell under the Acomas' blows. One Spaniard, his ribs smashed, sprawled on the ground, in the poet's words,

> When from the topmost of a house,
> From on its parapet, a mighty rock
> Was by a weak old woman thrust.
> This fell straight down in such a way
> As smashed his head into pieces.

Close by, a wounded mulatto servant boy snatched the dead Spaniard's dagger and sliced his Acoma assailant so severely that

Now tripping over their own entrails,

One to the other, both raging,

Fell each in the others arms, dying.

Five Spaniards jumped. Falling hundreds of feet, four landed in sand blown up against the base of the rock and lived. The fifth, "his flustered brains knocked out / Among the rocks, came down losing both eyes."[12]

Recalled to headquarters at San Juan Bautista by this setback, Oñate faced the first grim challenge to his proprietorship. Tens of thousands of Pueblo Indians watched. Unless the Acomas were swiftly and overwhelmingly punished, the Spaniards' rule was a farce. The Franciscan priests with the colony concurred, urging "just war" by a Christian prince to quell "rebellion" and preserve the peace. Had not the Acomas voluntarily sworn obedience just before their treachery? Oñate named his younger nephew (brother of the deceased Juan), Sargento mayor Vicente de Zaldívar, to humble the Acomas.

The governor first admonished Zaldívar to keep in mind the savage nature and incapacity of the Acomas and therefore "to make more use of royal clemency than of the severity that the case demands." Specifically, he must offer peace three times, demanding that the Acomas lay down their arms, surrender the leaders of the rebellion, and abandon their lofty pueblo for another site in the valley below. That accomplished, the sargento mayor was to send a large enough detail back up to the old pueblo, "burn it to the ground, and leave no stone on stone, so that the Indians may never be able again to inhabit it as an impregnable fortress."

If the Acomas chose to fight, and if, by God's grace, the Christians triumphed, Zaldívar was to take everyone prisoner. Those of fighting age, he might punish as he deemed appropriate, including public execution. If, on the other hand, the Spanish commander wished to show mercy, Oñate instructed, "you should seek all possible means to make the Indians believe that you are doing so at the request of the friar with your forces. In this manner they will recognize the friars as their benefactors and protectors and come to love and esteem them, and fear us. To execute this punishment as you may see fit, I grant you the same powers I myself hold from his majesty."[13]

In the gray dead of winter, some seventy armed and mounted Spaniards trailed out of San Juan Bautista upon what must have seemed an impossible mission: atop that formidable rock resided more than a thousand Acomas, who considered themselves invulnerable. To Acoma defenders looking down from their towering stronghold, the Spanish horsemen appeared absurdly puny. No one below mistook the mood of the tiny gesturing figures lining the edge, yelling, brandishing the swords of dead Spaniards, letting fly arrows and spears, hurling down rocks and chunks of ice. Whatever they were shouting, Zaldívar rightly took as insults. Despite their caution, several riders fell into the numerous horse traps.

The Spanish commander restrained his company, ritually offering peace three times in a manner that satisfied his officers. Camped a little way off, the Spaniards could faintly hear the Acomas' all-night war dance. The sweet pungence of juniper-wood smoke seemed out of place. Next day, a party of Indians sneaked down to attack Spaniards leading horses to water, killing two of the animals. That sealed the encounter. About three in the afternoon, Vicente de Zaldívar cried battle without quarter. Surely a good omen for the Spaniards, January 22 was the feast of San Vicente, the saint's day of their bold commander.

Not even in his most cherished fantasy could knight-errant Villagrá have imagined the battle at Acoma. Unfolding over five days, between January 21 and January 25, 1599, the drama captivated him. Having testified in the formal record immediately afterward, he later devoted more than a third of his *Historia* to the action, further developing characters, dialogue, and plot, from the time he fell into the Acoma horse trap until the battle's smoldering conclusion. There, his epic ended abruptly, before the prisoners' trial. Although he promised a sequel, it has never come to light.

Back at San Juan, there had been a scare. Rumor of an attack by neighboring Pueblos greatly upset everyone, Spanish colonists and natives alike. Oñate ordered musketeers and small field pieces to the four entrances. In his epic, Captain Villagrá told how the Spanish women, with so many of their men absent in the field, took the news. Their leader, doña Eufemia de Sosa—to the admiring poet's eye a woman of exceptional beauty, courage, and will—organized a wives' brigade. Earlier, when the expedition to New Mexico had been halted en route, doña Eufemia had harangued the weak-hearted who complained and spoke of turning back. Now, with the governor's encouragement, she sent the women to the rooftops. Hence, wrote Villagrá, "With gallant spirit they did promenade / The roofs and lofty terraces."[14] They were just as capable, after all, of dropping a heavy rock on an attacker's head as was the old woman of Acoma. This time, however, the danger passed.

At Acoma Zaldívar's clever strategy leveled the battlefield. As most of the Spaniards charged toward the base of the main trail up, drawing defenders to the mesa's edge above them, a dozen men, including Zaldívar himself and Captain Villagrá, scaled the less sheer, broken north end unopposed, taking cover behind the weather-worn rock formations. Volleys from their harquebuses turned back Acomas who sought to dislodge them. They fought till dark, then maintained their position all night long, shaking the Indians' confidence.

Other Spaniards gained the height. Carnage raged throughout the twenty-third, heightened by two small, swivel-mounted cannons loaded and reloaded with shot. Surrender appeared imminent, yet another night passed. Keeping up the siege on the third day, Zaldívar spurned a peace offering of turkeys and blankets. Finally, on January 25, the feast of the Conversion of Saint Paul, as attackers began herding Acomas

Acoma Pueblo, aerial view, *New Mexico Magazine* (December 1957).
Courtesy Palace of the Governors (MNM/DCA), no. 58320.

into a kiva under arrest, vicious fighting broke out again, and
Spaniards set what they could of the pueblo ablaze. Emerging
out of the choking smoke and confusion, some five hundred to
six hundred Acoma survivors, many of them women clutching
their children, clambered down under guard, bearing stupefied
witness to the Spaniards' improbable victory. The Franciscans
of New Mexico, recognizing the foundational import of this
singular event, adopted the Conversion of the Apostle as the
banner of their ministry to the Pueblo Indians.

Zaldívar's men marched the stumbling column of Acoma prisoners back eastward to the Rio Grande and then north upriver. Bystanders in other pueblos through which they passed may have felt less compassion than fear. Like the strong gateway pueblo of Pecos to the east, Acoma had lorded over its neighbors from its unassailable perch in the west. The people of both pueblos had earned reputations as bullies. Based on what other Pueblo people had conveyed to the Spaniards, Coronado's chronicler had characterized Acoma's two hundred warriors as "marauders feared throughout the land."[15] Having fought against them, Captain Villagrá testified that the Acomas "wanted nothing more than to kill all the Spaniards in the army, and after disposing of them to kill the Indians at the pueblos of Zía, Santo Domingo, and San Juan Bautista" for harboring the invaders.[16]

The notorious trial that shook the Pueblo world in 1599, and reverberated again four centuries later, took place at the centrally located Keresan pueblo the Spaniards had named Santo Domingo, forty miles south of San Juan Bautista. Governor Oñate presided. The Acomas' court-appointed Spanish defense attorney pled that not all the prisoners were present at Juan de Zaldívar's death. Neither, as an uncivilized people, did they understand Spanish law. Be that as it may, came the response, had their representatives not sworn in due form obedience as subjects of Felipe II? As a lesson to all residents of the Kingdom and Provinces of New Mexico, Pueblos and Spaniards alike, the Acoma prisoners must be made an example.

Acoma men who appeared older than twenty-five, the full legal age under Spanish law, would have one foot severed, then be bound to twenty years of personal servitude. Males twelve through twenty-four and females over twelve would serve without mutilation for twenty years. Two Hopi men who allegedly had fought alongside the Acomas would lose their right hand and be freed to convey this message to their people.

The crier droned on, echoed by interpreter Tomás. Acoma children under twelve the governor declared innocent of their parents' crimes. The girls he entrusted to fray Alonso Martínez, the Franciscan superior. (Years later, Captain Villagrá testified that he had accompanied sixty to seventy of these girls to Mexico City, where they were distributed among convents.)[17] The governor put the boys in Vicente de Zaldívar's charge. And finally, the old and infirm he sent to fellow Keresan-speaking pueblos with orders to care for them but not to let them go. The throng of Acoma slaves, whom the governor distributed among his men, surely strained housing at San Juan Bautista.

Dismemberment, a barbaric penalty routinely imposed by "civilized" Europeans, unquestionably struck fear into those who viewed the result. So, too, did the mere threat of it. Following the Spanish victory at Acoma, certainly a signal deterrent, why would Oñate not have acted upon the advice he gave to Vicente de Zaldívar, to demonstrate royal clemency and show mercy? After all, a slave with only one foot was of little value. The trial record does, however, contain a methodical note that the sentence was executed in Santo Domingo and other pueblos, "where the Indians whose hands and feet were to be cut off were punished on different days."[18] But just how was this intentionally harsh sentence actually carried out? In what way were the prisoners punished? There are no further details. Did armed Spaniards repeatedly gather the onlookers, raise high the sword or ax, then on cue have the Franciscans intercede, as Oñate had prescribed to Zaldívar? This was conquest theater, performed time and again throughout the Americas.

Another brief mention in the documents is ambiguous. Its author, twenty-five-year-old Ginés de Herrera Horta, arrived in the colony late in 1600 with viceregal orders to investigate Oñate's administration. The governor would have none of it, refusing to honor the viceroy's commission to Herrera. Hence, after listening in secret to the anti-Oñate vitriol of unhappy friars and colonists, the investigator left New Mexico in March

1601, having stayed only three or four months. Back in Mexico City, Herrera charged that Oñate had grossly mismanaged the colony. In his critical account of the Acoma battle and trial, he affirmed that Acoma men and women over eighteen or nineteen were serving twenty-year terms as slaves. "Others were maimed by having their feet cut off." Then, without clarifying which category, Herrera claimed that he "saw some of them at the said camp. He was told that most of the slaves had run away, that they had tried to reestablish the pueblo," a remarkable project for one-footed men.[19] Few, it seems, served Spaniards long enough to gain their freedom twenty years later in 1619.

Veteran Captain Luis de Gasco Velasco despised Oñate. Writing to the viceroy from San Gabriel in March 1601, he charged bluntly that "twenty-four Indians had their feet cut off as punishment; all those more than twenty years of age were taken as slaves; those younger were put under surveillance for twenty years. I assure your lordship that it was pitiful."[20] Both Gasco and Herrera wanted to defame Oñate. Although their testimony taken together sounds conclusive, passing mention of a one-footed Acoma slave in the subsequent record would help resolve any doubt, and no such mention is known to exist. Spaniards may indeed have performed the maimings, but a close reading of the documents raises reasonable doubt.[21]

As for Villagrá, whose missing sequel would also likely resolve any such doubt, he departed New Mexico in the spring of 1599. With him went Father Martínez, the captive Acoma girls, and Oñate's dispatches for the viceroy. A year later, Villagrá meant to rejoin Governor Oñate. Yet at the encampment of reinforcements for New Mexico in the valley of San Bartolomé, before marching northward in early September 1600, Captain Villagrá stumbled. In command of one of the companies, he got crosswise with Oñate's major financial sponsor. Whatever the specifics, charges ensued. Villagrá was said to be "rebellious and disobedient."[22] To avoid arrest, he sought asylum in a nearby Franciscan convento. Whether the fighting poet ever caught up with the New Mexico reinforcements or simply pursued his career elsewhere is uncertain.

To reward Villagrá's loyalty, whether he was present for the required five years or not, Governor Oñate bestowed upon him in 1603 the title hidalgo.[23] A veteran of the colony's first turbulent year, Gaspar Pérez de Villagrá had devoted little time to getting to know the Pueblo Indians. His epic portrayed them as classic pagans, worthy adversaries for Spaniards to conquer, bring to civil order, and teach to love God. In his mind, the miraculous Spanish victory of 1599 had been no accident.

Amid the chaos of the Acomas' surrender, Villagrá provided a script for selected survivors. Who, they asked in sullen earnest, was that invincible Spaniard, tall, bald, with long white beard? Astride a white horse, wielding his terrible broadsword, he had with him "a beauteous maid, / More beautiful than the sun or the heavens."[24] None other than Santiago, James the Greater, warrior saint of all Spain, accompanied by the Blessed Virgin Mary, had assured the Spaniards' triumph. And so, warned the poet, let the Pueblo peoples beware their return.

The pivotal battle at Acoma early in 1599 had assured the survival of Juan de Oñate's enterprise of New Mexico, though not its happiness. While the colonists insisted on prospecting for precious minerals, negative assay reports repeatedly disappointed them. Drought conditions and food shortages persisted. Relations with the Pueblo Indians remained tense. Yet reports reaching Spanish royal authorities in Mexico City and Madrid read like fantasy.

In 1605 Miguel de Cervantes saw published in Spain his *El ingenioso hidalgo don Quijote de la Mancha*. That same year in Mexico City, Viceroy Juan de Mendoza y Luna, the marqués de Montesclaros, writing to King Felipe III about Oñate's self-proclaimed kingdom of New Mexico, lamented, "I cannot help but inform your majesty that this conquest is becoming a

fairy tale. If those who write the reports imagine that they are
believed by those who read them, they are greatly mistaken."

That particular and grandiose fancy of Spaniards to perform
daring feats against all odds, so keenly satirized by Cervantes,
lived on in New Mexico. Don Quijote de la Mancha and
don Juan de Oñate drank from the same cup. "There is no
end to this business," fumed Montesclaros, "because they keep
expanding it by passing from one undertaking to another."[25]

Oñate, desperate to salvage his sinking colony, had picked
his way westward beyond the Zuni and Hopi pueblos, diago-
nally across present-day Arizona, down the Colorado River, to
a beach at the head of the Gulf of California. His ritual act of
possession in early 1605 echoed the behavior of don Quijote.
"Fully dressed and armed, with a shield on his arm and sword
in hand," recalled a Franciscan thirty years later, "he gallantly
waded into the water up to his waist, slashing the water with
his sword and declaring, 'I take possession of this sea and har-
bor in the name of the king of Spain, our lord.'"[26]

Oñate's chaplain at the time, a friar known for his gift of
languages, interpreted what he believed a loquacious Indian
was telling him by gesture, pantomime, and lines in the sand.
Strange beings lived along the lower Colorado. One tribe had
huge ears that dragged the ground. Another bounded along
on only one foot (perhaps a faint echo of Oñate's sentence six
years earlier). Others slept underwater or in trees or existed
solely on the smell of food, having no anuses. "Not far from
this nation there was another one, he told us, whose men
had virile members so long that they wound them four times
around the waist, and in the act of copulation the man and
woman were far apart." Pondering God's countless marvels,
the Franciscan convinced himself that He could indeed have
made such creatures. Furthermore, certain books told of
such and "even greater monstrosities, things of great amaze-
ment."[27] Viceroy Montesclaros scoffed.

The joy occasioned on Christmas Eve, 1600, at San Juan Bautista by the arrival of reinforcements had drifted off like smoke. Seventy-odd heads of household and their families and servants—a couple hundred people at least—had added a measure of security but also more mouths to feed. At least their coming satisfied Oñate's contractual obligation to outfit and transport to New Mexico two hundred soldier-colonists.

Anticipating the new arrivals, colonists of the first wave along with the few Acoma slaves who had not run away began renovating the mostly abandoned winter pueblo of Yunque, across the Rio Grande a quarter mile west of Ohkay Owingeh. They added familiar European floor-level doorways, even a few windows, and inside, raised cobblestone hearths for cooking. Another innovation, later mistaken as pre-Spanish, intruded gracefully on the built landscape: dome-shaped outdoor ovens for baking bread and pastries from the wheat the Spaniards had begun growing. They called their new headquarters San Gabriel. This early spatial division—Pueblos in Ohkay Owingeh, Spaniards in San Gabriel—reflected the Spanish notion of a republic of Indians and a republic of Spaniards. It eased tensions but failed to stanch the colonists' gripes. They cursed the bedbugs and lice, the cottonwood smoke that burned their eyes, the sickness and hunger of their children. "Eight months of winter," they muttered, "and four of hell."[28]

They knew by the Pueblos' reluctance to share dwindling reserves of corn that less rain than usual had fallen in recent years, severely limiting crop growth. Yet none knew how bad things really were. Oñate had chanced to launch his colonial migration into the American Southwest during the final decade of the most intense drought in a thousand years. Beginning in the 1560s, it had lasted two generations, long enough for the native peoples to adjust to thinner margins. Most Spaniards, however, did not care to adjust. And their complaint about eight months of winter was prophetic. The seventeenth century in New Mexico was unusually and over-whelmingly cold, a North American counterpart of northern Europe's "Little Ice Age."[29]

The governors who succeeded Oñate, hardly an exemplary lot themselves, often spoke ill of the kingdom's low-life colonists. Already in 1600, the roster of reinforcements reflected the lessening appeal of New Mexico, although the list did include the proper doña Francisca Galindo, wife of a captain from Castile. The couple's eighteen-year-old son was among Oñate's original colonists. Anticipating their reunion, doña Francisca suffered the endless jolting north, comforted by the knowledge that her crimson taffeta bedspread trimmed with lace lay folded in one of the trunks containing her satin and velvet dresses, hoopskirts, pearl headdress, silver spoons, "and many other things for the adornment of women and the home."[30]

In contrast, Isabel de Olvera, a resolute mulatta emigrant, secured certification attested by three witnesses because, in her words, "I . . . have reason to fear that I may be annoyed by some individuals, since I am a mulatto, and it is proper to protect my rights in such an eventuality by an affidavit showing that I am a free woman, unmarried, the legitimate daughter of Hernando, a negro, and an Indian named Madalena . . . that I am free and not bound by marriage or slavery."[31] As the century wore on, those tough settlers who stayed, raised children, and made New Mexico their home bid welcome to fewer and fewer refined doña Franciscas and more rugged Isabels, along with their male counterparts.

Doña Francisca hardly unpacked. Having experienced firsthand the rudeness and uncertainty of life at San Gabriel, her husband joined a cabal of six or eight other leading citizens intent on returning to New Spain. Recurring resistance from the distant Salinas pueblos, perceived as an immediate threat to the colony, strengthened their resolve.

Residing in the Estancia Basin with its salt flats, roughly 130 miles south of San Gabriel and east of the Rio Grande, these reluctant, Piro-speaking, so-called Jumanos had from the start begrudged Oñate's levies of corn and mantas (the Pueblos' emblematic cotton blankets about four feet square). Evidently, leaders at Cueloce, their largest town (today's Gran Quivira in Salinas Pueblo Missions National Monument), had claimed poverty in mid-1599. Rather than bread, they handed Vicente de Zaldívar stones instead. Informed of their defiance, Governor Oñate spurred south to confront them. Although details are sketchy and at variance, Oñate's troops apparently set fire to a corner of the pueblo, killed several Indians, and hanged two alleged war chiefs along with an offending interpreter. Months later, word reached San Gabriel that these stubborn Jumanos had slain two Spanish travelers and were now inciting a general Pueblo uprising. Worried colonists assembled in a town meeting and expressed their dismay.

Again, Zaldívar got the call. Again, conflicting details cloud the event. The Spanish force met and drove a diverse front of Indians back on Cueloce, where, according to Zaldívar's service record, the siege lasted five days and five nights, until his own "clever stratagem of taking control of their water supply" broke the defenders' spirit.[32] Zaldívar, wounded in action, boasted that he released the many prisoners and left the Jumanos grateful and submissive. As usual, someone else told a different story. Smuggling a letter to the viceroy from San Gabriel in March 1601, Captain Luis Gasco de Velasco, Oñate's archcritic, reported that Zaldívar and his men "killed more than nine hundred Indians, burned and leveled their pueblo, and took more than two hundred prisoners, who ran away a few days later."[33] The encounter must have been bloody, but the Jumanos, busy traders on the southeast fringe of the Pueblo world, did not go away. Their punishment, however, gave the knightly Oñate leave to resume his questing.

On June 23, 1601, eve of his saint's day, the Spanish governor led forth more than seventy chosen men-at-arms, hundreds of spare horses and mules, eight wagons of provisions, and four artillery pieces, along with essential scouts, herders, cooks, and other hands. While the Great Plains beckoned their miniature procession into the rising sun, consuming them for months, colonists left behind at San Gabriel quarreled.

Some questioned the governor's competence. Beset by disappointments and increasingly given to dark moods and rash outbreaks, Oñate appeared unstable. Was it not true that he had gone to the tent of an estranged captain with murder in his eye and delivered the final sword thrust himself? Few doubted that their governor had condoned Vicente de Zaldívar's ambush and disposal of another dissenting captain, a married father of five. Marshaling their accusations, trusted captains and most of the Franciscans argued fiercely that higher service to God and king demanded the abandonment of New Mexico. Others, fewer in number but equally impassioned, wanted to postpone any decision until the governor's return. The subsequent vote doomed Oñate's kingdom.

In early October 1601, observing the departure of a hastily formed, grim-faced stream of Spanish families, two-thirds or more of the colony—perhaps four hundred men, women, and children—the Pueblos may not have understood. Were the intruders withdrawing permanently, as had every previous Spanish entrada? That question hung in the air for several years. Returning to San Gabriel in November, weary and without gain, Governor Oñate called for the traitors' heads. But they had eluded his grasp, reaching Santa Bárbara in Nueva Vizcaya ahead of the pursuing Vicente de Zaldívar. Vastly conflicting reports crossed the desks of viceregal authorities in Mexico City, who chose neither to prosecute the mutinous colonists, considering them civilians rather than military deserters, nor to force their return to New Mexico. Thwarted, Zaldívar went on to the capital in person to press his uncle's case before the viceroy. When that official briefed his successor in 1603, flood control in the Valley of Mexico remained the high priority, while New Mexico's fate resided far down the list.

The cultured Viceroy marqués de Montesclaros, who wrote to the king about Oñate's folly late in October 1605, warned Felipe III, "When we least expect it, your majesty will be obliged to support something that is of no benefit to you, at incredible cost." The viceroy would act no further in the matter without specific orders from the crown.[34]

Oñate saved them the trouble. He resigned. Writing from San Gabriel in August 1607, the undone proprietor laid his lack of success at the king's feet. Since his majesty "has failed to support this undertaking as its importance demands," Oñate saw no alternative to surrendering his New Mexico estate to the crown. He and his family circle of investors had expended more than six hundred thousand pesos. The remaining colonists were "as exhausted, hard pressed, and in need of help as I am helpless to furnish it." They would hang on until the end of June 1608, after which he would release them. It infuriated Oñate that the mutinous colonists had gone unpunished, only to keep vilifying his conquest from wherever they had settled.

Like don Quijote, Oñate lamented the shortsightedness of other mortals. How could they abandon the enterprise, just when reports were "most promising and encouraging"? Would His Most Catholic Majesty truly turn his back on "the addition of great and rich provinces, which according to our information, are at our threshold"?

Lastly, Oñate appealed on religious grounds, presenting the crown with a dilemma. If every Spaniard withdrew from New Mexico, surely the more than six hundred Christian Indians would revert at once to the devil's idolatrous grasp. For the sake of their souls, should not these converts be removed to New Spain? But even he recognized the risk. If their Christian brothers and sisters were abducted, the remaining Pueblo Indians would never again submit to baptism. Worse, "seeing how few of us are left for this task," they would fight to prevent such an exodus.

In the end, the Kingdom and Provinces of New Mexico brought don Juan de Oñate to his knees. He could only repeat the lament of its every previous would-be conqueror: "What we have thus far discovered is nothing but poverty."[35]

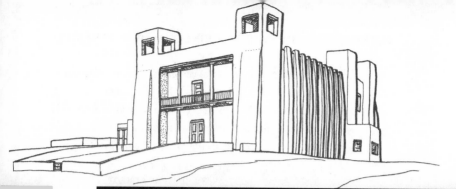

3 A Franciscan City of God on the Rio Grande, 1610s–1640s

Born of a deeply spiritual family in the mountain town of Ágreda in Spain, eight-year-old María Coronel on Christmas night offered herself to God. Eight years later, God spoke to María's mother in a vision, inspiring the family to dissolve their civil relations, turn their home into a convent, and all become Franciscans.

Tormented by her passions, the young nun anguished over the countless peoples of the New World who did not yet know her God. It seemed terribly wrong to María that their conversion depended solely on male missionaries. So God—she never understood how—took her up miraculously and flew her hundreds of times to preach among native peoples in their own languages and to instill in them a thirst for baptism. Franciscans in New Mexico swore that Jumano Indians, heartened by a mysterious sky-borne lady in blue, flocked to their missions begging to be baptized.

An object of ridicule and awe in Spain, María de Jesús implored God to withhold His special gift of bilocation, and three years later He did. The prepossessing nun went on thereafter to serve as abbess of her convent, to channel an autobiography of the Blessed Virgin Mary, and to correspond intimately with the king of Spain, Felipe IV. Investigated by the Inquisition in 1650, she

convinced its officials of the genuineness of her miraculous
experiences. Although physically never leaving her convent,
Mother María de Jesús de Ágreda, a woman, actively
participated in the Christian conversion of the Indians of
North America, emboldening thereby the men in charge.

BIOGRAPHICAL SKETCH OF SOR MARÍA
DE JESÚS DE ÁGREDA (1602–1665)

Poverty suited the Franciscans. Members of the mendicant
Order of Friars Minor founded in thirteenth-century Europe
by Saint Francis of Assisi, Franciscan missionaries throughout Spain's empire received subsidies from the royal treasury. Although Franciscans had accompanied earlier entradas,
the friars who came with Oñate saw the world of the Pueblo
Indians as a clean slate. Sharing the medieval worldview of the
first Franciscans who appeared among the teeming populations of central New Spain in the 1520s, they would do battle
with the devil and win the hearts of the native people. As their
exclusive ministry unfolded in the distant north, they would
be far removed from meddling bishops or competing religious
orders. The only Roman Catholic priests in the kingdom, they
envisioned a Franciscan City of God on the Rio Grande.

None of the several hundred Franciscan friars who served
in colonial New Mexico was born in the colony. All were
Spaniards either from the mother country (*peninsulares*) or
from some part of the Spanish Indies (criollos). The former at
times acted superior, and the two groups competed. Because
none of the friars could be ordained a Roman Catholic priest
until his mid-twenties after years of study in Spain or Mexico,
not one grew up among the Pueblo peoples as did the children of the colonists. While most were priests authorized to
administer the sacraments of the Church, a few came as assist-
ing lay brothers with trades such as carpentry, horticulture, or
medicine.

The great majority of New Mexico's missionary friars were humane souls who carried their lonely crosses with devotion and charity, if at times clumsily. Some struggled to establish any rapport with their Pueblo congregations, while others relied on their charisma or ingenuity to endear themselves to the native people. A few proved woefully deviant, sexually or physically abusing their charges. A missionary's effectiveness depended more on his persuasive personality, creativity, and willingness to learn from his neophytes than on formal knowledge of Christian doctrine. Collectively, the friars' insistence that New Mexico existed solely to save Pueblo souls clashed with the Spanish governors and colonists who vied for Pueblo labor, land, and loyalty. As a result, the Pueblo peoples received notoriously mixed messages.

Fray Alonso de Benavides, the New Mexico friars' superior in the late 1620s, became their apologist, providing in his writings not only a sampling of his own millennial religious fervor but also considerable ethnographic data about the Pueblo Indians. But reader beware. Because Benavides exaggerated in an effort to gain further royal and ecclesiastical support for the Franciscans' ministry in New Mexico, one must sort out rhetorical propaganda from simple observations. At the outset, for example, Benavides boasted that by the late 1620s the friars had "converted" more than five hundred thousand Indians in New Mexico—a clear impossibility. Yet if one adds up the numbers of "baptized souls" he estimated in each of the Pueblo communities, a sum less than fifty thousand complements other documentation.

While condemning as idolatrous, pagan, and diabolical everything he associated with the Pueblos' kachina religion— kivas, stone shrines, feathered prayer sticks and painted "idols" of wood or rock, offerings of sacred cornmeal, tests of endurance for entry into secret societies, and the ubiquitous native priests or "sorcerers"—Benavides nevertheless set down invaluable early written descriptions. He mentioned divisions of labor among Pueblo women and men, the former constructing the walls of their houses and presiding over life in the home and the latter weaving, farming, and hunting. Occasionally, Benavides approved of native ways, as in the case of Pueblo monogamy.[1]

Rearranging his New Mexico notes and revising his published *Memorial* of 1630 for the pope, the tireless Franciscan appeared to contradict himself. Proclaiming on the one hand the wondrous acceptance of Christianity among the Pueblo Indians, he could not resist eulogizing his Franciscan brethren murdered by these same people. One wonders if he saw the irony.

The Pueblos, who, to fray Alonso's mind, "had lived in the darkness of their idolatry from the time of the Flood," by the 1620s had seen the light. "Once the Indians have received holy baptism," he assured the pontiff, "they become so domestic that they live with great propriety. Hardly do they hear the bell calling to mass before they hasten to the church with all the cleanliness and neatness they can."[2] At the Zuni pueblo of Hawikuh, however, on a Sunday in February 1632, Benavides reported, when their impatient young missionary called "the converted and baptized Indians" to Mass, "they all rose in rebellion and attacked him in a body, smashing his head with their clubs in order to prevent him from preaching the word of God to them any longer, and they inflicted many cruelties on him." Five days later, another friar, who had earlier survived being hit over the head and dragged around the plaza of Picuris Pueblo, appeared at Zuni, and they killed him too.

Another older, more mature Franciscan who with several companions had volunteered for service on the Hopi mesas a rugged 250 miles west of Santa Fe also died a martyr. According to Benavides, this friar learned enough of the Hopi language to impress and convert many of the natives. Challenged to a test by hostile Hopi headmen at the pueblo of Awátovi, the friar was reported to have cured a Hopi boy blind since birth (here Benavides alluded to the gospel precedent of faith healing the

A Franciscan friar. After Diego Valadés, *Rhetórica Christiana* (1579); redrawn by Jerry L. Livingston. From Kessell, *Kiva, Cross, and Crown*.

blind), thereby winning over the crowd and exasperating the native priests. Since they dared not dispose of him openly, they allegedly resorted instead to poison.

In contrast, on the lonely rock of Acoma, fray Juan Ramírez had been well received, subsequently supervising construction of a church still considered miraculous. Even in the early twenty-first century, Acoma guides tell the story of Father Ramírez's arrival in 1629. Children, sighting a strange figure below, began throwing rocks. As more people gathered, an Acoma mother lost her grip on a baby girl, who plummeted down the cliff and was caught by the friar. Father Benavides recorded a different version. Already received peaceably among the Acomas, Ramírez got word one night that "sorcerers" had bewitched a baby girl at the breast who was gasping for life. Hastening to the scene, the friar besought the mother, not yet a Christian, to let him baptize her daughter. In so doing, "scarcely had she received the waters of holy baptism when she became well and healthy."[3]

Undeterred by the risks, the Franciscans had cleverly engineered their City of God on the Rio Grande. Calculating that Oñate's small count of several hundred baptized Pueblo Indians would not convince the crown, they swore one year later "that more than seven thousand had been baptized and so many others were ready to accept baptism" that New Mexico must not be abandoned.[4] Their stratagem worked. Don Luis de Velasco, the viceroy who had negotiated Oñate's original contract in 1595, was back for a second term. Neither he nor New Mexico's failed proprietor looked as foolish in light of so bountiful a harvest of souls. Yet Velasco had no illusions. "They say that the land is suitable for farming, but such distant discoveries, without gold or silver, will be expensive and difficult to maintain, for no one comes to the Indies to plow and sow, but only to eat and loaf."[5] And who, now, fancied New Mexico as a place to eat and loaf?

The prospect of favorable mineral assays in the future, vague suggestions of foreign rivals, and a reluctance to give up territory once conquered all figured in the crown's decision. Baptisms justified it. Straightaway, the Spanish government, at an unforeseen net cost of more than two million pesos throughout the seventeenth century, committed to underwrite a Christian ministry to the Pueblo Indians of New Mexico. Warding off possible encroachments by Dominicans, Jesuits, and bishops, the Franciscans, meantime, assured themselves a unique spiritual monopoly. Throughout the seventeenth century and for a good part of the eighteenth, they remained New Mexico's only Roman Catholic priests.

Early in 1610, a salaried governor, don Pedro de Peralta, relieved Oñate, who had resigned three years earlier but stayed on awaiting a successor. Peralta laid out a new capital at Santa Fe (a site upon which a Spanish settlement may have evolved several years earlier), symbolizing the changed status of the Kingdom and Provinces of New Mexico from a proprietorship funded primarily by Oñate's private consortium to a crown colony financed by the royal treasury. The stone- and mud-built complex (known as the *casas reales*) that rose on the north side of Santa Fe's plaza, eventually to two stories in places, housed offices, a jail, and the so-called palace of the governors, seat of royal authority in the kingdom.

The ceremonial reception at Santa Fe early in 1626 of Father Benavides and a dozen more Franciscans bespoke further change for both Pueblos and Spaniards. Benavides came fully invested. To officials of church and state in New Mexico's capital, he presented his credentials not only as *custos,* or prelate and superior of missionaries in the field, but also as local agent of the Inquisition. In the former capacity, he would greatly stimulate Indian missions. In the latter, he heralded to non-Indian colonists the consequences of unacceptable behavior such as bigamy, blasphemy, practicing heathen or Jewish rites, pacts with the devil, witchcraft, and solicitation of sex by a priest in the confessional. At the same time, broadly defining heresy to include lack of respect for representatives of the Church and utterance of evil-sounding words, he armed the friars with a formidable weapon to use against perceived adversaries. Indians alone, considered minors in Spanish law because of their presumed lack of sophistication, were exempt from prosecution by the Inquisition.[6]

As superior, Father Benavides listened to the hopes and fears of the fourteen Franciscans already laboring in the kingdom. Able, forthright fray Andrés Juárez (or Suárez) had come in 1612. Juárez had enlisted in Spain as a musketeer among thirty men recruited for New Mexico by Alonso de Oñate, Juan's brother. A native of Fuente Ovejuna in the province of Córdoba, he disembarked at Veracruz in the summer of 1604.[7] What changed his destiny as a soldier-colonist and scattered the rest of the recruits is not known, although continuing government investigations of Oñate's conquest may have dried up funds for the group's trek northward. Shelving his musket, Juárez entered religious life at the Franciscans' Convento Grande in Mexico City in 1608 at the age of twenty-six.[8]

By 1622 Father Juárez had taken over the eastern gateway pueblo of Pecos. He cannot have known the history, but sometime around 1450 (just before Christopher Columbus's birth in Genoa), the native people of the Pecos area, living then in rambling, connected, one-story dwellings, committed themselves to a monumental community building project: a single defensible structure large enough to accommodate everyone in the pueblo, some two thousand adults and children.

Juárez and his escort, having trailed over the pass east of Santa Fe, glimpsed the formidable gray-brown pueblo from a good way off. It rose to four and five stories at the wider north end of a rocky ridge in a mountain valley of brick red soil. The scattered piñon and juniper forest one sees today had been cleared for miles around for fuel and roofing poles. The air was clear. At an elevation near seven thousand feet, the growing season between last and first freezes averaged only a hundred days, barely long enough for corn to ripen—so prayers were constant. The Pecos River flowed swiftly a mile to the east, then bent southeastward to skirt a massive, multicolored mesa before breaking free toward the plains. To the new missionary, it seemed that the wind, which prevailed from the west, was always blowing. Hardly ever did the clouds stand still.

Both blessing and curse, location more than any other factor determined the prominence of Pecos Pueblo and in the end its decline. The people of Pecos guarded the natural route of trade and war between the agricultural Pueblo Indians of the Rio Grande valley and the buffalo-hunting nomads of the Great Plains. Although it was not a center of cultural innovation like Chaco Canyon or Mesa Verde, the fortress-pueblo of Pecos nevertheless dominated the frontier between two worlds. As gatekeepers, the pueblo's occupants profited from the export of crop surpluses, cloth, ceramics, and turquoise, as well as the import of buffalo hides, tanned skins, dried meat, Alibates flint knives and scrapers, bow wood, and human captives. Among the most exposed of Pueblo peoples, they also suffered fearsome attacks from the plains in times of famine and war. Both commerce and war drew Spaniards.

Juárez trod softly among the Pecos. He had inherited both the start of a massive new church and the ill-feeling caused by his predecessor. The previous padre had smashed Pecos "idols" and clashed with a traditional Pueblo religious leader named Mosoyo. Several foot-tall human figurines, unearthed by archaeologists in the twentieth century, had been carefully pieced back together by Pecos residents and hidden as sacred relics. A milder sort who immediately began learning words in their Towa language, Juárez swept the reluctant community up in his vision, vigorously renewing the ambitious building project.

At first he had only a "jacal" in which to celebrate Mass, but not half the people would fit into it. The grand permanent church would gather not only all the pueblo's two thousand souls but also the Plains Apaches who came every fall to trade and socialize. Writing from Pecos in October 1622, Juárez implored the viceroy of New Spain to provide an altarpiece featuring Nuestra Señora de los Ángeles (Our Lady of the Angels), the pueblo's patroness. Whenever an Apache entered the church, gaping in wonder at the altarpiece and begging to be baptized, His Excellency would share in the victory.

Unlike most New Mexican churches of stone, earth, and mud built right into or closely adjoining the existing pueblo fabric, the temple of Pecos would stand alone at the far southern tip of the ridge three hundred yards from the main pueblo. The plan mystified Pueblo Indians accustomed to building small rooms in horizontal layers. Raising eight- and ten-foot-thick walls straight up to a height of forty feet, enclosing so vast a vacant space in honor of the imported Christian God, evoked awe. There was little need of coercion. For three years, weather permitting, the Pecos church construction site was the best show in the colony.

Action rarely ceased. Yokes of straining oxen moved carts and sleds of boulders and field stone into position as the broad-set foundations took shape. Others, harnessed to a single axle of wagon wheels, dragged in seasoned ponderosa, spruce, or fir logs, fifty feet long and weighing as much as a ton, to be squared with adzes, planed, and decorated for roof beams. From stacks of heavy planking and poles, men lashed together scaffolding resting on putlogs sticking out from walls that mounted higher and higher with each course of adobes. Pulley blocks and ropes, likely hung from shears, hoisted finished beams into place.

Although Pueblo Indians had for centuries built with coursed earth and hand-molded mud loaves, the production of uniform, sun–dried bricks from wooden forms was an innovation. Shifts of workers dug pits in the soft black earth of a giant midden along the east side of the ridge where prevailing winds had dictated for generations the disposal of trash. Mixing the dirt with water from barrels and shoveling the mud into drying molds, they manufactured an eventual three hundred thousand adobes, roughly 20 X 9 X 3 inches and weighing forty pounds apiece. If the deep red mortar added a quarter again as much weight, the walls of the church and the adjoining one-story convento, or friar's quarters, would have weighed seventy-five hundred tons. Just south of the convento, Juárez had the Indians dig a round kivalike structure twenty-two feet across, lining it with the same adobes and mortar. This space, familiar to the Pecos people, may have served for transitional Christian instruction, part of the friar's dynamic program of evangelization.

Women, accustomed in the pre-Hispanic Pueblo world to building their families' homes onto communal structures, may at first have laid up the church walls of these heavy new blocks, but perhaps not. On this job, gender specialization may have broken down. If men constructed or helped with the walls of the huge church, women no doubt applied the yellowish-white exterior lime plaster and the interior whitewash, jobs they still perform in the pueblos today.

Pride in or resentment of the towering structure, as it slowly gained form, pervaded the pueblo. Here was power to change the landscape. Almost 150 feet long, ribbed outside with square, unevenly spaced, ground-to-roof buttresses, the monumental Pecos church proclaimed from every angle its European heritage, surely Father Juárez's intent. It was the grandest building north of New Spain.[9]

The friar's civilian partner in the project was Francisco Gómez, a native of Portugal. Gómez held the gainful Pecos encomienda, a royal grant from the governor entitling him to collect the annual tribute owed by each of the pueblo's several hundred Indian households. In return, Gómez swore to defend the colony, providing his own horses and weapons, and to promote the Christianity of his Pecos tributaries. Like all encomenderos in New Mexico, whose number the viceroy set at thirty-five, he further agreed to maintain a residence in Santa Fe. He and the others formed the officer corps of the colony's Spanish militia, composed of every able-bodied male.

An encomienda in New Mexico was by law a grant neither of labor nor of land, but of tribute, in effect a tax in goods imposed upon agricultural Indians. Nevertheless, irregular agreements were made for work in lieu of goods, and grantees sometimes illegally took up residence among their tributaries, thus customizing the system. Each Pueblo Indian household owed to its designated encomendero a standard annual tribute of one manta (the typical small Pueblo blanket) and one fanega of corn (between two and three bushels)—the cloth collected in May, the corn in October. At Pecos, with its access to the plains, Gómez willingly accepted the equivalent value in animal skins or, during years the trees produced, piñon nuts,

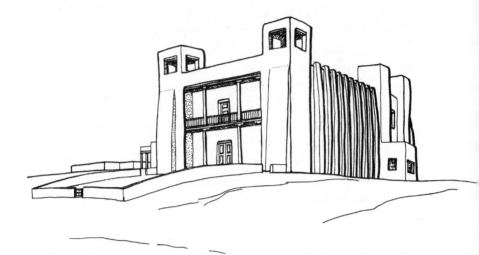

Fray Andrés Juárez's massive mission complex at Pecos, 1620s. Conjectural view by James E. Ivey. Courtesy of the artist and the National Park Service.

a commodity that sold in Mexico City for ten times its local value.[10]

Andrés Juárez and Francisco Gómez had known each other years before. As fellow recruits and shipmates, they had landed in New Spain together in 1604 with the others gathered in Spain by Alonso de Oñate. Gómez pressed on to New Mexico, married the daughter of one of the original loyal colonists, and became a leading citizen of the poor colony. His wife, Ana Robledo, was born at San Gabriel and personified the ideal Hispanic Catholic woman, not the loose sort mentioned more frequently in the documents. Doña Ana had charge of the tiny, richly adorned brocade dresses for the image of Our Lady of the Assumption, which arrived with Father Benavides aboard one of the supply wagons in 1626 and, as La Conquistadora, remains today Santa Fe's most cherished religious icon.[11]

As sargento mayor, Francisco Gómez had commanded the caravan escort from Mexico City that brought Father Benavides, himself a native of the Portuguese Azores (between 1580 and

1640, Spain ruled the Portuguese Empire). The two men got on well. In Santa Fe on the New Mexico friars' principal feast day of the Conversion of Saint Paul, January 25, 1626, at Benavides's request Francisco Gómez led the procession carrying the standard of the Mexican Inquisition. (Years later, Gómez would be implicated posthumously as a crypto-Jew.)

The grand Pecos church of fray Andrés Juárez and Francisco Gómez did not survive the Pueblo Revolt of 1680, and the words Father Benavides used to describe it seem greatly exaggerated. "A very magnificent church of unique architecture and beauty," insisted Benavides' 1630 *Memorial*.[12] Elaborating in 1634, he called it a "church of peculiar construction and beauty, very spacious, with room for all the people of the pueblo."[13] The ruins of a smaller, simpler eighteenth-century structure built right on top of its fallen predecessor had never measured up to Benavides' claims. Not until 1967, when National Park Service archaeologist Jean M. Pinkley troweled up against the foundations of the massive structure, was the friar at last vindicated.[14]

Neither did Father Benavides exaggerate when he told how avidly Pecos men had taken to carpentry, "since their minister brought them masters of this craft to teach them."[15] The same 1604 document listing New Mexico recruits Juárez and Gómez included a senior master carpenter, who applied to bring his family.[16] They too may have reached the colony. It is also likely that the missionary and encomendero hired a professional master builder, the sort who went where the work was, then moved on. As an intentional by-product of the project, Pecos became colonial New Mexico's carpenter pueblo. Colonists in need of lumber, doors, or a bed, or the missionary who wanted carved corbels and beams to embellish a new church ceiling, made arrangements at Pecos. As members of carpentry crews, some of the pueblo's men enjoyed unusual mobility. It is likely, for example, that Pecos carpenters, using saws, draw knives, planes, augers, and a wide array of chisels, prepared and carved the beams and much of the woodwork of the stone mission churches in the dry Salinas province to the south. El Carpintero, conspicuous as a Pecos leader in 1660, embodied the pueblo's pride in this trade introduced by the industrious Father Juárez.

Acknowledging his successes, Juárez's superiors left him at Pecos for thirteen years, longer than any other missionary in the pueblo's history. He was a stabilizing influence on the colony's eastern flank, ministering both to the Pecos and to their Plains Apache trade partners, who made him an honorary tribal elder. Juárez also learned the pueblo's Towa language, a rare accomplishment among New Mexico's Franciscan missionaries.[17]

Criticized time and again throughout the colonial period for not mastering Pueblo languages or publishing a single vocabulary list, the friars were hardly to blame. The kingdom possessed no native lingua franca like the Aztecs' Nahuatl in central New Spain. And although the Franciscans of New Mexico debated their policy—recognizing the folly, unintended hilarity, or mischief as Pueblo Indian interpreters rendered the friars' sermons or their admonitions in the confessional—they rarely assigned a missionary to a pueblo for more than three years, hardly enough time to master the intricacies of a Pueblo language.

Fray Andrés Juárez's unusual knowledge of Towa and his longevity at Pecos cut two ways. For generations, relying on their own interwoven family, kinship, and kiva relationships to control the internal dissensions endemic to walled communities, the Pecos had held together. Nevertheless, existing at the gateway between Pueblo and Plains peoples required a delicate balancing act. Tensions existed between traditional farming "summer people" and the hunting, trading, and warring "winter people." The latter, having long dealt with outsiders, gravitated more readily into the Spanish sphere, while Mosoyo, the native sacred leader who objected to the destruction of

Pecos "idols," and those who sympathized with him resisted and took the old ways underground.

The long-serving Juárez actually caused an intramural migration, separating Pecos architecturally into two distinct communities. Converts who participated in the new Christian ceremonialism or pursued carpentry flocked toward the mission, dismantling a large section of the original, Contact-period pueblo and rebuilding one long houseblock and then another in closer proximity to the soaring church. Until recently, archaeologists were perplexed by tree ring dates from these structures, which seemed much too early, and only of late recognized that pro-Spanish Pecos families were actually salvaging old timbers as well as masonry from the north pueblo to build their new homes.[18]

Such physical partition of Christian converts and nonconverts also took place in other close-built contiguous pueblos where certain sections, or quarters, became identified with factions. Two and a half centuries later, Anglo-American reformers would label them Progressives and Conservatives. At Pecos, the separation was plain for all to see. Unwittingly, Father Juárez had hardened the Pecos people's divisions. Then he left them.

⸺◆⸺

A shuffling of missionaries in 1634 finally transported Juárez from his longtime peripheral posting among the Pecos to the smaller Tewa-speaking pueblo of Nambe, two hours by horse or mule north of Santa Fe. With an ear to the capital, Juárez could hear Spaniards bellowing at Spaniards over what was best for the Pueblo Indians. What New Mexico's governors, bent on personal profit, proposed as legitimate use of native human resources the Franciscans labeled abuse. What the friars, with their easier access to Pueblo land and labor and their ever-increasing flocks of sheep, demanded in the name of Christian salvation, the governor and ambitious colonists saw as unfair and overprotective. The shouting grew louder in the late 1630s and early 1640s, reaching a crescendo over the outrages of a baldly avaricious governor.

The entire colony knew he was coming. Every three years, the lumbering mission supply caravan with its dozens of heavy freight wagons and rowdy escort brought a new governor. His first duty was to conduct the residencia of his predecessor, a thirty-day review period when creditors or aggrieved subjects might present their cases against the former governor before he returned to New Spain. In 1637 the Franciscans gloated. The outgoing executive, a scourge in their eyes, was sure to be charged with exploiting native workers, disrespecting the Church, and coercing colonists to falsely malign the missionaries. But they were wrong. Evidently, the new man took a bribe, and the former governor departed unbowed.[19] Soon enough, the friars would learn the true meaning of a scourge.

Irreverent, passionate, and devoid of scruples, Luis de Rosas wrestled the kingdom to the brink of civil war. For fifteen years, he had served loyally with the Spanish army of occupation in Flanders, rising through the ranks. He had heard of New Mexico's bad reputation "for mutiny and seizure of governors," yet he likely paid a sizable sum to the crown for his appointment. Now, by God, he would make the colony pay him back.[20] The governor's two-thousand-peso annual salary hardly counted. To recover his initial investment and the 50 percent royal tax on his first year's pay (*media anata*), plus the cost of items he had purchased in New Spain for resale in the colony at inflated prices, Governor Rosas turned businessman and bully, ignoring every legal obstacle.

Intensifying the former governor's petty industries, Rosas set more and more captive Indians and prisoners to weaving local cotton and woolen shawls, stockings, and other items in a filthy Santa Fe workshop. Through his district officers, he set up cottage production of similar textile and leather goods in outlying Pueblo Indian missions over the friars' protests. The campaigns he launched against Apaches and Navajos served less to protect the colony than to add Indian men, women, and children to his holdings or to sell them at the silver boomtown of San José del Parral in Nueva Vizcaya, sixty days to the south by wagon.

As merchant and retailer, the governor gouged whomever he could. By blatantly juggling access to grants of office, land, and encomienda, he encircled himself with a corps of henchmen among the colonists and at the same time amassed a growing list of unforgiving enemies. He vilified missionaries in front of their Pueblo neophytes. And to gain the Indians' favor, he promised that he would allow them to choose their own leaders and return to their idolatrous practices.

Blustering that he was on the king's business, Governor Rosas showed up at Pecos Pueblo in the fall of 1638, accompanied by armed men and pack animals carrying crates of trade knives. The governor had learned that Pecos served as an entry point for captives and hides from the plains. But he arrived too late. The fair was over, and the Apaches had traded everything. Furious, Rosas berated the missionary, then turned on the unwell, seventy-year-old lay brother who came to help, placing him under guard "to the profound scandal of the natives."[21] By warring on Plains Apaches and taking captives at random, Rosas imperiled the flow of hides to Pecos trade fairs and thus the ability of Pecos households to pay their annual tribute.

Yet never once did Pecos encomendero Francisco Gómez, sworn to uphold the pueblo's Christianity, fault hell-bent Luis de Rosas. An unswerving partisan of every royal governor since Oñate, Gómez had his reasons. His Portuguese birth suggested possible Jewish heritage. (After their expulsion from Spain in 1492, many Jews settled in Portugal.) More recently, efforts by Portuguese nationalists to end the "Spanish captivity" of their homeland (1580–1640) had gained momentum. Gómez meant to prove his loyalty regardless, which set him at odds with his old shipmate, fray Andrés Juárez, who found fault with Rosas at every turn.

Gómez in fact took it upon himself to inform the viceroy of what, in his partisan view, the Franciscans' City of God had become. The friars were stifling the colony. They controlled everything, charged Gómez, "and they proceed without a civil judge. The ecclesiastical one they do have here is for throwing the cloak over their faults."[22] When Governor Rosas, with obvious relish, demanded that the Franciscan superior investigate the missionary at Taos Pueblo, whom the Indians had accused of "cruelty, homosexuality, and assaults on Indian women," the case went nowhere, and the friar was reassigned to Sandia Pueblo. Later, a faction of Taos Indians, supposedly emboldened by the governor's hatred of the friars, murdered the accused missionary's successor along with two Spaniards and fled to the plains. Another Franciscan died violently at Jemez under obscure circumstances, killed either by the people of the pueblo or by Navajos or Apaches.[23]

The year 1640 began badly. Stung by slaving raids on their camps, Apaches and Navajos, who had transformed themselves since Oñate's time into admirable horsemen, retaliated with lightning attacks on pueblos and Spanish ranches. The avaricious Rosas and his henchmen—whom the Franciscan superior had excommunicated from the sacraments of the Church—kept on terrorizing missionaries until in early February the prelate summoned the friars to Santo Domingo for an emergency conference. Prominent armed colonists and their retainers joined the churchmen, purportedly to protect them. Aging, ailing fray Andrés Juárez eagerly put his name to their manifesto of grievances against the heavy-handed Rosas administration. The governor declared the lot of them traitors to the crown.

That year, too, an unnamed pandemic settled over the colony, killing an estimated three thousand Pueblo people, literally decimating their population. Temperatures dropped and stayed lower than at any previous time in this cold century.

A new governor appeared in the spring of 1641, encouraging the secular foes of Rosas, who gained control of the Santa

Fe *cabildo,* or town council. When this lately installed executive suddenly dropped dead, the anti-Rosas faction pushed aside Francisco Gómez, the designated lieutenant governor, and took over the government. They immediately confined Rosas to prevent his departure before another governor conducted his *residencia.* In response, fearing that these vengeful colonists might kill him, the former governor drew up a last will and testament, along with a ranting denunciation of the Franciscan regime in New Mexico.

Every mission, alleged Rosas self-righteously, was a stock-raising and mercantile enterprise run by friars at the expense of the Pueblo Indians. "During the time I have been in these provinces they [the Franciscans] have extracted seventy-five two-and-a-half-ton wagons of goods, which from a land so poor amounts to more than extracting millions from Potosí." So much for their vows of poverty. The friars' vow of celibacy, too, according to the ex-governor, was a joke. Yet these unworthy priests regularly withheld the sacraments from him, branding him a follower of Luther and Calvin and swearing that he practiced "an abominable idolatry with a goat." Hardest to believe, these false men of God, by fortifying Santo Domingo with 73 of the colony's 120 soldier-colonists, had openly defied their king, whose authority resided in the royal governor.[24]

Rosas was right to fear for his life. His enemies set him up. Early in January 1642, amid suspicious circumstances, a colonist, accompanied by witnesses, discovered his wife under Rosas's bed. She promptly confessed. All during her husband's long absence from Santa Fe, she and Rosas had been lovers, which of course had become the talk of the town. Next, in the frigid early hours of January 25, the supposed cuckold and four masked men crept up on the house where Rosas was being held. Sword unsheathed, the shamed husband burst in and stabbed the former royal governor to death.

Matters could not rest there. Prejudiced by earlier reports against New Mexico's Franciscans and their anti-Rosas allies,

viceregal authorities moved to punish the rebellious colonists who had fortified Santo Domingo and murdered Rosas.
Secrecy prevailed. Under cover of a calming general pardon, proclaimed on Epiphany, January 6, 1643, newly arrived
Governor Alonso Pacheco de Heredia quietly gathered damning evidence. The Franciscans appeared conciliatory, absolving
and burying in the Santa Fe church the mortal remains of Luis
de Rosas. Yet by midsummer, Pacheco had justified in his own
mind the most drastic action. It stunned the colony.

On the governor's orders, in front of carefully chosen witnesses who included Francisco Gómez, executioners beheaded
in rapid succession eight well-known New Mexican soldier-
colonists, all signers of the anti–Rosas manifesto. Later the
same afternoon, Pacheco summoned the townspeople to the
plaza. Through the strong voice of Jusepe, the crier, the crowd
learned in hushed silence of the executions and of the governor's secret instructions from Mexico City. Pacheco had
Captain Antonio Baca's head nailed to the public gibbet as
a warning and again proclaimed general amnesty. Word went
out to all parts of the kingdom, including Pueblo Indian communities, that every citizen, many of whom were relatives of
the victims, must swear allegiance by rallying to the royal standard. Few could believe what had just happened.

Pueblo Indian "*caciques* and captains" also bore witness
to this dark example of Spanish justice. Spaniards had long
applied the title *cacique* (Caribbean Arawak for chief) to whomever they perceived as the paramount leader. In New Mexico,
they used the term interchangeably with native "governor,"
an office introduced by the invaders. Elected or appointed
annually, often with the missionary's assistance or interference,
Pueblo governors headed a staff of lesser officers who kept
order in the community and dealt with outsiders. These native
governors, along with Pueblo war captains, would have traveled
to Santa Fe. In contrast, the headman whom Pueblo Indians

came to call "cacique" or "inside chief," who served for life or at the pleasure of the elders and who maintained the traditional ceremonial harmony and well-being of the pueblo, would have remained within its walls.

The multipartite world of the Pueblo Indians had shuddered and contracted during the 1630s and 1640s. The number of their towns along the Rio Grande and its tributaries —bedeviled by fatal diseases, internal conflict and desertion, Apache raiding, vagaries of weather and crops, and Spanish demands—had plummeted. Where eighty separate Pueblo communities had stood during Oñate's proprietorship, and seventy during the ministry of Father Benavides, not forty remained at midcentury.

The events of the 1640s left little doubt that unrest and dissension also pervaded the Franciscans' City of God on the Rio Grande. Writing to the king in 1647, fray Andrés Juárez, by then dean of New Mexico's missionaries, despaired of the governors he had known. With only one exception he could think of, they had not supported the government-subsidized missionary initiative, but instead had tyrannized and despoiled both Pueblos and Spaniards. "May I be cursed of God," he cried out, "if they have kept a single command of Your Majesty." As a result, restive Pueblos no longer obeyed the friars. They were returning to their kachinas.[25]

A cycle of sporadic outbreaks of Pueblo Indians allied with their seminomadic trade partners against Spanish rule had begun. As Juárez composed his diatribe, to the west natives of the Jemez pueblos and Navajos plotted an uprising. When word of their alleged scheme was betrayed, the Spanish governor ordered twenty-nine of the supposed conspirators hanged. A foiled Easter Week plot in 1650, again involving Jemez in league with Keresan and southern Tiwa neighbors, envisioned Apaches driving off Spanish horses while Pueblos fell upon Spaniards at Holy Thursday services. "Many Indians were arrested from most of the pueblos of this kingdom. . . . Nine leaders were hanged and many others were sold as slaves for ten years."[26]

These occasional but brutal acts of repression, combined with the anguished abandonment of depleted communities, drove Pueblo resistance further underground. While outwardly complying, Pueblo subjects found subtle ways to keep alive traditional practices. Pueblo women potters, as they produced new forms for trade to Spaniards—soup bowls, cups with handles, and candlesticks—might still decorate them with Pueblo symbols, or the seemingly obedient Christian cross, in which they saw a bird, a dragonfly, or the morning star that shone before the dawning of a new day.

Buried from view in interior rooms that served as kivas (sometimes called *cois*), knowledgeable elders instructed young men born at the time of Father Benavides in the esoteric ways of their ancestors. Small carved and painted images of the kachinas, much like Christian crucifixes, were believed to possess power both to teach and to implement action. Spaniards derisively called them idols; much later, fascinated tourists took them for dolls. Not for another generation, when these Pueblo youths were elders themselves and when the punishing forces of earth and sky emboldened them to take vengeance unto themselves, would they discover how much they risked and hoped in common with one another.[27]

The Franciscans, meanwhile, pressed on during the 1650s, enlarging and reinforcing their Pueblo ministry. The weather warmed notably. And when toward the end of the decade "another Rosas" sought to disrupt the missionaries' regime, they summoned and readily abused the awful authority of the Mexican Inquisition.

4 A Colony of Cousins, 1630s–1660s

Until Kastera [the Spaniards] arrived, each new group in turn had come in search of a land where the people could live in their own ways, honoring their own leaders and traditions. None, before Kastera, had tried to impose its rules or its ways upon its neighbors. The Spaniards, however, came with the intent to make the region's other peoples adopt Kastera's ways and beliefs, by choice if possible, by force if necessary. They were armed, not only with formidable weapons, but also with elaborate systems designed to allow a few men to enforce their way of life rapidly on peoples far more numerous, living in a vast land. Thus, in only twenty years, a few hundred Spaniards, led by a still smaller group of officials and friars, set up a network of government that reached from Taos to Zuni, supervised the construction of churches in many of the pueblos, saw that the people of those pueblos followed Kastera's forms of worship, and established the Spanish language as one all of the region's people must learn. With a force no larger than most pueblo groups, and much smaller than some, Kastera had an impact far beyond its numbers, and far different from those who had come before.

LAURA BAYER WITH FLOYD MONTOYA
AND THE PUEBLO OF SANTA ANA, *SANTA ANA* (1994)

The first Spaniards to gawk at the dark, slow-moving, shore-less oceans of buffalo (more correctly, North American bison) called them *vacas* (cows) and the Plains Apaches who shadowed them, *vaqueros* (herders of cattle, or cowboys). The principal chronicler of the Coronado expedition never forgot his impression of buffalo bulls:

> It is amazing that at first there was not a horse that looked them in the face that did not flee from their gaze. That is because they have a wide and short face. From eye to eye it is two *palmos* across the forehead. The eyes are protuberant from the side of the head, so that when they are running in flight they can see whoever is chasing them. They have very large beards, as billy goats have. When they run away they carry the head low, the beard dragging across the ground. From the middle of the body to the rear, they are narrow-waisted with very fine, dense, and short hair, like ewes. From the waist forward the hair is very long in the manner of a raging lion. It has a great hump, larger than that of a camel. The horns are short and stout; they are exposed only a little above the hair.... They have a short tail and a small brush at the end. They carry it high when they run, in the way a scorpion does.[1]

Although a mine developer by preference, proprietor Juan de Oñate thought he might raise buffalo. Sixty years earlier, one of Coronado's captains had visualized an insatiable market for buffalo hides skillfully tanned by Plains Indians. Why should Oñate not ship hides, meat, and fat not consumed by his colonists, or drive the animals like cattle down the camino real to the mining districts of northern New Spain? Trouble was, the buffalo refused.

In October 1598 Vicente de Zaldívar and his sixty men had tried valiantly to bring back alive from the plains some of the absurd-looking beasts. For three days, they constructed a massive corral of cottonwood logs "so large and with wings

Drawing of a buffalo from the Oñate documents.

so wide that they thought they would be able to enclose ten thousand head."

The drive started well. The buffalo appeared headed for the corral when suddenly they veered round in a fury, scattering the riders, unseating some and goring their horses. There was no turning them. "This is the most stubborn and fierce animal imaginable," observed Zaldívar, "and so cunning that if you chase it, it runs, and if you stop or slow down, it stops and rolls on the ground as if it were a mule, and after this short rest it runs off again." The buffalo calves they did catch, dragging some by their tails and slinging others across horses, struggled so frantically that all died within an hour. Thus it appeared to the Spaniards that "unless they are newborn and suckled by our cows there will be no way to capture them until they become tamer than they now are."[2] And they never did.

Zaldívar's hunters managed to kill and dress enough buffalo to convince Oñate's camp that the meat of the bulls was better tasting than the beef of Spanish cattle, and buffalo fat superior to pork fat. Yet for supplies of either, the colony henceforth relied, like the Pueblo Indians before them, on trade fairs at points of entry like Pecos or on the few individuals who for adventure, commercial advantage, or ceremony were willing to risk the perils of going to the source.

Captain Gaspar Pérez, a blond armorer from Brussels, was one such speculator. He seems to have come north in the train of Governor Peralta, the bureaucrat who replaced Oñate in 1609. In clashes with Franciscans, Pérez, like Francisco Gómez, always took the governors' side. Through the woman he wed, María Romero, a native of Oñate's San Gabriel, the immigrant found himself suddenly related to almost everyone in the colony's soldiering, landowning, and trading community. If the Pueblos were close knit inside their walls, with children addressing every adult beyond their immediate family as aunt or uncle, New Mexico's Spaniards were no less so. To one degree or another, everyone was your cousin.[3]

In 1634 Pérez and two cousins joined in a diplomatic and commercial venture that took them far out onto the buffalo plains. Fray Andrés Juárez of Pecos Pueblo, known for his rapport with the Plains Apaches, rode with them, likely accompanied by a delegation of Pecos Indians. Further details derive from testimony recorded in the 1660s. Somewhere between two hundred and three hundred leagues east of the Rio Grande (five hundred to eight hundred miles, which put them in present-day Oklahoma), the cousins came to the banks of a substantial river (perhaps the Canadian).

As the New Mexicans and Pecos Indians set to lashing rafts to cross over, their Plains Apache hosts protested, gesturing that beyond the river lay the lands of the Wichitas, their enemies. The traders desisted. In the interest of peaceful and profitable relations, they engaged in a Plains Apache ceremonial. Although the friar's part is obscured, Gaspar Pérez became a "captain" of the Apache nation, ritually having sex with a young woman and allegedly fathering a half-Apache son. Pérez's death a dozen years later in 1646 and Father Juárez's sometime after 1647 failed to erase the memory.

Gaspar Pérez's third son, Diego Romero, who preferred his mother's surname, told and retold that story about his father. Rude and heavyset, with curly black hair and beard, the semiliterate Romero nevertheless held the military rank of sargento mayor, served a term as Santa Fe magistrate, and enjoyed grants of tribute as encomendero of half the households of Zia Pueblo and all of Cochiti and Cuyamungue. In 1659 Romero, who had a large home on the Santa Fe plaza, served as the colony's *protector de indios,* obliging him to represent Christian Indians in legal matters.

He had, in fact, recently argued the case of Juan Zuni, actually a Hopi from Awátovi, and his accomplice Cristóbal el Meco (the Savage), two disreputable Santa Fe laborers accused of stealing shoes, chocolate, sugar, and silk ribbon from the stock of merchant Juan de Mestas stored in the casas reales. Romero's defense, in part that such Indians did not consider theft a crime, failed to spare them. Just as in Mexico City, each man was to be mounted on a pack animal and paraded publicly through the streets of Santa Fe as the town crier called out his crimes and a paid tormentor laid two hundred lashes across his back. Finally, at public auction, they were to be sold as slaves—Juan for ten years and Cristóbal for five—"in order that in this way they may purge themselves of their sins and that it may serve as a punishment for them and as an example to the rest."[4]

Romero's chance to emulate his deceased father while turning a profit came at last in the summer of 1660. Governor Bernardo López de Mendizábal had contracted with him to carry merchandise on consignment to the Plains Apaches. Besides prime buffalo hides and tanned skins, the governor had a particular interest in Wichita boys and girls the Apaches might have for sale. Almost every Hispanic family of property, as well as certain Pueblo Indian households, raised and relied on such servants who commonly bore the family's name. Besides, a healthy captive youth of whatever heathen tribe— Wichita, Apache, Navajo, Ute—brought thirty to forty pesos, the equivalent of a good mule.

Although Pueblo Indians, by outdated law, were not supposed to ride horses or carry Spanish arms, these proscriptions broke down in New Mexico. Since surrounding seminomadic Apaches and Navajos took readily to both, acquired by theft or as contraband, Spaniards turned to their Pueblo neighbors to help defend the colony. For planned campaigns, militia officers regularly called up quotas of Pueblo fighting men, who routinely outnumbered the colonists two or three to one. Likely El Carpintero, the Pecos headman who agreed to accompany Diego Romero in 1660, rode and carried Spanish weapons; a generation later, his successor most certainly did.

The intimate trade relations of Pecos Pueblo with Plains Apaches, which antedated the Spaniards, dictated that Romero enlist Pecos men as allies. The main body of these auxiliaries probably walked; they could easily cover on foot ten leagues or more a day (twenty-five or thirty miles). A dozen trail hands, who included a "half-mestizo" blacksmith, a Mexican Indian, and a mulatto, kept the slower Spanish pack-train in line and moving. If, as Romero later claimed, they traveled two hundred leagues, the column must have made and broken camp repeatedly for almost a month. Where wood was scarce, dried buffalo dung made for a hot, fast-burning fire. Meat roasted on a spit over such a fire took on a peppery taste.

Their rendezvous had been arranged. Romero, betraying an insider's knowledge of plains commerce, identified the large settlement of colorful tepees as the rancheria of don Pedro, named conceivably for an Apache leader or another known New Mexican trader. Romero called the river the Río Colorado (likely today's Red, Canadian, or Cimarron River). Eager Spaniards and Pecos pitched their tents a half mile from the Apaches.

Word of Romero's purpose had preceded him. The heathens would make him, as he imagined it, "chief captain of the entire Apache nation." If he embraced an Apache half brother, his father's son, no one recorded the scene. Late one evening, about thirty Apache warriors appeared at the traders' camp. They called for Romero, forming a circle around him.

Four stepped forward and spread a new buffalo hide on the ground. They picked up the trusting Spaniard and laid him flat on the hide. On another hide, they placed El Carpintero. A procession formed, and accompanied by reed whistles, flutes, and singing, the Apaches bore the two prone figures as if on stretchers toward their settlement. The rite, identified by an anthropologist in the late twentieth century as a calumet ceremony, had begun.

Lowered to the ground after what seemed about fifteen minutes, Romero and El Carpintero found themselves at the center of a ring of hundreds of seated, chanting Apaches. They felt themselves being swayed back and forth by Indian men who grasped their shoulders. A native orator began what could have been a eulogy, and four others joined in. These five next brought a pole with a scalp dangling from it, planting it in the ground before Romero. They placed a ripe ear of corn at its base. Amid this solemnity, forty or fifty warriors suddenly burst into the circle unannounced, brandishing shields and lances as if to attack Romero. Another Apache rushed out striking their shields with a stick, defending the Spaniard. Three times his assailants attacked; three times this protector beat them off. The chanting never stopped.

Near midnight, two Apaches took hold of Romero and laid him on his back as if he were a corpse. He could not remember how long he lay there. The two Indians then stretched out his arms and raised him up. A third approached with a lighted pipe of tobacco on a long wooden stem. The bearer smoked it first, then held it low to the ground, "as if for the devil to smoke," and handed it to Romero, who repeated the ritual three times. The pipe slowly made its way from hand to hand around the circle. Someone stuck the shaft of a pure white feather into the ear of corn, then put the feather in a leather band on the Spaniard's head as the insignia of their "chief captain."

The Apaches also understood Romero's desire to consummate the act as his father had. Accordingly, they put up

Plains Apaches. From a painting on hide, Segesser I, Museum of New Mexico; detail redrawn by Jerry L. Livingston. From Kessell, *Kiva, Cross, and Crown.*

a new tepee, smoothed out a hide inside, seated Romero on it, and performed what he assumed was a kind of marriage dance. (He did not say if Apache women joined in this part of the ceremony.) After the dance, they brought to the tepee a young virgin. Next morning, verifying that he had known her carnally, Apaches anointed the Spaniard's chest with her blood. They made him a gift of the bed and the new tepee.[5]

If only Romero and his men had kept their mouths shut, but they boasted. And soon word of their participation in heathen Apache rites became Inquisition testimony, another exhibit to incriminate the close associates of Governor López de Mendizábal, "the new Rosas."

Although more cultured and urbane, Governor Bernardo López de Mendizábal squeezed profits from the colony as vigorously as his predecessor had two decades earlier. For his leisure and that of his cosmopolitan wife, doña Teresa, López brought along not only their elegant household furnishings but also books, among them the earliest documented copy in New Mexico of *Don Quijote*. Before leaving the viceregal capital, he had invested in a thousand decks of playing cards for resale on the trip north. His store in Santa Fe's casas reales, which he stocked with European textiles, shoes, and hats, along with quantities of sugar and chocolate shipped from New Spain, was only the beginning of his private enterprises.[6]

It had been an unpleasant journey north. In addition to the tedium of six months in carriages, from early January to early July 1659—sixteen hundred stop-and-go miles through mostly hostile scenery in maddening slow motion—López and his wife had been sick. The governor quarreled incessantly with the Franciscan superior, each accusing the other of overstepping his jurisdiction, and ten of the twenty-four missionary recruits abandoned the caravan in disgust.

Travel on the Camino Real del Norte, dubbed early on the Camino Real de Tierra Adentro (romantically the Royal Road to the Interior, more prosaically the Inland Highway), had by López's day evolved into a routine. Northward bound, everybody and everything going to New Mexico—from the new governor and his entourage to a ragged stable hand, along with mail, consigned merchandise, gifts, eight spare mules per

wagon, meat on the hoof, together with the entire missionary supply contingent—came together on the outskirts of
Mexico City or, like the freighters of Parral, joined the train
en route.

As far as Zacatecas, the well-worn road, graded and sur-
faced with paving stones, was not so bad. Beyond, mostly
through high desert all the way to El Paso del Norte, the route
kept changing. Unstable geography—a washout, shifting sands,
or altered river course; as well as seasonal conditions; enough
water, pasture, and firewood; successive mine discoveries and
movable settlements; even a native revolt or bandit gang—
could set traffic off on a somewhat new *ramal,* or branch road.
Communities, shrines, and roadside inns competed for the
transient business.

People of means and those subsidized by the government
bounced and swayed aboard wagons, coaches, or carts. Others
rocked in the saddle or trudged on foot. Bags, barrels, and
bundles of provisions plodded along, ingeniously balanced
on mules, mules, and more mules. While never as tidy as the
government contract stipulated, the every-third-year New
Mexico mission supply service aspired to good order: two
squadrons, each containing sixteen two-ton, four-wheeled,
eight-mule freight wagons. The lead wagon of each traveled
under a wagon master's whip and flew the royal banner, its
mules decked out in ornamental harnesses, trappings, and bells.
The triennial cost came to more than sixty thousand pesos.
The crown paid for an armed escort, while the Franciscans
agreed to service the wagons and replace spent mules.[7]

Cultural baggage too—ideas, language, lifestyles, songs,
and prayers—enlivened travel. Not all the traffic was welcome.
While the camino real wending toward impoverished New
Mexico rarely served as an emigrant trail, thieves, vagabonds,
microbes, burrs, and other bad seeds also hitched rides.

Recovering from his illness and the trip, Governor López
de Mendizábal tore into New Mexico's self-serving Franciscans,

who still believed that the colony existed primarily to support their ministry to the Pueblo Indians. Jesuit educated, he relished affronting friars. Within weeks of his arrival, he attacked their cherished entitlement to Indian labor and denounced the suppression of Pueblo ritual practice.

Once during his term, a governor was obliged by law to tour his jurisdiction, informing himself about local administration and defense, hearing complaints, and rendering justice. On López's visitation in 1659, the governor did not scruple to interrogate Pueblo Indians through interpreters about their missionaries' treatment of them, even about the friars' personal lives and habits. Such prying, he claimed, served to ensure Indian rights.

At Tano-speaking Galisteo Pueblo in the basin just south of Santa Fe, Governor López, in front of his retinue of Spaniards, questioned the Indians so eagerly about possible excesses of their missionary that the friar stood aghast. "No prelate of mine," a fellow priest objected, "would have made such a rigorous examination of any religious [i.e., friar], and with so many and such exquisite questions, as His Lordship made of each of the natives."[8] Meddling further in mission affairs, López told the Indian women who baked the missionary's bread to stop doing so. He later sent the friar's trusted Tano interpreter away, ordered several mission aides dismissed, and forbade any Indian to carry messages for the minister.

Pay for Indian workers, irregular at best, had stood for some time at a half-real per day or its equivalent in produce. López by decree doubled the base pay to a full real (the eighth part of a peso) plus food, then challenged the missionaries' right to free Indian labor. They defended themselves, citing a previous governor's ruling that exempted at least ten essential Indian helpers from payment of tribute: the Pueblo governor, interpreter, sacristan, first cantor, bell ringer, organist, shepherd, cook, porter, and groom. Since such Indians owed no tribute, they were in effect being paid. López disagreed.

The arithmetic spoke for him: force fifty Franciscans to pay five hundred Indians the required one real a day, then put the latter back on the tribute rolls. A single unit of tribute—one Pueblo manta, valued at six reales, and one fanega of corn, at four to six reales, or their value in piñon nuts, hides, or salt—times five hundred came to about seven hundred pesos. Landholding colonists, some of them women, who did not also enjoy grants of Pueblo tribute naturally protested the increased cost of Indian laborers.

Unlike their sisters in much of British America, Hispanic women in colonial New Mexico could and did own property. North of Socorro, en route to New Mexico's capital, Governor López had enjoyed the hospitality of rancher doña Luisa Díaz de Betansos and her daughter, Isabel de Salazar. A number of early ranch properties and land grants bore feminine place-names. To empower themselves in a man's world, such women of property routinely got their way through male relatives: fathers, uncles, brothers, and of course, cousins.

But López held the upper hand. Every New Mexico governor relied on his appointed *alcaldes mayores* (district officers) in the colony's six or eight subjurisdictions, which corresponded roughly to different Pueblo language groupings. These officials publicly announced the governor's orders throughout the kingdom. As had governors before him, López also employed them as business agents to amass quantities of hides, cotton and woolen mantas, piñon nuts, and salt for the governor to export on his account. López chided his man responsible for Pecos Pueblo to hurry up with the boards he had ordered to repair the casas reales. Serving unsalaried at the governor's pleasure, such officials dispensed petty justice, heard land and water disputes, supervised Indian labor, rallied the local militia and Pueblo auxiliaries, and kept an eye on mission discipline. The worst of them set themselves up as petty tyrants, extorted goods and services, and lived scandalously.

Encomendero Francisco Gómez Robledo, eldest son of the late Portuguese-born royalist Francisco Gómez, also backed López. A thick-set man in his early thirties, Gómez Robledo held the rank of sargento mayor and mayordomo of the religious confraternity of Nuestra Señora del Rosario. He was unmarried, but he had fathered two children, who lived with him and his servants in a corner house on the Santa Fe plaza. Gómez had been taught to read and write by his own father for lack of teachers in New Mexico; he also possessed a remarkable knowledge of Indian languages and customs.

Curious about their new surroundings, Governor López and his wife inquired of Gómez Robledo about Pueblo Indian dances. The couple had traveled widely, and to them, such ceremonials sounded like the colorful folk festivals of Europe and other parts of the Americas. How could such harmless rites be incompatible with Christianity, at least from an educated point of view?

A good question, agreed Gómez. Since he held the encomienda of Tesuque, along with Pecos and several other pueblos, Gómez arranged for Tesuque Indians to perform for the Spanish governor in the plaza at Santa Fe. Pueblo Indians from Tesuque, the Tewa community closest to Santa Fe, were a familiar sight around the capital as *semaneros* (paid Indian servants at the casas reales who rotated on a weekly basis). Although present-day anthropologists doubt that the clownish, masked performance the Indians put on was truly a kachina dance, López found it good fun. "But for the fact that I am the governor," he supposedly quipped, "I would go out and dance myself."[9]

Based on his own brief observance of such entertainment, Governor López at once ordered his alcaldes mayores to announce in their districts that henceforth Pueblo Indians were free to resume their kachina ceremonials. The friars gasped. What was the royal governor thinking? Taking quick advantage of this decree, rowdy, low-life colonists, according to one Franciscan, "had got themselves up in the manner of the Indian kachinas and had danced the dance of that name."[10] Pueblo Indians, who were masters of parody (especially of their missionaries), may have laughed at this reversal of roles. Whatever they thought, it appeared that the Franciscans were losing control. As scandalized reports piled up in Mexico City, the order's superiors appealed to the Inquisition.

As tough as Father Benavides and twice as strict, fray Alonso de Posada also wielded dual authority as prelate and agent of the Inquisition. Working his way up the Rio Grande valley in the spring of 1661, he could scarcely believe the stories he was hearing. He had ministered previously in New Mexico and was now convinced of the colony's rapid perdition under the López regime. Yet during the 1650s, Posada himself had stood accused, scurrilously he claimed, of immorality, even of covering up a murder, while he ministered at the Hopi pueblo of Awátovi.

Back then, the Hopis had enjoyed mimicking the intense Father Posada. Juan, the same Indian whom Diego Romero would later defend, had staged a burlesque in Posada's absence from the mission. Summoning the people of Awátovi into the pueblo's imposing church, Juan donned the missionary's vestments, lighted the incense burner and censed an altar, chanted the Salve, and made as to sprinkle holy water "in the manner priests do it." For his spontaneous impersonation and alleged voracious sexual appetite, Juan was placed in the convento of Santa Fe. Until his trial in 1659, the incorrigible thief kept pilfering items for resale, including forceps for pulling teeth, probably from the convento's infirmary.[11]

Now, in the early 1660s as Franciscan superior, Father Posada countermanded Governor López's permissive decree. He banned further kachina dances, ordering the missionaries to destroy all confiscated Pueblo ceremonial artifacts—masks, prayer sticks, effigies, and other paraphernalia. Sixteen hundred such objects, among them a dozen especially "dia-bolical" masks from Isleta Pueblo, were burned at the friars' bidding.[12] Certain Pueblo Indians would remember the prec-edent twenty years later, as they torched wooden images of Christian saints and the Blessed Virgin Mary.

Much as he might have wished to take matters into his own hands as local agent of the Inquisition, Posada was not empowered to conduct trials or sentence anyone. That author-ity resided in Mexico City not far from the cathedral in a gray stone building housing the Holy Office of the Inquisition. There sat the only tribunal for all of New Spain, Guatemala, and the Philippines. In New Mexico, Posada, aided by a scribe and a constable, gathered testimony, denounced alleged offend-ers in cover letters to the Inquisition, and quietly forwarded their files to Mexico City. Upon examination, the inquisitors, if they saw cause, could order the accused summarily arrested and brought before them.

As his scribe took down declaration after declaration from friar and layman alike, Father Posada categorized acts of dis-respect for the Church and its ministers by four of Governor López's partisans: Francisco Gómez Robledo, his first cousin Diego Romero, and two others. All appeared vulnerable, especially Gómez, who was rumored to be Jewish. The New Mexico agent sent a batch of such testimony to Mexico City at year's end in 1661 to be added to files already implicat-ing them. The Inquisition's panel of experts in theology and canon law had in fact already voted to arrest the four and have them conducted under guard to the viceregal capital for trial. Printed arrest warrants, with the name of the accused handwritten in ink, reached Father Posada at Santo Domingo on April 1, 1662. Gloating, he wasted not a moment.

What was this? How dare anyone pound on the door of Francisco Gómez Robledo's Santa Fe home at five o'clock in the morning, jarring him awake? Paterfamilias of the extensive Gómez clan and pillar of the Hispanic community, he had long ago dismissed rumors that he was under suspicion. This only happened to others. "Open, open in the name of the Holy Office!" He did not resist. While zealous friars stood by, the chief constable, who chanced to be a former governor and enemy of López, served the warrant. Then they hustled him across the plaza in semidarkness to a cell in the Franciscan convento.

Two days earlier, downriver at Isleta Pueblo, they had waited for Gómez Robledo's cousin, the unsuspecting sargento mayor Diego Romero, and one of the others. The two officers had been escorting a vigorous new governor, don Diego de Peñalosa, on his visitation of the mesa-top Hopi pueblos to the west. The last of the four marked men fell into the constable's hands at Sandia Pueblo soon after, and within weeks each occupied a cell at Franciscan headquarters in Santo Domingo. Here they languished for five months, "seeing neither sun nor moon."[13] Meanwhile, their captors auctioned off enough of their personal property to cover expenses for food during their imprisonment, the impending journey to Mexico City, and their trial.

As the returning supply train formed up in early October 1662, Father Posada reviewed provisions to transport not only the four accused New Mexicans but also, incredibly, the furious, cursing former governor López de Mendizábal—each man shackled in a wagon—with López's wife, doña Teresa, also in custody following in a carriage. Posada had seen to every detail. A well-paid guard for each prisoner had posted bond guaranteeing delivery of his charge to the Inquisition prison in Mexico City. Gómez Robledo's keeper, like the others, had sworn not to allow him "the least communication, nor that he be given letter, ink, or paper, nor that said prisoner be permitted to leave his wagon."[14] None escaped, and by April 1663 all resided woefully in the Inquisition's *cárceles secretas*.

The least intimidated, Francisco Gómez Robledo fared best—despite charges that his family practiced Judaism. One

New Mexico witness, for example, claimed to have over-
heard Governor López de Mendizábal asking Gómez about
the rumor that "your father, Francisco Gómez, was a Jew,
and that he died with his face turned to the wall," an alleged
crypto-Jewish practice.[15] More incriminating were innuen-
dos that he and his brothers had been circumcised. Surgeons
in the Inquisition's employ twice confirmed that Francisco
had marks on the foreskin of his penis that looked like tiny
cuts from a sharp instrument, yet they could not rule out the
defendant's assertion that these were scars from small ulcers.
Brought from his cell with maddening infrequency, Gómez
Robledo looked his inquisitors in the eye and answered force-
fully, citing time and again his father's long and distinguished
royal service as a believing Christian. In the end, these judges
were less vindictive than the Franciscans of New Mexico.
Their verdict: acquittal on all counts.

At the same time, the inquisitors broke Gómez's cousin.
Diego Romero at first tried to be brave, stating repeatedly that
he had no idea why he had been arrested. Week after week in
his solitary cell, he struggled mentally to anticipate the charges,
implicating himself further at each successive hearing. Then
they read to him the formal twenty-three-count indictment.
Charges ran from scandalous utterance to incest, but the most
serious, the one "that showed him to be an apostate of the
Catholic Religion or at the least vehemently suspect in the
Faith," centered on his alleged heathen "marriage" among the
Plains Apaches three years earlier, in the summer of 1660.[16]

As he answered the allegations one by one, Romero pleaded
with his inquisitors. He loved the Church. Whatever he had
done resulted from ignorance not malice. He did manage to
fend off one common charge: that of incest. Juana Romero,
supposedly the mother of his child, was not his cousin, he
swore, but "a native of Pecos, of whose issue he does not know."
Considering her a mestiza, Romero's mother had raised her
from infancy in Santa Fe. Later, young Juana had come under

Seal of the Mexican
Inquisition. From
Kessell, *Kiva, Cross,*
and Crown.

the influence of an accused madam and, according to Romero, had slept with the Franciscan friar at the Santa Fe convento. Her blond boy was not Romero's but the friar's, as their resemblance would prove.[17]

As the proceedings continued, Romero grew more and more frightened, finally heeding counsel and throwing himself on the mercy of the court. The result was pitiful. Contradicting himself repeatedly, he began to implicate the others, denouncing them for their alleged anti-Christian behavior. He was but a worm, led to sexual perversion in thought, word, and deed by the devil. He meant no harm. Admitting sexual favors of heathen women, he insisted over and over that there had been no marriage. He begged for God's pardon.

To extract the last ounce of contrition, the inquisitors routinely handed down an unduly severe sentence, fully expecting to lighten it on appeal. Romero's attorney did appeal, and instead of forced labor on the royal Philippine galleys, his client would be banished from New Mexico for ten years to the mining district of Parral. Learning subsequently that his wife in Santa Fe not only refused to join him in exile but also sought to have their marriage annulled, the despondent Romero fantasized about how free his life might have been among the Plains Apaches. Foolishly, in 1673 at Guanajuato, he married again under an assumed name. Back before the Inquisition as a bigamist, he underwent the entire process again, suffered ritual humiliation, and heard himself sentenced to six years on a galley without pay. At Veracruz, in a musty cell of the public jail as he awaited his first galley, the hapless "chief captain of the entire Apache nation" cheated the Inquisition and died of natural causes.[18]

So did former governor Bernardo López de Mendizábal, during the proceedings of his trial in 1664. Since the inquisitors had not yet established his guilt, they buried the body in the prison's corral. Thanks to later efforts by doña Teresa, who had been released without prejudice, the Inquisition dropped its case against the memory of her husband and raised the embargo on what was left of his property. Lastly, they dug up his bones and gave him a Church burial.[19]

In the dirt streets of Santa Fe, the people hailed Francisco Gómez Robledo. After an absence of more than three years, he had come back from the dungeons of the Inquisition a free man. Although his neighbors had never put much stock in rumors that the family was secretly Jewish, he had finally lifted that cloud of suspicion. He had argued the issue before the inquisitors and won. Neither smug nor cocky, Gómez signed a release of all claims against Father Posada and stipulated that the value of encomienda tribute usurped during his absence, 831 pesos, be turned over to the Holy Office of the Inquisition and donated to its chapel in Mexico City. He recovered his unsold personal belongings, his house on the plaza, his titles to lands and encomiendas, as well as some accrued tribute.

Gómez Robledo's widely scattered encomiendas—bequeathed, granted, or traded to him—covered to a remarkable degree the entire extent of the Franciscans' cruciform Pueblo Indian apostolate, horizontally from the isolated Hopi mesas in the west to Pecos in the east and vertically from Abo in the south to Taos in the north. His father had arranged by contract with the Indians of Tesuque to provide services in lieu of tribute. Elsewhere, Gómez Robledo collected from half the households in the Hopi pueblo of Shongopavi; half of Acoma minus twenty houses; all of Pecos except for twenty-four houses held by a cousin, brother-in-law, and compadre; half the pueblo of Abo, which he had traded for half of Sandia; and some portion (two and a half shares) of Taos. Gómez Robledo's annual total of 610 units of tribute, if valued at a peso and a half per unit, came to 915 pesos, almost half the two-thousand-peso salary of the Spanish governor.

The Franciscans' greatest sway in the early 1660s—close to sixty of them were in the field, attending fifty churches—overshadowed a Pueblo world reduced in population by at least a third, from the estimated sixty thousand of Oñate's day to fewer than forty thousand. Pecos, for example, had thinned from the initial two thousand souls to about twelve hundred. Although disease and recurrent epidemics took the grimmest toll by far, an undetermined number of Pueblo Indians and Pueblo mixed-bloods blended into Hispanic society, as had the infant Juana Romero of Pecos.

During Governor Peñalosa's visitation in 1661, he counted no more than some forty Pueblo communities in all New Mexico. It had never been easy for Spaniards to establish the number of distinct households in a given pueblo, because of their close quarters and varying family relationships. Father Benavides had thought it only right that an encomendero willing to collect tribute from houses added to a pueblo "should also be ready to lose and cease taking tribute from abandoned houses, even though the owners live in someone else's house."[20] Although some were slow to adjust their rolls to reflect the declining number of Pueblo tributaries, the Franciscans rarely complained about such abuses by encomenderos.

During the forced absence of encomendero Francisco Gómez Robledo, fray Alonso de Posada had done battle with the avaricious, womanizing Governor Diego de Peñalosa over the impounded assets of the four New Mexicans and former governor López de Mendizábal. Father Posada insisted that he, as agent of the Inquisition, should take charge, even approving *escuderos* (literally, shield bearers), that is, proxies who held an encomienda temporarily, rendering substitute military service and collecting the tribute. But Peñalosa defied the friar. He appointed his own retainers and sequestered on his own account the tribute they collected. He had five wagons loaded with New Mexico products and personal effects extorted from López. And he laughed about it. At one point, according to testimony gathered by Father Posada, the governor in a rage had boasted that if the inquisitors opposed him the way their New Mexico agent did, "he would scour all their assholes!"[21]

Late on a Sunday evening, September 30, 1663, Father Custos Posada, who had taken refuge at Pecos earlier in the year seemingly to avoid Peñalosa, had gone out on a second-story balcony. A successor of fray Andrés Juárez had enlarged the convento, superintending construction of an upper floor. Posada heard rustling below and called out. Learning it was Peñalosa, the friar hastily called for the door to be unbolted and chocolate prepared, leading the governor and his party of armed men directly into the guest cell. He later recalled in minute detail their shouting match, which lasted for hours. Finally, Peñalosa sarcastically invited the Franciscan superior to honor the casas reales in Santa Fe with his presence. They rode for the rest of the night.

Having made good on the first half of his threat to arrest and exile the father custos, Governor Peñalosa rethought his position. While friars and colonists held their breath, negotiators came and went during nine tense days. Finally, the governor released the prelate. How he hated this place. Could captivity by Barbary pirates be any worse? Writing to a friend a year earlier, Peñalosa had implored, "Someone come and get me out of this Algeria of New Mexico."[22] When no one did, he left.

Ever swaggering, still casting friars as protagonists in his dirty jokes, Peñalosa knocked the muck of Santa Fe off his boots early in 1664 before a successor arrived to take his residencia. But he was not quick enough to outdistance the Inquisition. They arrested him in Mexico City. Father Posada had been thorough; the charges against the ex-governor numbered 237 and required two days to read. At the end of proceedings that dragged on for two and a half years, his final sentence only deepened Peñalosa's passion for revenge. Made to appear in an auto-da-fé (the Inquisition's public spectacle of sentenced prisoners), fined five hundred pesos, excluded for life from political or military office, and banished from New Spain and the West Indies, any other man might have given up in despair. Not Diego de Peñalosa.

He reinvented himself as the Count of Santa Fe de Peñalosa and showed up among cavaliers at the court of Charles II in Restoration England with whispered schemes of attacks on Spanish America. Spain's ambassador in London failed to entrap him. Proceeding to France, he married a Frenchwoman, gaining access to Versailles. Yet his falsified documents of a mighty expedition across the plains of North America, which he claimed to have led in 1662, did not sufficiently impress the minions of Louis XIV. He found little support for his plans of revenge, and in 1687, still scheming, Diego de Peñalosa expired in Paris.[23]

The Franciscan who replaced fray Alonso de Posada, scourge of governors, tried to fill his predecessor's sandals and "make every affair and case an Inquisition matter."[24] The Santa Fe cabildo fought back, protesting effectively enough to shake the Holy Office in Mexico City. The friars of New Mexico, the inquisitors concluded, were indeed abusing the authority of the Inquisition to perpetuate their ecclesiastical stranglehold on the colony; they should be restrained. Orders went north from Mexico City admonishing the New Mexico agent to cooperate with local officials. During the late 1660s, the Holy Office, in an effort to dilute Franciscan power in the colony, forbade the father custos to serve simultaneously as agent of the Inquisition. Almost apologetically, fray Juan Bernal took up the agent's cross in early 1669. By then, shriveling drought and famine had settled over the colony.

In forty scattered Pueblo towns, infants baptized at the time of Father Benavides were now coming of age. Although many had adopted certain Catholic practices—forming factions within their communities—most of the thirty thousand surviving Pueblo Indians remembered who they were. Even as they coexisted with the Spanish colony of cousins—who with their servants and farm hands numbered perhaps two thousand by the late 1660s—Pueblo elders did not forget the wisdom of their ancestors.

As well as they could improvise undercover, traditional leaders initiated Pueblo children into their culture's intricate web of ceremonial obligations. They told and retold the creation stories of emergence from the underworld, breathing life into the supernatural beings who helped or hindered their ancestors and taught them about life-sustaining corn and animals and the weather. They explained about the kachinas and how the various social and religious organizations interacted. Such schooling never ended. One way or another, the elders kept alive Pueblo beliefs and knowledge, influencing a new generation of leaders, men like Tompiro-speaking Esteban Clemente of Abo, the cautious Popé of Tewa San Juan, and the adolescent Bartolomé de Ojeda at the Keresan pueblo of Zia. Thrust to the fore during the coming years of crisis, each would take a different path.

5 Troublous Times, 1660s–1670s

In the year 1670 there was a very great famine in those provinces [of New Mexico], which compelled the Spanish inhabitants and the Indians alike to eat the hides that they had and the straps of the carts, preparing them for food by soaking and washing them and toasting them in the fire with maize, and boiling them with herbs and roots. By this means almost half the people in the said provinces escaped [starvation]. There followed in the next year of 1671 a great pestilence, which also carried off many people and cattle; and shortly thereafter, in the year 1672, the hostile Apache who were then at peace rebelled and rose up, and the said province was totally sacked and robbed by their attacks and outrages, especially of all the cattle and sheep, of which it had previously been very productive.

FRAY FRANCISCO DE AYETA TO THE VICEROY, MAY 10, 1679

Among Pueblo Indians who adopted Spanish ways, none stood taller than the man they called Esteban Clemente. Colonists addressed him as don Esteban, a title of esteem, or by the diminutive don Estebanico (Stevie), a long-established custom among Spaniards meant to keep exalted native leaders not too exalted. "Native governor of the pueblos of Las

Salinas and Tanos, very capable interpreter of six languages of this kingdom," he also spoke and wrote Spanish.[1] Spaniards referred proudly to such Indian Spanish-speakers as *indios ladinos*. Because Clemente was literate and in their eyes a good convert, the Franciscans had sought his services in the kachina wars against Governor Bernardo López de Mendizábal, asking him to make a statement repudiating the kachinas. Wherever his deepest loyalties lay in 1660, don Esteban agreed to do so.

That late fall day, youthful fray Diego de Santander, clad in the characteristic floor-length, dark-blue habit of his order, awaited Clemente in the portal of the convento at Las Humanas, a hundred miles south of Santa Fe. The Pueblos had grown used to seeing Franciscans in blue. A century earlier, Coronado's friars had worn the gray of humble, undyed wool. The change, to a dark denim blue, was a show of advocacy. Theologians in seventeenth-century Europe, marshaling scripture and church fathers pro and con, loftily contested the doctrine of the Blessed Virgin Mary's immaculate conception, which held that God had preserved Mary free of original sin at the time of her own conception. About 1621, when Franciscans in general convocation elected the Immaculate Mother as patroness of their order, the Mexican province adopted blue for their habits.

Toward the end of Father Benavides' fervent New Mexico ministry in the 1620s, he too had come under the spell of a mystic woman in blue, María de Jesús de Ágreda, a Franciscan Conceptionist nun in Spain. Esteban Clemente, then only a small boy, likely learned her story. Jumano hunters and traders from the south plains who had developed close relationships with the Salinas pueblos had shown up in the 1620s imploring Franciscan missionaries to visit their camps, or so Benavides tells us. A beautiful young white woman robed in blue had descended miraculously among them, imploring them in their language to seek friars to teach and baptize them. Later at her convent in northeastern Spain, Benavides interviewed the dark-eyed, statuesque Mother María, who allegedly possessed the rare gift of bilocation—of remaining bodily in her cell yet trans-porting herself spiritually to the Americas. The friar convinced himself that it was she who had appeared earlier to the Jumanos, obviously a sign of God's favor toward the Franciscans of New Mexico. The story made grand propaganda.[2]

Apparently a native of Tompiro-speaking Abo, Esteban Clemente must have been baptized, either as a newborn or as a child early in the 1620s, on November 21. The officiat-ing friar, likely fray Francisco Fonte, Abo's mission founder, had consulted his *santoral,* a calendar of saints' days, where he found for that day the names of two minor martyrs, San Esteban and San Clemente. The youth proved precocious, just the sort the friars hoped to indoctrinate fully as examples to their families. Probably an acolyte at services, he was given access to the convento, where the friars taught him prayers in Spanish. He had a remarkable knack for languages, not that unusual in the polyglot Pueblo world.

Father Benavides in his writings may have portrayed the mission boys' schools more as an ideal than a reality. Nonetheless, Esteban Clemente is proof that certain Pueblos did learn Spanish subjects. Benavides wrote of teaching prayers, read-ing and writing, arts and crafts, choir and music. Certain friars gained reputations as music teachers. Although the Franciscans probably exaggerated the size and skill of native choirs, practi-cally all the missions had them. Mission Indians also learned to play European trumpets, dolcians and shawms (early double-reed woodwinds), sackbuts (the medieval trombone), and small organs that may have been maunfactured in situ by the friars. These the Pueblos accepted willingly as complements to their own traditional percussion and wind instruments.

The most promising boys lived in the convento, and bells governed their daily routine. "Promptly at dawn, one of the Indian singers goes to ring the bell for the Prime, at the sound of which those who go to school assemble and sweep the rooms thoroughly." The missionary of course had to be

María de Jesús de Ágreda preaching. From Alonso de Benavides, *Tanto que se sacó* (1730).

present, according to Benavides, to see that all went smoothly. "When everything is neat and clean, they again ring the bell and each one goes to learn his particular specialty." Older students as sextons had the duty "always to have a dozen boys for the service of the sacristy and to teach them how to help at mass and how to pray." Although Father Benavides did not mention the familiar kivalike structure built in the convento patio at Abo, it may have served as Clemente's transitional schoolroom.[3]

As an adult, with his tutors' blessing, don Esteban Clemente became governor of his pueblo and chief war captain of Indian auxiliaries in the Salinas district—the dry, hilly, piñon-and juniper-stippled basin east and south of the Manzano Mountains. On contract with Spaniards or to substitute as tribute, the people of its five pueblos harvested salt—essential for drying meat or for export in processing ore—from the shallow saline lakes that gave the province its name. Clemente, with his sons and other hands, operated a profitable trading business, running packtrains of varied goods to the Apaches of Los Siete Ríos, ancestors of today's Mescaleros. Trusted even by Spanish governors, he at times carried their commodities on consignment.

Clemente's dilemma centered on his dealings with Governor López de Mendizábal, the Franciscans' nemesis, and with the mestizo alcalde mayor in the Salinas district, Nicolás de Aguilar. The friars, deeply offended by Aguilar's utter disrespect and scandalous behavior, dubbed him "the Attila of New Mexico." In charges forwarded to the viceroy, the missionaries accused López and his henchmen of organizing slaving expeditions to the plains. One such foray in 1659, the friars alleged, involved forty colonists and eight hundred Indians, who brought in seventy captives. Pueblo captains like Esteban Clemente who marshaled quotas of fighting men shared in the spoils. Later, during López's residencia, Clemente entered a private claim as a creditor of the governor.

Whatever inducements or threats the friars used in November 1660 to persuade him, Clemente took pen in hand and denounced the kachinas. Father Santander stood nearby, almost certainly coaching him. What could he say about the dances? There were many kinds. "Some are done with ugly painted masks," Clemente wrote, by which the dancers made the people believe they were from the spirit world. He remembered numerous details: fasts, symbolic feathers and corn meal, observance of the four cardinal directions, ritual whipping, and ceremonial drinks. Sometimes men impersonated women, for what reason Clemente could not say. Certain rituals required an idol to which people offered gifts. "These are the kachinas I know—which are evil—although I have heard that there are others." Like most Pueblos, especially those who had adopted Spanish ways, Clemente may not have known much more. Only the caciques possessed such esoteric knowledge.

And what about Alcalde mayor Nicolás de Aguilar? Father Santander asked. Clemente understood the missionary's prompt. Yes, Aguilar had ordered the people of the five pueblos of his district to dance the kachinas. Moreover, he had demanded that all the missionaries' Pueblo Indian helpers ignore whatever offenses or wrongs anyone committed. In Clemente's presence, three unmarried individuals living in sin had been brought before an Indian magistrate and sent away without punishment. Dating his declaration at Las Humanas, November 30, 1660, he signed crudely "d. esteban clemente," complete with rubric. Satisfied, Father Santander, as secretary and apostolic notary of the Franciscan custody, swore that the statement "is genuine and original and wholly in the hand of don Esteban Clemente."[4]

For as long as he could remember, he had lived almost as a Spaniard, and in this way he and his family had fared well. Clemente came to understand the colonial system, its strengths and its flaws, as keenly as any Pueblo Indian. He had long been willing to cooperate, at whatever cost to his inner being. Then, during the horrors of drought and famine that lay ahead, don Esteban Clemente experienced a change of heart that would cost him his life.

—————◆—————

The Jumano Pueblo Indians of Cueloce, or San Buenaventura de las Humanas, where Clemente pronounced kachinas evil in

1660, had always lived on the edge. Population and water supply balanced precariously atop the hill where they had built.
No perennial stream flowed closer than the Rio Grande, two
long days on foot to the west. Their lives depended on springs
and catch basins and the rich alluvial soils washed down from
the hills. In years of average or above-average rain and snowfall,
they could dry farm. For drinking water, they dug *pozos* (wells)
by hand, some thirty or more feet deep. Evidently, Vicente de
Zaldívar had seized these when he assaulted the pueblo in
1601. Even after Father Benavides had dedicated the pueblo
in 1627 to San Isidro, patron of farmers, its unreliable water
supply forced subsequent Franciscans to withdraw to Abo
with their thirsty livestock. Father Santander's arrival in 1659,
with his plans to erect a proper church and convento, had
signaled the friars' renewed efforts to defy the environment
at Las Humanas.

Defending himself before the Inquisition in Mexico City
in 1664, former governor López de Mendizábal had claimed
that on his visitation in 1659, a drought year, he had suggested
a reclamation project to Santander and the Indians of Las
Humanas. It made sense. If they would build longer and higher
check dams of rock to catch the silt running off down the hill-
sides, they would soon have small artificial fields in which to
plant supplemental crops. Whatever Father Santander thought
of the governor's idea at the time, the outspoken Franciscan
resented López de Mendizábal's antimissionary regime. While
the friar's work crews laid up rock-and-mud walls of a church
never completed, a little more precipitation fell in the early
1660s, but later in the decade even the silt dried and cracked
and corn plants shriveled.[5]

From Pecos, fray Juan Bernal called heaven to witness that
neither Pueblos nor Spaniards had harvested a decent crop in
three years. Of course he exaggerated, but the end time seemed
so near. Fields parched under a merciless sun. Another friar
spoke of swarms of locusts in 1667, followed by famine. "Last

year, 1668," lamented Father Bernal, "a great many Indians perished of hunger, lying dead along the roads, in the ravines, and in their hovels. There were pueblos, like Las Humanas, where more than four hundred and fifty died of hunger." No one could afford to import foodstuffs. Domestic animals were dying. "As a result the Spaniards, men as well as women, have sustained themselves for two years on the cowhides they have in their houses to sit on. They roast them and eat them."[6]

The worst drought in memory drew lamentations and prayers for rain not only from communities along the Rio Grande's channel, wherein the weakened flow no longer reached the headgates of their ditches, but also from less settled folk on the kingdom's outer edges. Apaches and Navajos, too, saw caked mud where water had always stood. The corn they planted barely came up, then withered. Driven by their own hunger and hard times, these peripheral, independent, non-Christian peoples struck at the kingdom ever more often as marauders.

Governor Juan Rodríguez de Medrano y Mesía, who assumed the office late in 1668 and immediately set about retailing four wagonloads of goods from Mexico City, reported that during his first seven months Apaches killed six Spanish men-at-arms and 373 Christian Indians, stealing thousands of head of sheep and other stock. The numbers kept mounting. At Acoma in June 1669, Western Apaches abducted two residents alive, murdered a dozen, and drove off eight hundred sheep, sixty cattle, and every horse. "No road is safe," said Father Bernal. "One travels them all at risk of life for the heathens are everywhere. They are a brave and bold people. They hurl themselves at danger like people who know not God, nor that there is a hell."[7]

Don Esteban Clemente must have looked on in horror, questioning what had possessed him to condemn the kachinas. They were obviously punishing the Pueblos. No rain fell. Prayers to the Blessed Virgin Mary offered no relief. Neither did the Franciscans' favored San Buenaventura at Las Humanas or San Gregorio at Abo intercede to bring rain, nurture the corn, or hold off plains raiders. Clemente must win back the kachinas.

At one time there had to have existed in the Spanish archives at Santa Fe a documentary record of what Clemente tried to do. His plan was too large in scale not to have generated folio after folio of testimony among defensive, legal-minded Spanish authorities. Two respected witnesses would have been sworn in by the governor to attest the proceedings, since no authorized notary resided in New Mexico. A further statement would have affirmed that the record had been set down on blank sheets because of the perennial lack of official stamped paper. Yet the documents have gone missing. Not even the year is known. All that remains today is the brief testimony in 1681 of tall, beady-eyed Sargento mayor Diego López Sambrano, a Hispanic native of the kingdom accused repeatedly of oppressing Pueblo Indians.

In the late 1660s, Spaniards discovered a treasonous Pueblo plot to overthrow the kingdom. To deter further unrest they hanged six of Clemente's prominent Piro neighbors. Far from cowering—the intended response to such punishment—he swore to avenge them. Runners carried word of his resolve throughout the Pueblo world. To maintain secrecy, Clemente counted on the cover and fame of his reputation as governor and chief war captain of the Salinas pueblos. He sought to enlist Pueblo leaders everywhere to rise against the Spaniards. Certain caciques in the north may have held back, but according to López Sambrano, "the whole kingdom secretly obeyed." Esteban Clemente staked his future on nothing short of a general Pueblo revolt.

Previously, Pueblos and Apaches had conspired but failed to catch Spaniards off guard during the activities of Christian Holy Week. Clemente believed he could get the plan right. As inconspicuously as possible, Pueblo herders would move the colonists' horses into the mountains to prevent the Spaniards' escape. Then, at a time agreed to in all the Pueblo communities —Maundy Thursday night—while the colonists were at services, Pueblo fighting men aided by Apaches would spring the trap simultaneously throughout the colony. The obvious goal, declared López Sambrano, was "to destroy the whole body of Christians, not leaving a single religious [i.e., friar] or Spaniard."

But the Spaniards found out. López Sambrano did not say how, but with earlier attempts at rebellion fresh in their minds, some of the colonists must have been wary. After three generations of coexistence, they knew who among the Pueblo Indians would inform about such a conspiracy. About 1670, although details are lacking, "they hanged the said Indian, Don Esteban Clemente, and quieted the rest." Breaking in to confiscate his property, Spaniards "found in his house a large number of idols and entire kettles full of idolatrous powdered herbs, feathers, and other trifles."[8] All to placate the kachinas.

Despite the drought, the daily round of survival in Pueblo houseblocks and Spanish ranchos was still broken by laughter, if not so often. During the 1670s, however, calamitous events came on so rapidly that they ran together in a blur. If Spaniards who viewed Clemente's dangling corpse were quickly distracted, believing that this public execution had "quieted the rest," they would have cause to mourn soon enough.

At Ohkay Owingeh (San Juan Pueblo), an Indian who undoubtedly bore some Christian saint's name devoted himself secretly to the sacred knowledge of his ancestors. After he had made his mark, Spaniards called him a medicine man or sorcerer, identifying him only by an approximation of his Tewa name, El Popé (Po'pay is the preferred form today), loosely meaning Ripe Corn. They never found out who he was, although the native name suggests a cacique of the Summer People. At the same time, downriver at Santa Ana, a robust and promising Keresan lad whom the friars had baptized Bartolomé de

Ojeda learned to speak, read, and write Spanish while training as a war captain. These two, along with other Pueblo elders-in-the-making, kept alive the memory of Esteban Clemente's sacrifice. And they waited.

In 1670, a year after he had defined the colony's twin calamities as drought and godless Apaches, fray Juan Bernal was feeling sorry for himself. Sunburned and "suffering other afflictions of this country," the friar held one arm awkwardly because of running sores. Even so, he assured the Holy Office of the Inquisition in Mexico City, "I carry on gladly, ever confident that Your Illustrious Lordship will protect me and take me from this country." An unobtrusive sort, Bernal nevertheless recognized the perils of his appointment as agent of the Inquisition. Resentful colonists looked for any excuse to malign him. He lived in seclusion, mostly at Pecos, and carried out Inquisition business with extreme caution, "fraternizing with no one since they attempt to stain my reputation."[9]

The most notorious case Father Bernal inherited ended either in tragedy or a clever faked demise. It involved a German peddler who had wandered over from the province of Sonora, one Bernardo Gruber. Accused of hawking little slips of paper said to make buyers who chewed them invulnerable for twenty-four hours, Gruber had been summarily locked up by Bernal's predecessor. When Bernal inquired what should be done with him now, response from the Holy Office stung: no local agent had authority to arrest anyone without specific orders from Mexico City. Moreover, the colonists' disrespect for New Mexico's Franciscans was no concern of the Inquisition.

Gruber, meanwhile, after two years in confinement suddenly decided to act. Ripping out the bars of a window with the help of an Apache servant assigned to guard him, the German galloped off down the Camino Real. A squad of militiamen with forty Pueblo Indians gave chase in vain.

Later, northbound travelers spotted the bones of a dead horse tethered to a tree, with bits of torn clothing strewn about and a skull and scattered human bones. No matter who murdered whom, the Holy Office told Father Bernal to auction the peddler's wares, bury the bones in consecrated ground, and say Mass for repose of his soul.[10] Case closed, but not forgotten. On later maps, a water hole near the crime scene bore the label *Alemán,* "the German." Even today, a well-informed tour guide will tell Gruber's story to passengers on air-conditioned coaches from Interstate 25, pointing eastward to a shimmering desert expanse known as the Jornada del Muerto (Journey of the Dead Man).

The decade of the 1670s in the kingdom of New Mexico brought to mind the Old Testament plagues of Egypt. And all the woes touched fray Juan Bernal. In 1671 he and his brothers carried what remedies and solace they could to the many malnourished Pueblos and Spaniards laid low in one of the colony's recurring epidemics, probably smallpox, often accompanied by flu and measles. The missionaries' heroic efforts to distribute provisions could be read in the dole of food stores and livestock on inventories demanded by their father custos in late summer 1672. The friars, along with more fortunate colonist families, responded as well, not always without protest, to the Spanish governor's constant levies of rations and animals to keep armed squads patrolling the roads and guarding remote communities. As always, campaigns taking the field against Apaches and Navajos counted three, four, and five times as many Pueblo fighting men as Spaniards.[11]

In mid-1672 Father Bernal had wished his former secretary well as the young priest left for the distant western pueblo of Hawikuh. The avid friar would minister to descendants of Zunis who, forty years earlier, had martyred one of his predecessors. His turn came swiftly, in October. Combined bands of Western Apaches overran the pueblo so completely that one suspects collusion with a Zuni faction. The attackers took women and children captive, killing their men, as other Zunis fled to Dowa Yalanne (Corn Mountain), their traditional mesa-top refuge. A pious chronicler, writing in the 1690s, supplied the usual gruesome details of a proper martyr's death. Amid the killing, burning, and looting, the missionary had run into the church, embracing a cross and an image of the Blessed Virgin. They dragged him outside, stripping off his blue habit. At the foot of a large patio cross, his tormentors stoned and shot arrows at the writhing nude body, finally smashing his skull with a heavy bell.[12]

After 1672 fray Juan Bernal ministered to the Tanos of Galisteo, observing the colony's agonies from there. South of him, the Salinas pueblos, especially Las Humanas, debilitated by disease, famine, and flight, absorbed blow after blow from Siete Ríos Apaches, former trade partners of don Esteban Clemente. Within a few years, all the sites lay deserted. At depleted Galisteo, Father Bernal took in refugees from Clemente's former pueblos. Along with native Tanos, these disillusioned and displaced persons prayed for a return of the kachinas.

Meantime, an ominous drama was unfolding among the Tewas north and west of Santa Fe. These were the people among whom Oñate's colony had originally settled, "the first to be baptized." "This nation," wrote Father Benavides in the early 1630s, "is very attached to the Spaniards, and when a war breaks out they are the first to join and accompany them."[13] They did not require coercion. For Pueblo males, who upheld a proud tradition as skilled fighters, service as military auxiliaries continued to offer manly challenges against old enemies, as well as wide mobility and a share in the spoils of war. Even though at times their missionaries objected when campaigning took them away from mission fields and flocks, Pueblo fighting men eagerly filled the quotas summoned by Spaniards.

New to the kingdom in 1675, Governor Juan Francisco Treviño impulsively heeded a trio of New Mexico veterans, each of civil and military rank: forty-five-year-old Spaniard

Mounted Pueblo auxiliaries fighting unidentified Apaches. After a painting on hide, Segesser I, Museum of New Mexico; detail redrawn by Jerry L. Livingston. From Kessell, *Kiva, Cross, and Crown.*

Francisco Javier from Sevilla, who had come to New Mexico in Governor López de Mendizábal's train and since prospered; the younger, pockmarked Luis de Quintana, another Spaniard from the Basque country; and the tall, New Mexico–born Diego López Sambrano. The three agreed: the governor must act swiftly to quash a resurgence of Pueblo religion among the Tewas.

Signs abounded. The old and ailing missionary of San Ildefonso Pueblo swore that Tewa sorcerers had bewitched him and done worse to others who opposed them, reputedly with fatal results. His complaint was not alone. Elsewhere among Tewas and at outlying Taos, Acoma, and Zuni, the friars were disconsolate, unable to turn back the tide of idolatry. Hence, the inexperienced Governor Treviño charged his three advisers to summon a sufficient force and sweep through the Tewa towns, rounding up suspected sorcerers and confiscating all the heathen paraphernalia they could lay hands on. This they did, evidently with relish, and allegedly helped themselves to the Indians' horses as well. And the Tewas never forgave them.

By the Spaniards' count, they abducted forty-seven Tewa men, including Popé of San Juan, and impounded, according to López Sambrano, "many idols, powders, and other things . . . from the houses of the sorcerers and from the countryside." This witness later referred to legal proceedings against those arrested. Again, the trial record is gone without a trace, lost in the maelstrom to come, but not Treviño's sentence. The governor decreed that four Indians be hanged as warnings, each among distinct language groups. López Sambrano saw personally to the execution of one in Tewa-speaking Nambe and another in Keresan San Felipe. A third was strung up to chasten defiant Towas of the Jemez pueblos. The last, left alone, hanged himself. And the rest Treviño condemned to lashings and servitude.[14] The scars on the back of Popé's seven-foot-tall likeness in the National Statuary Hall of the United States Capitol in Washington, D.C., are a permanent testament to Treviño's verdict.

Deliberating in emergency council, Tewa elders set a bold course. They would come in peace unbowed, bearing gifts of "eggs, chickens, tobacco, beans, and some small deerskins," but armed and more menacing than their erstwhile Spanish allies had ever seen them. They would convey demands: pardon and release all the prisoners or else. They were prepared to kill the Spanish governor, or so his minions believed. Leaving an ambush in the hills above Santa Fe in case of forced retreat, more than seventy Tewas carrying war clubs and leather shields pushed their way into Governor Treviño's quarters, filling two rooms.

Reading the Tewas' faces, Treviño's advisers urged him to accept their gifts and offer them woolen blankets in return. López Sambrano, present during the tense encounter, agreed with other Spaniards. For now, give them what they wanted.

"Wait a while, children," the governor stalled. "I will give them [the prisoners] to you and pardon them on condition that you forsake idolatry and iniquity."[15]

———•◦•———

Hardy fray Francisco de Ayeta, custos and supply man for the Franciscan custody of New Mexico, had proven an apt beggar at the viceroy's court. He had ridden to Mexico City in the returning supply caravan of 1676 with the anxious blessings of Treviño, the Santa Fe cabildo, and his fellow friars. His message was clear. Unless a special royal grant of aid could be secured for the afflicted colony, little hope remained for its survival. Another churchman, fray Payo Enríquez de Rivera, viceroy and archbishop of Mexico, heard Father Ayeta's supplication. He and his *fiscal,* or chief legal counsel, agreed that the crown should pay the costs of relocating to New Mexico a commander, a sergeant, and fifty soldiers, mostly convicts. This established European imperial practice—clearing jails to provide security in undesirable places—made better sense at the core than on the periphery.

Besides the regular, previously contracted, triennial mission supplies, Ayeta signed receipts for a hundred harquebuses, a hundred sword and dagger hilts, fifty saddles and tack, and 3,000 pesos to purchase horses in Durango, all covered by a special appropriation of 14,700 pesos. The custody's syndic (or business agent) posted bond for safe delivery. One of the convicts, freed of his fetters because of epileptic attacks, deserted near Parral. While the wagons were halted at El Paso by the swollen Rio Grande, six more got away, stealing fifty-seven horses, six saddles, and three harquebuses. Each of the remaining convict soldiers, along with the three volunteers among them, received a payment of 18 pesos upon arrival at Santa Fe. The 126 pesos not disbursed to the deserters would be refunded to the treasury.[16]

Governor Treviño delighted in news that Father Ayeta and the combined mission and relief caravan of 1677 were at last approaching the capital. He could leave now. With minimum ceremony and little regret, Treviño transferred the colony's government assets and archives to his officious successor, don Antonio de Otermín. Whatever advice, verbal or written, the outgoing governor offered during the transition, it surely contained a warning about the defiant Tewas. Among New Mexico's veteran colonists, Francisco Javier, Luis de Quintana, and Diego López Sambrano had a history with the Tewas and could be counted on to keep them in their place. Governor Otermín's decision to appoint Javier his secretary of government and war proved a grave misjudgment.

On the last day of 1677, Ayeta stood before Governor Otermín and the Santa Fe cabildo in open council attended by the leading men of the colony. By formal petition, the friar reviewed his disposition of the royal largesse and requested formal approval of his actions. Only with such certification would treasury officials in Mexico City cancel the bond against the custody's syndic. The picture the Franciscan superior painted had to demonstrate to viceregal authorities the good accomplished with the previous appropriation, as well as convey the continuing distress of the king's New Mexico subjects, Pueblos and Spaniards alike.

Long-suffering Juan Bernal persevered that winter of 1678 among the uneasy Tanos at Galisteo. A ready witness to Pueblo dislocations and emergency aid, he had acceded to Father Ayeta's plan. To block Apaches raiding from the south, the governor with the friars' blessing stationed ten of the recently arrived soldiers at Galisteo, twenty miles south of the capital. Ayeta then redistributed to storerooms and corrals at Bernal's mission more than four hundred fanegas of foodstuffs, two hundred goats, and forty head of cattle to feed the guard and succor two hundred refugee families from the ruined Salinas pueblos.

A year later, the tireless Ayeta was back in Mexico City at the viceroy's court, both to verify how the previous relief had been applied and to beg for more. He provided as well a state-of-the-colony summary. By his reckoning, within the kingdom—from Nuestra Señora de Guadalupe at El Paso (founded in the late 1650s) upriver as far as San Gerónimo de Taos, and from the eastern frontier to the farthest western Hopi town of Oraibi—there remained forty-six pueblos of Christian Indians, twenty-five of them staffed missions and the remainder, visiting stations. By census, the total mission population stood at seventeen thousand, "men and women, but only six thousand of them can use the bow and arrow, the rest being old men, children, and women." The friar did not estimate the number of Hispanic residents, saying only that among them scarcely 170 were capable of bearing arms. That ominous ratio of fighting men, Pueblos to Spaniards, seemed of little concern at the time.[17]

To hold off Apaches and keep the Pueblos Christian, New Mexico desperately needed another fifty irregular soldier-colonists on the same terms as the previous contingent, but more urgently a formal fifty-man presidio at Santa Fe, armed and paid like the one that had previously been authorized for the coastal province of Sinaloa. This time, however, Viceroy fray Payo hesitated. His fiscal recommended that Ayeta's new request be forwarded to Madrid without recommendation, a familiar delaying tactic. The Council of the Indies in Spain, of course, sent it back, admonishing the archbishop viceroy to assess the need and cost of the project and "the injury that may result if it is not done." He might also thank Father Ayeta in the king's name. By then, many months had passed and the year was 1680.[18]

———— ❖ ————

Francisco Javier, the governor's secretary, made enemies easily. Certain Spanish citizens had begun quietly asking who was governing the kingdom, resentful of the authority the detached Governor Otermín had bestowed on Javier. As secretary of government and war, Javier enjoyed constant and ready access to the governor. Possessing further civil and military titles—*alcalde ordinario* of Santa Fe, one of two municipal magistrates; and *maestre de campo,* highest rank in the colony beneath the governor as captain general—Javier was untouchable. His enemies, shifting any blame from themselves, portrayed the governor's favorite as a lightning rod for trouble that summer of 1680.

Javier and his associates, Quintana and López Sambrano, both *sargentos mayores,* had kept pressure on neighboring Tewas. The furtive San Juan sorcerer or medicine man whose name they did not yet know had slipped out of their circle of persecution, however, taking refuge in the north at Taos, home to a tradition of violent defiance and farther from the Spanish capital.

To the east on the other side of the mountains from Santa Fe, the gateway pueblo of Pecos remained deeply divided. Still among the most populous Pueblo communities, with perhaps four hundred families, it had turned in on itself. Men of knowledge and power spoke on both sides of the schism. Had their acceptance of Spaniards brought down upon them the curse of the kachinas? According to subsequent testimony by his detractors, Francisco Javier gave the anti-Spanish party cause for resentment. "A man of bad faith, avaricious and sly," Javier and his bullies had approached a camp of Plains Apache traders at Pecos under a flag of truce and taken them and their families prisoners. Some of them Javier distributed to his men, and others he sent off to Parral to sell on his own account.[19]

Meanwhile, word of an impending uprising by Tewas, Taos, Jemez, Tanos, and who knew how many others had reached Pecos. Weighing the implications, Juan de Ye, a Pecos who suffered no doubts about his allegiance to the Spaniards, promptly informed the pueblo's longtime encomendero Francisco Gómez Robledo of the rumors. The latter reported in person to Governor Otermín.

Other warnings had begun to flood the governor's office: from aging fray Fernando Velasco of Pecos; from the Spanish alcalde mayor of Taos; and from the recently elevated Franciscan superior, dolorous fray Juan Bernal at Galisteo. Whatever their purpose, certain Tano headmen from the Galisteo Basin betrayed a couple of Tewa messengers from Tesuque. Delaying until Francisco Javier arrived, Otermín sent Gómez Robledo, who was encomendero of Tesuque as well, to bring in the messengers for questioning, at the same time dispatching warnings to his scattered district officers. Respected by the people of Tesuque, Gómez Robledo was able to identify the two messengers and escort them to the casas reales in Santa Fe that same day, August 9, without incident.

A Spanish colonist in his early twenties interpreted. Francisco Javier took down the testimony, recording the Tesuque pair's names as Nicolás Catua and Pedro Omtua. Under interrogation, they confirmed that the Pueblos of the kingdom were poised to destroy the Spaniards. Other Tesuque Indians had charged them to carry to the Tanos a deerskin thong with two knots signifying the days remaining until the uprising.

What had gotten into the Pueblos? Otermín demanded. The two runners were too young to know, offering only that their elders had held many juntas. It was, however, common knowledge among their people that word had come from the distant north, from a representative of the Pueblo savior god Poseyemu, urging annihilation of the Spaniards and threatening death to Pueblos who failed to comply. This representative, if the interpreter heard the young Tewas correctly, "was very tall, black, and had very large yellow eyes, and . . . everyone feared him greatly." The speakers would have associated a dark personage from the north with a mythic being from the Tewas' creation story, while their listeners conjured up a wholly European image of the devil.[20]

At about seven the next morning, August 10, 1680, feast day of San Lorenzo, Pedro Hidalgo, a literate native New Mexican, rode hell-bent into the Santa Fe plaza, disheveled and gasping for breath. Fear shone in his eyes. Hidalgo had left the capital that morning at dawn for the pueblo of Tesuque with fray Juan Pío to assist at Mass. Surprised to find the pueblo deserted, they came upon the people evidently headed up into the mountains, many wearing war paint. Impatient to say Mass, the friar confronted them in an arroyo, signaling Hidalgo to go around on a ridge. Although he lost sight of Father Pío, the blood-spattered torso of the pueblo's interpreter convinced Hidalgo to spur his horse and flee, dragging his assailants until they let go. The Tesuques, who had watched Gómez Robledo ride off the day before with Catua and Omtua, had drawn first blood. The revolt was on.[21]

Sympathetic Pecos Indians had warned fray Fernando de Velasco, who set off on the wagon road around the mountains to Galisteo, where Tanos assaulted and killed him within sight of his destination. Pecos of the opposing faction, meanwhile, murdered lay brother Juan de Pedraza along with a resident Spanish family. Custos Juan Bernal, who had suffered so stoically, died with others at Galisteo before the mob rushed off to besiege Santa Fe. Their cry, Otermín's critics told his successor, came down to "Give us Francisco Javier, who is the reason we have risen, and we will remain in peace as before." Yet even had Javier, scapegoat or archvillain, fallen into the hands of the Pueblo mob, the killing was already beyond any turning back.[22]

Although certain Spaniards' reckless exploitation may have goaded the Pueblos to action, years of dryness, want, and Apache marauding, particularly in the south, had created the stage upon which their eventual rebellion played out. Spaniards had written the script. They had first conceived of a single kingdom of all Pueblo Indians under one governor; they had regularly sent Indian runners conveying common messages to every corner of New Mexico; and they had taught quotas of Pueblo fighting men from different language groups to come together for joint campaigns. Now, so much hardship, compounded by recent outrages, galvanized anti-Spanish caciques and war captains in dozens of pueblos, swung most of the undecided, and brought on—a decade after don Esteban Clemente was executed for imagining it—the holy war of Pueblo revitalization that finally drove Spaniards out of the kingdom.

6 The Pueblos' Holy War, 1680s

Before the discussion went further, a Hemish [Jemez]
man, Luis Conixu, got up to urge that the delegates first
decide on a general leader. "Leadership was the flame that
enabled my people to stand up against the Uta-ong and
the K'elatosh [Utes and Navajos]," he told them. "If the
flame of leadership burns low, the Castyilash [Spaniards]
will take advantage of us. My council at Walatowa advised
me to say that good leadership alone will be the decisive
force in this great struggle between faiths of sunshine
and darkness. This much I say with the thoughts given
me by Maseway [one of the Twin War Gods]. Dabesh
[Enough]."

When he had finished speaking, a Tewa man took the
floor. "As you know, we Tewas have been involved in the
planning from the beginning. In our meetings we have all
agreed without acting on it that our brother, Po'pay, from
Ohkay is the leader that we are looking for."

This prompted the host war chief to say, "As my
brother from Ka-'p-geh has indicated, we have watched
our brother Po'pay for a long time and agree that he
would be an excellent choice. Since we have many more
things to discuss, why don't we make this selection of a
leader short by agreeing on Po'pay?"

IMAGINATIVE RE-CREATION BY JOE S. SANDO, PUEBLO OF JEMEZ

Santa Fe, August 14, 1680. Terror hung in the air. Unnerved, don Antonio de Otermín, twenty-fifth Spanish governor of the Kingdom and Provinces of New Mexico, stuttered in disbelief. Franciscan missionaries and whole families of Spaniards lay dead. Two Indian servants the governor had bribed to verify the rumors now fled back to Santa Fe ahead of an angry mob. More than five hundred grimly determined Pueblo fighting men were just one league from the capital, impassioned "to attack it and destroy the governor and all the Spaniards." Had they gone mad? "They were saying that now God and Santa María were dead . . . the ones whom the Spaniards worshiped, and that their own God whom they obeyed never died."[1]

Pueblo attackers could be seen next morning in the fields of the San Miguel chapel on a rise across the Santa Fe River. They were ransacking the homes of Mexican Indians in the barrio of Analco and preparing for a siege. Governor Otermín recognized their leader. He was a Spanish-speaking indio ladino named Juan, a Christian who had gone over to the rebels. On horseback, Juan wore a piece of red cloth stolen from the Galisteo mission, in the style of a priest's sash. Yet he came armed as a Spanish fighting man with harquebus, sword, dagger, and *cuera* (protective leather jacket), and the implication was that he knew how to use such weapons.

Otermín sent for him. Boldly, the Indian entered the plaza. With the blood of so many friars and colonists already on their hands, exclaimed Juan, there was no way to call his people to a halt. They were only awaiting others. "They were bringing two crosses, one red and the other white, so that his lordship might choose. The red signified war and the white that the Spaniards would abandon the kingdom."[2]

The Spanish governor pleaded. It was still not too late. If the rebellious Pueblos would put aside their weapons and retire peaceably, he would pardon their crimes. He did not want war. When Juan carried this word to his companions, they hooted in derision. Ringing the bell of the San Miguel chapel, they set the structure afire and kept up their tumult. Otermín, fearing that reinforcements would soon swell their numbers, sent out a troop to dislodge them. That failed.

The governor himself then took the field, and the fighting lasted all day. Just as the Spaniards appeared to be getting the best of it, hundreds of Tewas and Tiwas assaulted the opposite side of the town, forcing Otermín and his men back inside the plaza. Now the casas reales, the government complex on the north side of the plaza, became the Spaniards' last defense and their prison, as more and more survivors from outlying areas crowded in.

Captain Francisco de Anaya Almazán, whose protruding eyes gave him a look of perpetual astonishment, had barely survived. Suddenly militant, Indians from the Tewa pueblo of Santa Clara had assaulted him and his herders utterly without warning, killing two of them. Although his paternal grandparents had emigrated from Salamanca in Spain to Mexico City, the rugged Anaya, born in New Mexico about 1633, had little in common with Oñate's knightly, Salamanca-educated Gaspar Pérez de Villagrá. An adventure for Villagrá, New Mexico was home to Anaya. Whereas the poet depicted the Pueblos as noble savages, these were Anaya's neighbors. He learned their language, a badge of trust, and some were blood relatives. Yet before the violence ended, the New Mexican captain would lose every member of his immediate family. The battle for Santa Fe had become a hellish nightmare.[3]

As days passed, the Indians grew bolder. Tightening the noose, they overran ripe Spanish fields, burning homes, even the Franciscan church. Then they cut the ditch supplying the casas reales; without water for two days and a night, the trapped Spaniards watched their animals begin to die. In the eyes of the children, sleepless and terrified by the endless drumming and chanting of their besiegers, the governor and his council saw desperation. The Pueblos showed no signs of tiring. There appeared no other way: the Spaniards must gird for a surprise breakout at dawn. Better, they agreed, "to die fighting than of hunger and thirst, shut up within the casas reales."[4]

Early on the morning of August 20, hailing the Blessed Virgin Mary, every man and boy capable of bearing arms burst through the gate into the open. Otermín, wounded in the face and through his cuera on the chest, boasted later that they killed more than three hundred of the Pueblo rebels. His fighters seized eleven enemy firearms, eighty animals, as well as desperately needed provisions, withdrawing again inside the casas reales. They admitted the deaths of a ranking officer and four soldiers, along with many wounded, but they had temporarily broken the siege. The forty-seven Pueblo prisoners they interrogated and summarily executed left no doubt about the revolt's origin.

All the Pueblo peoples were obeying an Indian who lived to the north, a representative of the Pueblos' savior deity Poseyemu. At this point, though the Spaniards had still not yet heard the name Popé, the Indians' intent was clear. Not a single Spanish male was to be spared, not even baby boys at the breast. The Pueblos meant to take back New Mexico. At least for the time being, Governor Otermín, advised by the surviving Franciscans, Captain Anaya, and other leading citizens, must order a strategic withdrawal from Santa Fe before the Indians redeployed their siege. Of the thousand or more souls huddled in the casas reales, scarcely a hundred were fit to fight. Hence, on August 21, 1680, Governor Antonio de Otermín led forth from the kingdom's smoldering capital a terror-driven Spanish refugee caravan.

And the Pueblos let them go. At the ranch headquarters of Francisco de Anaya's brash older brother Cristóbal, the owner, his wife and children, and servants lay heaped up at the threshold, grotesque, naked, and dead.

———⋄⋄———

No Spaniard saw it happen. No Pueblo described it. Yet in terms of sheer determination, it had to have been the Pueblos' single most dramatic act of defiance: throwing down adobe by adobe the Spaniards' emblematic icon of Christian occupation, fray Andrés Juárez's monumental Pecos church. Not until twentieth-century archaeologists excavated the fallen remains could anyone form a picture of the massive temple's violent deconstruction.

Not surprisingly, fifteen or sixteen years after the act, the stronger, pro-Spanish Pecos faction denied responsibility for it. Father Custos Francisco de Vargas doubted their claim that they had not killed fray Fernando de Velasco, their minister in 1680. This restraint they considered "a meritorious act. They do not say a word, however, should you ask about fray Juan de Pedraza, a lay brother ... or a Spaniard who was at Pecos Pueblo with his wife and children at the time. If they are asked about the church they had then ... they make excuses by saying that the Tewas burned it."[5]

Probably Tewas did take part, perhaps even initiating the demolition during Popé's triumphal post-Revolt tour, but the manpower required to bring down the grandest structure north of New Spain suggests that not a few Pecos Indians themselves got caught up in the frenzy. According to an eighty-year-old indio ladino captive from San Felipe Pueblo who testified late in 1681 before Governor Otermín and Francisco Javier,

> the said Indian, Popé, came down in person, and with him El Saca [or El Jaca] and El Chato from the pueblo of Los Taos, and other captains and leaders and many people who were in his train, and he ordered in all the pueblos through which he passed that they instantly break up and burn the images of the holy Christ, the Virgin Mary and the other saints, the crosses, and everything pertaining to Christianity, and that they burn the temples, break up the bells, and separate from the wives whom God had given them in marriage and take those whom they desired.[6]

As for "burning" the Pecos church, as in the case of mud-and-stone Acoma in 1599, the bulk of the materials withstood flames, yet the billowing gray smoke of fired roof timbers,

along with brush and other flammables heaped inside, gave
the most conspicuous proof of destruction. Afire, the building
became a giant blast furnace. "A strong draft," the archaeologists surmise, "was created through the tunnel of the nave from
the clearstory window over the chancel thereby blowing ashes
out the door."[7] So much more visible than Pueblo smoke
signals announcing the synchronous rising of distant communities in August 1680, this great, cleansing bonfire offered
up smoke that the Pueblos believed the kachinas would turn
into rain-bearing clouds.

To bring down the towering blackened walls, however,
demanded heavy, anticlimactic labor by many, many hands,
Tewa or Pecos. Dragging ladders from the pueblo or lashing
together longer ones on site to reach up forty feet, the demolition crews must have competed for days or weeks. They had
to have used iron crowbars or something similar. Hacking and
prying loose adobes by the thousands, they all but leveled the
buttressed south and north side walls and the twenty-foot-
thick apse or west end, which supported two of an apparent
six towers.

The facade, facing east toward the plains, shadowed the
layer of ash blown out the front doors and, again by the
archaeologists' reckoning, "must have fallen to protect it [the
ash] very shortly after the fire and is represented by the stratum
of charcoal and adobe."[8] Although this last unsupported wall
had toppled on its face, the adobes still stood vertically on
their outer edges. Sandstone slabs, thrown forty to forty-five
feet out from the foundation, probably formed a decorative
coping. The eager spoilers left standing some rooms of the
convento, which lay along the church's south side, but as close
to the friars' quarters as bedrock would permit, they dug a
kiva, facing it with black adobes from the dismantled church.

Former neophytes at other missions, swept along by the
same purgative wave, wrought what horrified Spaniards saw
as sacrilege and doom. The effect varied from place to place.

The Acomas, in deference to parents and grandparents who had carried the dirt for the miraculous Acoma church up from below on their backs, left the structure standing. Elsewhere, Pueblos recovering from the rush of rebellion put the gutted, roofless shells of their churches to practical use as supplemental living, storage, or work space, or more frequently, as corrals or stables. At Isleta Pueblo, on his ill-fated attempt at reconquest in the winter of 1681, Governor Otermín raged at the Indians for penning cows inside the burned church nave, demanding that they be driven out into the cold. The Isletas, like the Pecos, blamed the destruction on the Tewas, Taos, and Picuris who had descended from the north.[9]

Just upriver at deserted Sandia, Spaniards found that Pueblos had turned the standing rooms of the convento into "a seminary of idolatry," with rows of kachina masks hanging from the walls "arranged very carefully, after their barbarous custom, . . . representing both men and women, and other small ones representing children." Otermín's men burned them all. In another room, the Sandias had set up "a forge with very good bellows and with a ploughshare for an anvil." Just as with carpentry, the Pecos specialty, other Pueblos refused to abandon ironwork and similarly useful arts.[10]

The devastation at Pecos had been the centerpiece, an extreme. When Spaniards next rode out from Santa Fe over the mountains to the gateway pueblo in September 1692, the fortress church of fray Andrés Juárez lay in an enormous, non-descript mound not worth noting in the record.

––––––•◦•––––––

During the Pueblo Revolt and its aftermath, motives and passions got terribly jumbled. Survival strategies—saying what might mollify or mislead one's interrogators—as well as the vagaries of communication and translation from Tewa to Spanish and vice versa and the desperation of both Pueblos and Spaniards to evade the onus of what had happened, all colored the testimony of several Pueblo captives heard by

Governor Otermín and set down by Francisco Javier. Themes emerged, nevertheless. Obviously Popé, however pivotal his role, did not act alone.

Allusions in the captives' statements to allegorical beings in a kiva at Taos, especially a big black man who claimed to represent the Pueblo deity Poseyemu, may have had bases in fact. One hypothesis posits a dark-complexioned, fully accul- turated Tewa war captain named Naranjo from Santa Clara Pueblo, descended on his mother's side from Pueblos and on his father's from a freed mulatto slave among Oñate's rein- forcements.[11] Such a mortal, skilled in contemporary war- fare, transformed kachina-style into the spiritual emissary of Poseyemu and conjoined with archcacique Popé, raised a common insurgency to the level of holy war. Whoever the other beings may have been, mortal or supernatural, they aided these two in convincing dozens of spiritual and tactical head- men across the polyglot Pueblo world that now, at last, the time was ripe.

The brilliant timing of Popé and his advisers lay at the heart of their stunning success. Previous revolts had been planned for the spring, a time of scarcity after the long months of winter had depleted food reserves. By waiting until high summer, when the spirits of agricultural peoples everywhere in the Northern Hemisphere rose in anticipation of harvest time, they caught the Spaniards totally unawares. August was a month of gathering in the crops, not a time for war. And 1680, unlike the preceding drought years, promised to be a good year. Moreover, among the Pueblos, it was the season of the summer leaders, who were likely to be more conservative and less tolerant of Spaniards than their winter counterparts.

A prevalent theme in statements taken from the captive Pueblo witnesses was fear. Not only did it serve them to shift blame, swearing that their people had joined the revolt only because of the leaders' threats to kill them if they did not, but their testimony also served Spaniards eager to cast Popé in an evil light. Tewa-speaking Juan from Tesuque testified through two New Mexico–born Spaniards who swore "to interpret in the Tegua and Castilian languages, accurately, loyally, and legally, without adding to or omitting anything." Asked why the people held Popé in such terror, Juan swore that Popé conversed regularly with the devil. Indeed, the devil had alerted Popé that his son-in-law, Nicolás Bua, native governor of Ohkay Owingeh (San Juan Pueblo), was about to inform the Spaniards. Bua's swift murder happened under Popé's roof. Although this story appeared only once more, Juan assured Otermín that it was common knowledge throughout the kingdom.[12]

Leadership of the revolt rested more on cultural loyalty, vengeful hatred of particular Spaniards, or the prospect of spoils than on blood purity. Several of Popé's prime collaborators came from mixed-blood marriages, however thoroughly Pueblo they had grown up. The nickname of Pueblo leader El Chato, who descended on Pecos with Popé and El Saca, can mean "flat nose," perhaps a hint of mulatto features and a shadow of the mysterious black man. Alonso Catití of Santo Domingo and Francisco el Ollita of Cochiti, who together coordinated the revolt of the Keresan pueblos, both had Spanish half brothers.

Whatever motivated the captured informants and their Spanish interpreters, they depicted Popé as self-deceived. Even while exhorting the Pueblo world to cast off every vestige of Spanish rule, he did so as only a Spaniard would. His victorious procession through the Pueblo communities, demanding tribute and compliance by decree, resurrected the memory of Governor López de Mendizábal. Yet during a banquet held at Santa Ana and served on a long table with Spanish fare, Popé resorted to the Pueblos' long tradition of sacred parody. He had two Christian chalices brought. Directing Alonso Catití to seat himself at the other end, Popé took his place at the head of the table. They drank. Then, in mock solemnity, Popé rose and offered a toast as if Catití were the father custos,

"'To your health, your Paternal Reverence!' And the other answered, 'The same to your lordship, Sir governor!'"[13]

While Popé and Catití bid the Spaniards a biting farewell in burlesque, far down the Rio Grande 1,946 Spanish survivors—householders and servants, grandparents, girls and boys—trudged into a chaotic, teeming refugee camp ten miles above El Paso. Because this was war, Governor Otermín's counters listed animals and firearms before dependants. They reckoned that no more than 155 men were capable of bearing arms. Some New Mexican families had escaped almost intact, while other familiar surnames were barely noted.[14]

Maestre de campo Francisco Gómez Robledo, married soon after his acquittal by the Inquisition, passed muster with eight horses and five mules "lean and worn out," and four guns. A crowd in tow, he had one grown son, five female and two male children, an unmarried sister, a sister-in-law with seven small children, and twenty servants.[15] In sorry contrast, Gómez Robledo's cousin with the bulging eyes, Captain Francisco de Anaya Almazán, on foot with nothing but the weapons he carried, had lost his whole family. Two years after the fact, a captive Indian deposed that he had recognized the nude body of Anaya's wife, Francisca Domínguez, "out on a field, her head bashed in, and a very small infant dead at her feet."[16] The final body count of New Mexico colonists and their servants killed in 1680 exceeded 380. Moreover, nineteen priests and two lay brothers of the thirty-odd Franciscans died at their Pueblo missions.

Either coerced by the retreating Spaniards or fearing Pueblo reprisal for their inaction, three hundred or more Southern Tiwas and Piros had joined the Spanish exodus in 1680. One of them, Alonso Shimitihua, a Christian indio ladino from Isleta who spoke Tiwa, Tewa, and Spanish, evidently secured Governor Otermín's license almost immediately to lead a small Pueblo peace delegation back upriver. It was a bold mission. Fellow Isletas Baltasar and Tomás, four Piros, and a Jemez traveled north with him, but Shimitihua began to suspect that his companions did not share his desire to bring the rebellious Pueblos back to the Christian God. The Piros dropped off en route, as the other two Isletas rushed on ahead.

When Shimitihua reached Isleta, he was met by a garishly dressed unnamed rebel captain from Alameda on horseback at the head of a large retinue and preceded by a yellow banner. This conspicuous Pueblo headman wore Christian ecclesiastical vestments: alb and surplice with red sash and a maniple as headdress. In welcome, the Isletas lined up in two rows and fired a salute. Like some reigning potentate, the honored visitor had other Indians lift him down from his horse. Immediately, this unidentified personage had Shimitihua and his remaining three companions tied up and escorted under guard to Santo Domingo.

When they were left alone for a time, Baltasar pressed Shimitihua about his mission, boasting that he and Tomás had come north to rally Tiwa and Piro allies for a massacre of Spaniards in the El Paso district, for which the local Manso Indians were already poised. Before Shimitihua could answer, guards hustled them off to the house of Alonso Catití, where the rebel leader received the prisoners amid furnishings and carpets from the pillaged church. A Navajo who had come to negotiate peace with the Keres sat in alb and chasuble on a cushion nearby. When Catití heard Shimitihua's plea to return to the Christian God, the Santo Domingo headman thundered that such a god no longer existed.

Three days later, Popé arrived and, according to Shimitihua, the scene repeated itself. In a fury, Popé, "who governed all the rebels despotically and supremely," lunged at Shimitihua with a dagger and would have stabbed him to death had Catití not intervened. Baltasar and Tomás explained their plan to attack refugee Spaniards. That delighted Popé. Discussion then turned to Pueblo leaders who opposed further war. Popé especially hated Lorenzo Muza of Jemez, whose warning had enabled the Spanish alcalde mayor and the missionary to escape death. Catch Muza, urged Popé, "and bring him here so we can gouge out his eyes." On Popé's orders, they paraded Shimitihua through various pueblos and eventually to Taos, where he spent the uncommonly cold winter observing idolatrous abuse of Spanish corpses and an image of the Virgin Mary. Finally escaping, he made his way back to El Paso, reappearing in March 1681.[17]

Whatever had really happened on Alonso Shimitihua's strange odyssey, certain Spaniards wanted to believe him. The clever native messenger portrayed Popé as a cruel warlord doing the devil's bidding. Although Governor Otermín bewailed the revolt to Father Ayeta and professed rhetorically that God had "permitted it because of my grievous sins," he chose not to elaborate. To his way of thinking, he bore no responsibility for oppressive labor practices or the campaign to stamp out native religion. Aware of mounting criticism among fellow Spaniards and ignoring Pueblo grievances, he insisted he had done his best to administer "this miserable kingdom."[18]

Father Ayeta and the surviving friars did the same. They blamed the devil for the insurrection. To have admitted that their self-denying, eighty-year Christian ministry to the Pueblo peoples was flawed or in any way had caused their beloved neophytes to revolt would have called into question their devotion to Jesus Christ, the very reason for their being. Twenty-one of their brothers had won crowns of martyrdom. The living dared not doubt their ministry. Satan, continuously striving against God, had temporarily ensnared and misguided the Pueblo Indians.[19]

The Pueblo–Spanish War, flaring first at Tesuque and fanned swiftly into a conflagration that drove the Spaniards before it, now entered a smoldering, decade-long second stage between 1681 and 1691. Both peoples suffered want, dissension, and uncertainty about the future. Upriver were the Pueblos, rid of their common enemy but breaking once again into contending groups, and far to the south in refugee camps milled the Spaniards, a colony in exile. Juan of Tesuque knew that the Pueblo Indians "were of different minds" regarding the Spaniards' return. Some would fight to the death to prevent it, while others accepted its eventuality. Obviously, the Spaniards, more than 80 percent of whom had been born in the kingdom, would wish to come home, for as Juan observed, they too were "sons of the land and had grown up with the natives."[20]

———•◦•———

A product of two cultures, Pueblo Indian Bartolomé de Ojeda lived with doubts. His mestiza grandmother, Juana Maroh, was a Christian, and as a boy, Franciscan missionaries at Santa Ana or Zia Pueblo had favored Bartolo, teaching him to read and write Spanish. He had a commanding presence, earning the Keresan elders' trust and becoming a war captain. And when the call came, despite any misgivings he may have felt, Ojeda joined the insurgency.

Long after the flames of 1680 had gone out, Bartolomé de Ojeda kept informed of events in the separated worlds of Pueblos and Spaniards. Keenly observant and sociable, he listened to fellow Pueblo Indians tell of the cruel deaths they had inflicted on their missionaries at Jemez, Acoma, Zuni, and the Hopi towns. His own Christian grandmother, stripped and tied between two naked friars, paraded and whipped, stoned and stabbed, had perished at Acoma. Ojeda watched as shifting coalitions of Pueblo communities, as well as internal factions, splintered whatever unity ever existed.

The highhanded Popé lost favor early on, yielding to the less passionate Luis Tupatu of Picuris. Apparently, as Ojeda remembered it, Tewas restored Popé locally for a time around 1688, probably in response to a Spanish thrust upriver the year before, but soon after—since no more was heard of him—the recognized prime mover of the great revolt probably died. Although his people everywhere retained Spanish seeds, horses, guns, and crafts, no other Pueblo resistance leader

Cliofi Arquero, Keresan Pueblo Indian, by T. Harmon Parkhurst, ca. 1935. Courtesy Palace of the Governors (MNM/DCA), no. 46990.

before or after Popé gained enough authority, as he had, to appropriate the mantle of sovereignty with which seventeenth-century Spaniards had vested the Pueblo world.[21]

Living now in wretched exile, Spanish survivors who did not desert to New Spain also split into factions reminiscent of the days of Luis de Rosas. One group coalesced around a tall, graying native of Mexico City who had been raised in the kingdom, Maestre de campo Juan Domínguez de Mendoza, who had his eye on the governorship. However much he may have embellished his service record, his withered left shoulder, cleft hand, and limping gait—all battle scars—reinforced his claim as New Mexico's most meritorious soldier of the 1660s and 1670s. On numerous campaigns against Navajos, he had led forces composed of many more Pueblos than Spaniards, unwittingly further preparing the Indians for 1680. His detractors among the refugees charged Domínguez de Mendoza and his enormous extended family, along with the Durán y Chávez clan, of profiteering in foodstuffs and animals while other people were starving.[22]

Finally in midautumn 1681, Governor Otermín headed a disgruntled column north, with Domínguez de Mendoza as second-in-command. They meant to reconquer the Pueblo world. By the governor's count, he had 146 Spanish men-at-arms, along with nearly a thousand horses and mules, some pulling wagons. He did not trust his 112 Manso and Pueblo Indian auxiliaries. Father Ayeta (hailed in September 1680 for his appearance once again at the head of an emergency supply train) and his secretary went as chaplains. Apache smoke signals marked the column's progress. Poking about in the successive, long-deserted pueblos of Senecú, Socorro, Alamillo, and Sevilleta, Spaniards gathered up broken Christian relics before setting fire to whatever would burn.

The smoke of home fires rose above Isleta, the first occupied pueblo they came to. The Indians' halfhearted defense and their decision not to abandon the pueblo revealed the residents' ambivalence. The Isletas allowed Governor Otermín to lecture them. When Father Ayeta set up his portable altar aboard a wagon and had it wheeled into the plaza, 511 of them consented to Christian absolution or baptism. Governor Otermín stood as godfather of the first boy baptized, whom they called Carlos in honor of the Spanish king. Even as fierce December weather closed in around the expedition, the repossession of Isleta appeared to bode well.

Sent ahead with sixty soldiers and some of the Pueblo allies, Domínguez de Mendoza nearing Cochiti came face-to-face with a tense, mixed gathering of Pueblo leaders and fighting men. At one point, according to Spanish accounts, Alonso Catití and Francisco el Ollita feigned tears as they begged forgiveness for their grievous sins. Their Spanish half brothers embraced the two seemingly repentant headmen. The Indians pleaded for more time to bring others to the peace gathering. Spanish-speaking Bartolomé de Ojeda must have accompanied Keresan war chief El Pupiste when a delegation from Zia and Santa Ana came down from their freezing refuge in the Jemez Mountains to treat with Domínguez de Mendoza.

While the Spaniards huddled against the cold at Cochiti, the Pueblos schemed. Luis Tupatu of Picuris, overall rebel leader, sent out a summons, even to the deposed Popé. The ruse, later disclosed by captives, was to have the prettiest young Pueblo women bathe, put on their finest, and appear at Cochiti as if to prepare a celebratory meal. That night, while the women seduced the Spaniards, Ollita and Tupatu would make off with their horses, while Catití and hundreds of armed Keresan and Jemez men descended in full fury. But too many Indians of mixed loyalty knew of the plot and risked death to alert Domínguez de Mendoza. Under heightened security and swirling snow, the Spaniards withdrew.

Otermín fumed that his second-in-command had not punished the rebels, burned their kivas, or kept him better informed. Each blamed the other for their deteriorating situation. The half-frozen men took sides. The Spanish governor's eyes smarted from personally torching kivas and wet piles of Pueblo ritual paraphernalia. Ultimately, a reckoning came at a council of war held on New Year's Eve 1681 in the vicinity of Alameda, Puaray, and Sandia—each of which Otermín's command had sacked and "burned." The hope cherished by

Father Ayeta that most Pueblo peoples, abused by their rebellious leaders, would welcome Christian absolution had been dashed. Bitter cold and snow numbed the men's morale, and the horses and mules were spent. The army must turn back.

The council further recommended that the Isleta Indians who had capitulated be taken south for their own safety. If left behind, the rebels would kill them, or they would again revert to idolatry. Therefore, as the Spaniards retreated, Governor Otermín decreed that 385 Isletas, carrying whatever they could of their personal belongings, join the exodus under guard. He then had Isleta torched.[23]

Amid swirling charges of incompetence, Governor Otermín retired in ill health to Mexico City in 1683. From that safe haven eight years later, he vented his doubts about recolonizing New Mexico.[24] The able Domingo Jironza, a professional soldier fresh from Spain in 1680, assumed the governorship after Otermín and tried to regularize the feuding colony, earning enmity for himself from disgruntled colonists. Troublemaker Juan Domínguez de Mendoza, whom Jironza late in 1683 sent on an expedition to the Jumanos of west-central Texas, departed El Paso illegally in 1685 with some of his circle to pursue appointment as governor even in Spain, only to die in Madrid a decade later.[25] Jironza, meanwhile, dealt vigorously with local native unrest, but before he could mount an expedition to gauge Pueblo sentiments upriver, a former underling replaced him.

Brash, ruddy-faced Pedro Reneros de Posada must have had connections at court. The young Spaniard had enlisted as a soldier in the fifty-man El Paso presidio authorized by the crown in the wake of the 1680 revolt and risen uncommonly fast to the rank of captain. Sent by Jironza to Mexico City with dispatches in 1684, Reneros reappeared two years later as governor.

Documents surviving from his undistinguished, less than three-year term reveal more about Reneros's alleged embezzlement of the El Paso presidial payroll than about the reconnaissance in force he led north up the overgrown Camino Real in 1687. The first serious penetration of the Pueblo world in more than six years, it met stiff resistance by Bartolomé de Ojeda's Keresan kinsmen at Santa Ana and Zia. According to one brief account, Reneros ordered his men, almost certainly including Tiwa and Piro Pueblo expatriates, to "burn" Santa Ana, probably located then atop the vast red mesa that rises sharply behind its present site in the Jemez River valley.

Judging from later charges against him, Reneros likely employed deceit to take four Keresan headmen and another ten Indian males captive. Back in El Paso by early October, the governor promptly condemned the four leaders to public execution. The other ten he accused of murder, sacrilege, and active participation in the 1680 revolt, sentencing them to ten years of slavery. Taken to Nueva Vizcaya for sale, these Pueblo Indians would never be allowed to return to New Mexico, lest they reveal to other natives the weakness of Spanish defenses. Money from their sale was to be deposited in the Spaniards' war chest.

A less somber public spectacle developed in front of the makeshift casas reales in February 1689. Recipients of unexpected rations of sugar and chocolate, happy soldiers from the El Paso presidio competed in a *juego de gallo*—galloping full tilt, swinging low out of the saddle, and trying to grab a rooster buried in sand up to its neck. Other soldiers bet on their favorites. A conspicuous, recently returned Spaniard cheered them on, according to one observer, loaning money to those without. Governor Jironza, having made the rounds in Mexico City and settled accounts from his previous term, was back to recoup the governorship.

Jironza brought food, clothes, weapons, ammunition, and livestock to succor the destitute exiles. The unpopular Reneros de Posada, at the conclusion of raucous residencia proceedings, left with the returning wagons. In Mexico City during legal wrangling over the El Paso garrison's pay, the damning residencia went missing. Reneros lost the court battle anyway. Although he apparently never returned to New Mexico, his discredit did not prevent him from serving again as a presidial captain in Nueva Vizcaya.[26]

———————

Unhindered by his doubts, war captain Bartolomé de Ojeda labored alongside hundreds of Pueblo fighters that summer of 1689 hastily throwing up barricades of adobe and earth to fortify Zia Pueblo. With the punishment of Santa Ana seared in their minds, they meant to make a stand. Although the site, on high ground farther up the Jemez River, presented little in the way of natural defense, the Indians were counting on numbers. Their women and children had carried provisions to shelters in the Jemez Mountains, rising to the west. Spies kept the men informed of the Spaniards' progress.

Although no detailed campaign journal has survived describing Governor Jironza's 1689 assault on Zia, there is little doubt of its ferocity. During their miserable exile, Spaniards had commemorated vengefully each year the feast of San Lorenzo, August 10, the day so many of their relatives had fallen under Pueblo blows in 1680. Jironza fanned the fervor of that anniversary. Outfitting eighty men-at-arms with the new and reconditioned weapons he had transported to El Paso, and attended by 120 Indian allies, Jironza advanced up the gentle valley of the Jemez River in late August, the slope-shouldered Sandia Mountains looming at their backs. Animals dragged at least one bronze cannon, which had been repaired but proved of little use. With Zia in sight, the commander called for an *alborada,* which some of the men knew as an *albazo* or *albada,* a dawn attack from all sides.

They fought all day August 29. The acrid smell of black powder and burning homes, the screams, and the exhaustion of the hand-to-hand combatants recalled Acoma ninety years earlier. Based on Jironza's similar estimate of six hundred Indians killed, some preferring death in battle to surrender, one suspects that the Spanish governor had read Gaspar Pérez de Villagrá's *Historia* and elevated his own feat to a par with that legendary action. Fifty of his eighty men suffered wounds, one apparently fatal. Between seventy and ninety Pueblo defenders fell into Spanish hands. Four of them, somehow identified as especially prominent rebel leaders, Jironza executed in the plaza of Zia (perhaps only an echo of Reneros de Posada's earlier act). Among the other prisoners was Spanish-speaking Bartolomé de Ojeda.[27]

Spaniards recalled how valiantly Ojeda had fought against them that day. Bloodied twice, once by a musket ball and again by an arrow, "thinking that he could not survive with such wounds," the Indian "surrendered, impelled by fear of hell, in order to confess before dying."[28] The victors complied. Chaplain fray Francisco de Vargas, father custos of New Mexico's exiled Franciscans, probably heard Ojeda's confession. Providing medical attention on the battlefield, Spaniards carried the wounded Keresan war captain back to El Paso, where he recovered.

Although such prisoners were subject to the standard ten years of servitude, Jironza's nephew, writing five years later, claimed that his uncle established a community of ninety repentant Pueblo Indians at El Paso with a missionary, surely Father Vargas. Ojeda became their leader. Earlier, Piro and Tiwa refugees, who had carried with them the names of their original towns, lived below El Paso in Senecú, Ysleta, and Socorro (to each of which they appended the suffix "del Sur," [of the south]).[29]

A faint memory of Bartolomé de Ojeda as culture hero persisted at Santa Ana Pueblo as late as 1980, when an informant recalled that after the battle "a Zía man who spoke Spanish" had withdrawn voluntarily with Jironza's force to El Paso. He would watch over the Keresan child captives. As agreed, this individual later reappeared, informing the people that their children "were all doing well and growing up and learning to speak Spanish and learning whatever they were taught to learn." Before rejoining the Spaniards, this Zia man said he would visit them again, but he never did.[30]

When he appeared before Governor Jironza in September 1689, Bartolomé de Ojeda needed no interpreter. The Indian swore by the sign of the cross to tell the truth. Governor Jironza, who had forwarded to the viceroy news of the Spaniards' triumph at Zia and his desire to lead an immediate, full-scale reconquest, wanted to know the general condition of the apostate Pueblos. Would they unite again to oppose the Spaniards' return?

Ojeda began with his fellow Keresan-speakers. People from Zia, Santa Ana, San Felipe, and Cochiti, allied with Jemez, Taos, and Pecos, fought continually with Tewas and Picuris. As Jironza already knew, the zealot Alonso Catití had dropped dead in his house at Santo Domingo in 1684. The Keres of Acoma had split, some remaining on the mesa top and others settling at Laguna with families from Zia and Santa Ana. Bad feelings existed between Laguna and Acoma. Zunis and Hopis were also at war. Apaches had made peace with some of the Pueblo apostates but committed hostilities against others. Since 1680, Utes from the north, who previously had grown used to trading with the Spaniards of New Mexico, raided any Pueblo town they could, but especially those of the Taos, Picuris, Jemez, and Tewas. Luis Tupatu of Picuris still figured as the rebel Pueblos' most conspicuous leader.

Evidently prompted by Father Vargas, Ojeda proceeded to relate in grisly detail what eyewitnesses had told him about the martyrdoms of seven Franciscans killed in the western Pueblo towns. He had heard vague talk about the deaths of other missionaries, but nothing he could report with any certainty.[31]

Redirected by Jironza, the witness may then have gone on to relate the willingness of certain Pueblo towns not to oppose Spanish reentry. According to a subsequent version of his testimony, Ojeda provided a description of specific geographical features marking the traditional league of land of each community. This, purportedly, enabled Governor Jironza to reconfirm Pueblo land grants in advance of the Spaniards' homecoming.

It is possible, though, that a well-informed, nineteenth-century con man with access to the archives put words in Ojeda's mouth with intent to defraud. Shortly after New Mexico became a territory of the United States in 1850, a number of Pueblo communities presented documents to the U.S. surveyor general purporting to be land grants issued in 1689 by Governor Jironza on the basis of Ojeda's testimony. Congress in due course conveyed such lands to the Pueblos. Still later, in the early 1890s, William M. Tipton, an expert with the U.S. Court of Private Land Claims, pronounced these so-called Cruzate grants (from the governor's full name, Domingo Jironza Petrís de Cruzate) forgeries. Already patented, however, pertinent Pueblo lands were not affected. But Tipton was right. The slipshod documents he examined were spurious. Yet just how and why they came to be—or if at one time genuine originals existed—remains a mystery.[32]

During the eighteen months from September 1689 to February 1691, Bartolomé de Ojeda underwent a transformation. As the Keresan war captain recovered from his wounds and regained strength in El Paso, fray Francisco de Vargas counseled him. The Indian remarried. Surely he replayed in his mind the Spaniards' brutal assault on Zia Pueblo, where so many of his kinfolk had perished. And for what? One thing seemed certain to Ojeda, as it did to Juan of Tesuque. Sooner or later, the Spaniards would return to the kingdom. New Mexico was their home too. Heeding whatever gods that now gave meaning to his life, Bartolomé de Ojeda resolved to join the pending Spanish reentry, perhaps to ease his people's suffering.

———•◆•———

No relation of Father Vargas, don Diego de Vargas, the confident, forty-seven-year-old Spanish nobleman from Madrid

who took over from Jironza early in 1691, embraced Bartolomé
de Ojeda quite literally. Spaniards introduced the Indian
to Vargas as don Bartolomé, more familiarly as Bartolo or
Bartolillo—once an apostate, now an ally. The new governor,
a keen negotiator, had previously administered mining districts
among Indians in southern and central New Spain. He considered himself an especially good judge of character. And he
trusted Ojeda from the start.[33]

Although the king had reappointed Domingo Jironza as
governor on the strength of his victory at Zia, the decree had
not reached Mexico City in time. Jironza's term, assumed to
be the standard three years, rested instead on the pleasure of
the viceroy. Because Vargas, through an agent at court in Spain,
had purchased in 1688 the future on a five-year term as governor of New Mexico, Viceroy conde de Galve, Vargas's neigh-
bor from Madrid, conveyed the office to him in 1690. Vargas
acceded at El Paso on February 22, 1691. He would direct
the third (or resettlement) stage of the Pueblo–Spanish War.
Jironza dutifully accepted appointment as alcalde mayor and
military commander in the province of Sonora.

After maddening delays, on August 10, 1692, twelfth anniversary of the Pueblo Revolt, Diego de Vargas finally proclaimed by the strong voice of African drummer and herald
Sebastián Rodríguez an armed reconnaissance. He would test
the Pueblos' resolve. Three squads from the presidio, along with
pack animals, wagons, a bronze cannon and mortar, livestock,
and a hundred Indian allies, departed El Paso on the sixteenth
to await Vargas upriver at Robledo. Bartolomé de Ojeda went
as emissary and interpreter to an arc of Keresan-speaking pueblos: Zia, Santa Ana, San Felipe, Santo Domingo, and Cochiti.
When the fifty promised soldiers from Nueva Vizcaya failed
to show, the governor and his party set out on the twenty-first
to overtake the others.

Hastening through deserted pueblos en route, purposely
doing no harm, Vargas planned a dawn assault on Cochiti,

where his guide Ojeda believed they would find Keresan Indians willing to talk. Yet Cochiti and nearby Santo Domingo lay lifeless, and Indians were seen abandoning San Felipe. Vargas ordered that nothing be disturbed. A mounted Indian from San Felipe approached the Spaniards, giving them to understand in broken Castilian that the Tanos and Tewas who occupied Santa Fe were enemies of the Keres. Hence, his people "celebrated the coming of the Spaniards and would help them and go kill the Tewas."[34]

As the first light of Saturday, September 13, 1692, gave looming form to the fortress pueblo that Tanos and Tewas had erected over the former palace of governors at Santa Fe, Diego de Vargas approached cautiously with his men in close formation. On signal, all cried out in unison, "Praise be to the holy sacrament of the altar!" That brought crowds to the flat roofs and terraces, the ramparts, as Vargas described the scene. The moment was critical. Four New Mexican Spaniards who knew the closely related Tano and Tewa tongues shouted up from the semidarkness that the Spaniards had come in peace to pardon them in the name of the king. The occupants did not believe it. This must be some trick of enemy Pecos or lying Apaches.

Urging calm, Vargas had bugle and war drum sounded. Now the Indians within began a furious shouting that lasted an hour, screaming "many shameful things in their language," which dutiful interpreters translated for the governor. Still he refused to be drawn into battle. After sunrise, the angry dialogue continued. If he were indeed the new Spanish governor, he should come forward and take off his helmet so they could see him. This he did, removing even the kerchief from his head. He displayed his banner with the Virgin on one side and the arms of Spain on the other. The vocal Pueblo tenants responded with a litany of earlier abuses committed by Spaniards. They demanded to know if Francisco Javier, Luis de Quintana, and Diego López Sambrano, their despised tormentors, were among Vargas's company. He swore that they were not, and, dead or alive, would never return to New Mexico.

While the tense negotiations continued, Vargas quietly had his small force of men-at-arms and Indian auxiliaries take up siege positions around the fortress and cut off its water supply. At the same time, outside the fortress he greeted other Tewa delegations drawn by the confrontation, physically embracing them. No one doubted this new governor's courage. Despite their urge to fight, Pueblo leaders inside the fortress noted that these Spaniards had not brought their women and children. They had not come to stay. Why not then let them perform their ritual acts and be gone?

Hence, on Sunday the fourteenth—a date still commemorated in Santa Fe's annual Fiestas amid mixed emotions—Diego de Vargas brushed aside his advisers' warnings and entered the fortress dressed in court finery without weapons. His bravado won the day. Gradually, women and children crowded into the plaza to join their men. Before this assembly, the Spanish governor and three blue-robed friars presided over the ceremonial repossession of Santa Fe and the absolution of hundreds of apostate Pueblo Indians, relying at every turn on the interpreters. Vargas cautioned his honor guard to shout "¡Viva el Rey!" ("Long live the King!"), throwing their hats in the air, but not to fire their harquebuses in salute for fear that Indians outside the walls would assume that war had broken out.

Don Luis el Picurí, alias Tupatu, put around his neck the rosary Governor Vargas had sent him as a safe-conduct. The paramount Pueblo leader appeared on horseback with his armed escort the next afternoon. He wore on his head like a diadem a plaited band set with a heart-shaped shell. The two leaders embraced in front of Vargas's tent, talked of peace and war, and exchanged gifts. The following morning, don Luis and other principal men knelt to accept absolution by the friars. After Mass in the fortress on September 17, parents and guardians presented 122 infants and children born since 1680

Diego de Vargas as a young man, Capilla de San Isidro, Madrid,
Spain. Courtesy of J. Manuel Espinosa.

for simple baptism. José, captain of the fortress, and his wife, Juana, asked Governor Vargas to stand as godfather to their three girls. Half a dozen mothers brought babies to him, the governor recalled, "so that I might carry them in my arms, as I did, to receive the water of holy baptism." Whatever the ceremony of water meant to the infants' parents, Vargas came away with more Pueblo compadres. He rarely missed a diplomatic opportunity.

Throughout that fall and into the winter, pueblo by pueblo, from Pecos in the east—where restraint won him allies in future battles—to the Hopi pueblos in the west—where bluster failed to impress—Diego de Vargas staged similar scenes, then moved on. Among the Zunis, the Spanish reconqueror experienced an epiphany. Since 1680, the people of the several Zuni pueblos had taken refuge on a great, one-thousand-foot-tall mesa known as Dowa Yalanne, or Corn Mountain. Vargas led a force unopposed up a foot trail from the valley floor below. The friars baptized 294 persons of all ages, after which the Zuni governor guided his new compadre to a small upstairs room.

The Spaniard stared, incredulous. There stood a well-kept Christian altar flanked by lighted tallow candles, with silver chalices, a monstrance (a vessel in which the consecrated host or a sacred relic is viewed), three images of Christ, and dozens of other religious objects and books, all carefully preserved. Overcome, Vargas knelt and kissed the images, giving thanks for the discovery of "such a divine treasure." In every other pueblo, the Spaniards had found accoutrements of Christian worship fouled, broken, or torn to bits.[35]

Generations later, Zunis told the intriguing story of "fray Juan Grayrobe" (a curious twist since the friars wore blue habits). Whatever its basis in fact, it explained the trove of Christian paraphernalia discovered by Vargas in 1692. The so-called fray Juan Grayrobe, according to Zuni tradition, had gone native, choosing adoption instead of martyrdom in 1680. One version had fray Juan writing a message of peace in Spanish with charcoal on an animal hide that the Zunis had dropped down to Vargas's men. And even while two women, captives of the Zunis since 1680 and sisters of Spanish soldiers with Vargas, revealed their identity and were ransomed with their five children, fray Juan in his Zuni disguise kept quiet. The Franciscan roll of friars killed in 1680 did list fray Juan de Bal, allegedly martyred at the principal Zuni village of Halona, although Bartolomé de Ojeda had heard that fray Juan perished while visiting Acoma. Whatever the circumstances, Diego de Vargas saw the Christian persistence among the Zunis as a miraculous example of God's grace.[36]

Vargas's 1692 campaign journals and letters to Viceroy Galve, which presented the reconquest of New Mexico as a fait accompli, inspired unrelieved praise and celebration in Mexico City, which Vargas made no effort to dispel.[37] Galve's court chronicler published a laudatory, thirty-six-page "news flash," or *mercurio volante*. The statistics resounded: numerous peoples and an entire kingdom restored to the Church and King Carlos II; seventy-four captives ransomed; 2,214 children baptized. Not a sword had been drawn, not an ounce of powder wasted, and most marvelous to relate, this peaceful Spanish victory had cost the royal treasury not the thinnest copper coin. Grand propaganda indeed![38]

But Vargas dissembled. A veteran administrator and military man, he understood the difference between a short-term truce and the renewed coexistence of Pueblos and Spaniards, between symbolic acts of repossession and actual reoccupation. Even at that, he gave too much credence to the compliance of Pueblo leaders in 1692. Don Luis el Picurí and other principal men had repeatedly lectured him that some Pueblos were good and others bad. Some had fallen in with Apaches and Navajos. Everywhere the Spanish governor went, Pueblo negotiators wanted Spaniards as allies to punish their enemies. Governor Vargas, admonishing his interpreters, had tried to impress upon the Pueblos with whom he parleyed that by

A ceremonial dance at Zuni Pueblo, *Century* (December 1882).

renewing their obedience as vassals of the Spanish king, they would all be protected. Peace would return. That, many Pueblo adults recalled, had not been so in the years before 1680.

Few Pueblo Indians, after experiencing Vargas's bold excursion through their towns in 1692, doubted that Spaniards would soon reappear with all their baggage. But because gathering, outfitting, and heading up a new wave of returning colonists and newcomers took the Spaniards so long, Pueblo summer and winter councils had a full round of seasons during which to discuss their response. Divisions ran deep, nowhere more so than at Pecos, still one of the largest Pueblo communities. Younger men, especially warriors and plains traders of the winter people, saw benefit in the Spaniards' return. Their leader, Juan de Ye, spoke for the largest party. The venerable cacique Diego Umviro refused to listen: Spaniards were vermin.

No one had to explain to Vargas that Pueblo factionalism favored resettlement, not only of Spaniards but also of temporarily displaced Pueblos. Thanks to Spanish-speaking Bartolomé de Ojeda, he knew for certain of divisions among the Keresan people. "Because he was trustworthy and had his wife in the pueblo of El Paso," Vargas hung a rosary around Ojeda's neck in late September 1692, after Spanish "repossession" of Santa Fe, and sent him to treat with Keresan headman Antonio Malacate.[39]

A month later, Bartolomé interpreted for Vargas and Malacate at the refugee pueblo where survivors from Zia, along with other Keres from Cochiti and Santo Domingo, had taken refuge on Mesa Colorada. As was his custom, the Spanish governor acted as godfather at the baptism of Malacate's son, approving another namesake for the Spanish king. Vargas told Malacate through Ojeda to move his people back down to their pueblo in the valley. The Spanish governor would provide a saw so that they might cut timbers and reroof the church damaged in Jironza's assault. After the meeting, Ojeda warned Vargas that Malacate was not to be trusted.

Whatever faults don Diego de Vargas exhibited—arrogance and impatience prominent among them—the veteran Spanish administrator had learned to heed the counsel of trusted Indians. Without Bartolomé de Ojeda of Zia, Juan de Ye of Pecos, and others like them, the Pueblo–Spanish War—begun in 1680, mostly on hold between 1681 and 1691, and renewed by Vargas in the 1690s—might have dragged on into the new century. Its earlier resolution, however, resumed the dance of Pueblos and Spaniards in the Kingdom of New Mexico.

7 | Resettlement, 1690s

*Asked whether they [the Pueblo Indians] thought that
perhaps the Spaniards would never return to this kingdom
at any time, or that they would have to return as their
ancestors did, and in this case what plans or dispositions
they would make, and what else he knew about this matter, he said that they were of different minds regarding it,
because some said that if the Spaniards should come they
would have to fight to the death, and others said that in
the end they must come and gain the kingdom because
they were sons of the land and had grown up with the
natives. Thus he replies.*

JUAN OF TESUQUE, DECEMBER 18, 1681

It seemed to don Diego de Vargas like a good idea, converting
a Pueblo Indian kiva into a temporary Christian church. The
Franciscan priest newly assigned to Santa Fe, fray José Díez,
thought so too. Resembling a squat tower, the kiva protruded
from one corner of the sprawling hive the Tewas and Tanos
had superimposed on the former governor's palace. Along
with outlying Spanish homes, they had torn down the previous Santa Fe church and planted corn in the ground where it
had stood. While the gutted chapel of San Miguel might have
been repaired, Indian leaders told Vargas that the snows lay too
deep in the forests to cut new roof timbers. They invited him
to use the kiva.

The Spanish governor went in person on December 20, 1693, to inspect the structure. "Having gone down the wooden ladder, I entered it and saw that it was round, and although its ceiling was low, it could serve for the winter." He accepted the Indians' offer and directed them to break a door through the wall at ground level for outside entry, make enough adobes for an altar, and whitewash the interior (an indication that kiva murals may have adorned the walls). They objected to cutting an additional door into the interior of a resident's house to provide an adjoining two-room sacristy and priest's quarters with fireplace, but Vargas convinced them to do so. He loaned them crowbars, and two days later the space was ready.[1]

Only then did Father Custos Salvador Rodríguez de San Antonio object. Since the Pueblo occupants of Santa Fe had used this structure for their "diabolical rites," the holy sacrifice of the Mass must not be performed within its walls. But the remodeling was complete, insisted Vargas. No matter, said the friar, there were other reasons as well why Christian worship could not take place in a Pueblo kiva, reasons the Franciscan superior did not elaborate. Recognizing the futility of further argument, the frustrated Spanish governor nevertheless reminded fray Salvador "that the main cathedrals of Spain had been Moorish mosques." Vargas also harbored an unspoken reason: if the Spanish reoccupation of Santa Fe came to war, the remodeled kiva offered a sure way into the fortress. With that in mind, the governor ordered Miguel Luján, a presidial soldier who understood Tewa and Tano, to move with his family into the unconsecrated kiva church and use it as a spy post.[2]

The ragged migration north from El Paso of a thousand Spanish men, women, and children during the fall and winter of 1693—the second phase of Diego de Vargas's recolonization—had set new standards of misery. Experienced New Mexicans had told their impatient governor that early October was too late to head up the caravan. Given the overgrown and deeply eroded Camino Real, the inevitable breakdowns of

Restored kiva, Pecos National Historical Park, by Fred E. Mang, Jr.
Courtesy Pecos National Historical Park.

wagons and carts, and the plodding pace of livestock on the
hoof, they could not possibly reach Santa Fe before winter set
in. Vargas had not listened. Now in mid-December, huddled in
wagons, frozen tents, and makeshift lean-tos, "within view of
the villa of Santa Fe, about two harquebus shots away" (several
hundred yards), mothers struggled to comfort their babies in
the fierce cold and blowing snow. At least twenty-two children died. Grieving fathers begged Governor Vargas to cease

negotiations and force the Indian occupants to vacate Santa Fe and return to Galisteo or whatever pueblos they came from.

A majority of the adults in the Spanish camp were return-ing survivors of the Pueblo Revolt. They carried with them two venerated icons: don Juan de Oñate's original royal ban-ner and the small image of the Blessed Virgin that Father Benavides had transported to New Mexico in 1625, renamed La Conquistadora and temporarily housed in a wagon. Such symbols meant less to several dozen soldiers Vargas had recruited in and around Zacatecas earlier in the year, a few with families, who were new to the kingdom. Yet everybody in the snow-blanketed encampment was anxious. Members of Santa Fe's town council in exile, along with the ailing father custos, requested an open town meeting, and the governor agreed. Although he and his men-at-arms were sworn "to suf-fer all kinds of weather and misfortunes on campaign," Vargas recognized that such hardship was not incumbent on the friars or the colonists' families.

Hence, on the two days following Christmas 1693, the colony's leaders crowded into Vargas's campaign tent to hear their earlier pleas read and to ratify them. Third to do so was sixty-year-old Sargento mayor Francisco de Anaya Almazán. He, as much as any Spaniard, personified the prerevolt, native New Mexicans who had come home to resume their inter-rupted lives. Anaya had buried his first wife in New Mexico as a young man. He had lived through the siege of Santa Fe in August 1680, losing his second wife and his children to the fury in the countryside. Married a third time in El Paso, he had come back; for the next twenty years he would forge a link in the chain that bound pre- and postwar New Mexico. This day in December 1693, Anaya stood with the rest. The Indian occupants of Santa Fe, "shameless and sneering at the Spaniards," must evacuate their stronghold at once.[3]

Vargas had feared trouble, despite the Indians' token wel-come and gift of tortillas. He doubted the sincerity of his compadre José, the Pueblo Indian captain whose three daughters had become his godchildren the previous year. He particularly distrusted the cunning, Spanish-speaking Antonio Bolsas, spokesman for the Pueblo occupants of Santa Fe, who "can easily sway the people of the villa to his will with persuasive words."[4] No Spaniard saw signs that the Indians were preparing to move out; in fact, others appeared to be moving in.

On December 27, after the town meeting had adjourned, distressing reports reached Governor Vargas. The Indians were arming. Before dawn on the twenty-eighth, the young son of Miguel Luján, housed in the remodeled kiva, carried messages through the snow to Vargas's tent. All night, the Indians had been working themselves up around bonfires inside the walls. Other multilingual informants had heard cries for war. Finally at first light, Spaniards observed that the Indian residents had taken up the ladders, barred the main gate, and manned the ramparts, shouting their defiance. Through a hail of arrows and stones hurled with slings, Miguel Luján and his family barely escaped, leaving their belongings behind in the kiva.

Vargas moved the camp forward, facing the main rampart, so that his men might more easily surround the fortress and prevent other Tewas and Tanos from entering. He and his secretary advanced from the siege line and Vargas shouted up to Antonio Bolsas that "they should come to their senses and come down; I would pardon them." But they kept screaming at him, until the Spanish governor gave up. Bolsas yelled that his people would talk and he would bring their decision out to the Spaniards. Vargas waited all day, but the Indian never came. That night, with the shouting and war chants reaching a crescendo, the Spaniards laid plans for a dawn attack. Mounted patrols kept circling the stronghold all night.

On this occasion, Vargas's earlier diplomacy strengthened the Spaniards' hand in battle. Pueblo reinforcements counted on by the defenders did not arrive in sufficient numbers to break through the Spaniards' line or in time to affect the outcome. Moreover, the Spanish governor's restraint the year before at Pecos had brought him Pueblo allies willing for their own reasons to risk death or victory shoulder-to-shoulder with Spaniards. Refusing to sack the abandoned pueblo in 1692, Vargas had given the Pecos time to return and to welcome him. Now, on the eve of armed conflict, their governor, Juan de Ye, and 140 Pecos fighting men put themselves under Vargas's command.[5]

The assault lasted just over twenty-four hours, from the moment Diego de Vargas shouted the charge "Santiago!" early on December 29 until the next morning when the defenders' women and children began streaming out of the war-torn complex. The Spaniards, seeing that their firearms had little effect from below, had built shielded ladders and clambered up them, taking one high position after another. As the besiegers sought to mine under the walls, Indians inside melted snow in iron kettles and poured boiling water down on them. Hacking and burning the heavy wooden gate and also breaking in through the remodeled kiva, the attackers gained the lower levels and overran the two interior plazas. Vargas ordered the royal standard and flag affixed to the highest rampart and a cross placed over the main entrance.

A room-by-room search yielded fifty-four Tewa and Tano fighters. Vargas's compadre José, his right wrist broken, had hanged himself at dawn on the thirtieth, according to Antonio Bolsas. Governor Vargas condemned the male prisoners to death by firing squad, interpreter Bolsas among them. Not only had they risen against the Spanish king, but they had also smashed to pieces the patio cross and an image of the Virgin, uttering countless blasphemies. Later, another sixteen men discovered hiding in the recesses of the fortress met the same fate. By Vargas's reckoning, "seventy were shot; nine died from the skirmishes; and two, without hope at the thought of defeat, hanged themselves."[6]

No one sketched this strange building, rising in isolation from an open space the Indians had cleared by razing every adjoining Spanish structure. It was unique in all the world, this pile occupied first by Spaniards, then by Pueblos, and again by Spaniards who began at once punching holes in the lower walls so they could breathe and let in light. In the last days of 1693, they had retaken their capital. Reporting to the viceroy, the Santa Fe cabildo evoked a picture in words of the stronghold. "There are so many dwellings, which they have built on the top of the casas reales (which we here call the palace), that it took twenty soldiers and thirty Indian allies the whole blessed day until nightfall to search the fortress and the dwellings."[7]

The Pueblo–Spanish War, waged between 1680 and 1696, had entered its third and final stage, the Spaniards' hard-fought reentry into the Pueblo world. Although temporarily successful, Vargas's motley company of returnees had little cause to celebrate. Months removed from cousins in El Paso, holed up in the fouled casas reales, they doubted how they could possibly survive as snows swirled outside. But Governor Vargas, while acknowledging the urgent need for food, defense, and Pueblo Indian allies, appeared undaunted.

The four thousand fanegas (some ten thousand bushels) of corn, beans, and dried vegetables collected from the deepest corners of the building, no matter how carefully distributed among a thousand settlers and their four hundred captive Tano and Tewa women and children, would not last the winter. Arriving in mid-December, the Spaniards had planted nothing. They must exact provisions from Pueblos beyond the walls of Santa Fe, by negotiation or by force. Those natives who had escaped the siege had to be seen as enemies. Many Pueblo Indians who had nodded in token obedience in 1692 were now preparing to resist, laying up supplies, making arrows, and piling rocks at defensive sites atop steep-banked mesas. Rumors already circulated of Pueblo confederations forming to attack Santa Fe. Priding himself as a diplomat, Diego de Vargas believed he too could count on other Pueblo Indians as allies.

While en route north from El Paso, the Spanish governor had sent his trusted Indian compadre Bartolomé de Ojeda among the Keresan people to enlist their allegiance. Now, on December 31, 1693, one day after the Spaniards had settled the matter of Santa Fe, Ojeda and a Keresan delegation arrived at the fortress. Their message was ominous. As Vargas fingered the four knots on the cord Ojeda handed him, the Indian recounted its significance: four days remained before a planned enemy convocation of Jemez, Navajos, and the faction of his own people from Cochiti and Santo Domingo swayed by old Antonio Malacate. Because the principal men of Zia, Santa Ana, and San Felipe had refused Malacate's invitation to march on Santa Fe, preferring instead to side with the Spaniards, they had become enemies. Somehow Ojeda had persuaded his Pueblo kinsmen, brutalized by Spaniards five years earlier, to stand with him and ease the colonists' return.

Ojeda had a plan. If Malacate and two other agitators could be captured and brought to Santa Fe, their following would surely disperse. Characterizing Ojeda as "brave and cunning," Vargas concurred. "I promised him I would reward him, and he promised me he would effect the capture." Next, Juan de Ye came to Santa Fe on January 4 to warn through an interpreter of a large encampment of Tewas, Tanos, Picuris, Taos, and Apaches about two leagues (five or six miles) from Santa Fe. Ye thought they might assault Pecos and asked Vargas for help. Unable to go himself at this critical juncture, the Spanish governor dispatched Captain Roque Madrid, a native New Mexican conversant in Ye's Towa language, and thirty men-at-arms. They were back the next day. No attack had come, but Juan de Ye and his faction at Pecos had tested their pact with Vargas, "remaining assured of having the Spaniards so much on their side."[8]

Malacate proved elusive. The literate Ojeda wrote to Vargas, and the Spanish governor's secretary copied the letter into his campaign journal. Malacate and his Jemez comrades intended to make war on the pro-Spanish Keres before attacking Santa Fe. Ojeda had heard that Malacate was "worshiping the things of the devil every night in order to kill your lordship and the Spaniards." The Keres of Santa Ana, who were guarding some of the Spaniards' horses, begged "for the love of God to send them some soldiers." Addressing his reply to Bartolomé de Ojeda as "son and compadre" (also copied into the record), Vargas suggested the residents of Santa Ana withdraw temporarily to the more secure sites of Zia or San Felipe. He could not send soldiers until he had first reconnoitered the Tewa pueblos in force. Tested time and again, this pivotal alliance of Vargas and Ojeda—Spaniard and Pueblo—held strong throughout the restoration.[9]

Nor could Vargas put a price on the support of don Juan de Ye. While some Pecos traditionalists murmured against his leadership, Ye saw in the Spaniards' return a revitalization of his pueblo as a trade center. He led Pecos fighters in Vargas's initial, unsuccessful February and March assault on the embattled Tewas of San Ildefonso (or Black) Mesa, twenty-odd miles north of Santa Fe. He escorted Plains Apache leaders to Santa Fe to drink chocolate with the Spanish governor and talk of renewed trade fairs. Late in June 1694, Vargas called for a major military action to punish the Jemez confederation that had been harassing Zia, Santa Ana, and San Felipe. Ye and his scouts reported that the Rio Grande was running too high to cross safely even on rafts. Rather than disband the force, Governor Vargas added a packtrain and led the cavalcade northward, intent on bargaining for food or simply removing stores from abandoned pueblos.

Four days out, the Spaniards made camp near Taos. Unwilling to parley with Vargas, the people of the pueblo streamed toward their refuge in a nearby mountain canyon. A band of Plains Apaches, friends of Juan de Ye, volunteered to arrange a meeting at the mouth of the canyon with Francisco Pacheco, Indian governor of Taos. Ye finally ventured too much, arguing passionately that the Taos return to their pueblo and accept the Spaniards' pardon. Pacheco feigned friendship. Since the sun was setting, he invited Ye to spend the night with him and talk more, and Ye agreed.

Veteran Sargento mayor Francisco de Anaya Almazán, sensing a trap, urged the Pecos governor not to go. Ye, insisting that he knew Pacheco well, dismounted from his mule, took off his spurs and the powder pouches from his belt, and handed over the harquebus that belonged to Vargas. He embraced the Spanish governor, Sargento mayor Anaya, and the others, "which the Taos Indians and their governor, Pacheco, closely watched." "God be with you," shouted Vargas. He would await them in his tent early next morning with chocolate. It was the last time any Spaniard saw don Juan de Ye. Later in Santa Fe, Governor Vargas tried to explain through interpreters to Ye's son Lorenzo. Presented with his father's cape and other effects, the Indian went away "satisfied, although sad."[10]

From communities in disarray, native residents of the Pueblo world closely watched Spaniards taking up homes again in the Kingdom and Provinces of New Mexico. Their reactions were not so different from those of their ancestors nearly a century before. A conspicuous few gave aid and comfort, more stood in angry opposition, and most kept to themselves their doubts about Spanish colonists as neighbors.

In 1694 three brooding citadels, one north and two west of Santa Fe, symbolized Pueblo resistance. Tewas and Tanos, who repulsed assaults in February and March, manned fortifications atop San Ildefonso Mesa; dissenting Keres of Cochiti and Santo

Domingo, whose leader Malacate had been replaced by El Zepe, occupied the mesa of La Cieneguilla de Cochiti (Horn Mesa, Potrero Viejo); and defiant Jemez fighters defended their refuge on Guadalupe (or San Diego) Mesa. All fell in 1694, each stormed by combined forces of Spanish soldiers, militiamen, and Pueblo Indian auxiliaries. As they overran Guadalupe Mesa, the assailants captured 361 Jemez noncombatants. Vargas offered their return if surviving Jemez warriors joined his army to besiege San Ildefonso Mesa a second time. This they did, and the Spanish governor released the hostages. Tewa and Tano holdouts, observing Spaniards and other Pueblo Indians uprooting their crops in fields below, at last came down from the heights in September to be pardoned by Vargas. But they did not forget.[11]

Having forced the evacuation of the three mesa strongholds, Governor Vargas and his entourage toured the restored Pueblo communities, reinstalling native officials and assigning missionaries. They traveled first to Pecos, home of the vanished Juan de Ye. In September 1694, with familiar pomp, the Spanish governor addressed the assembly through two prerevolt colonists. He introduced fray Diego Zeinos. Pecos carpenters had already rebuilt living quarters for the friar and sawed beams to roof a temporary place of Christian worship between the standing north wall of the old convento and the mound where their former monumental church had stood.

Vargas asked the pueblo's principal men to confer and then present to him the individuals they wished to be their officers. The Spaniard bestowed on each a staff of office and administered the oath of loyalty. As Pecos governor, Diego Marcos headed a list of eighteen. Among the nine war captains, Vargas recognized Lorenzo de Ye, whom he dignified as "don." The newly legitimized Pecos leaders then requested that the Spanish governor appoint as their alcalde mayor old Francisco de Anaya Almazán, who had warned Juan de Ye of the danger at Taos. Vargas swore in Anaya. Last, asked who they

wished to be the patron saint of their renewed mission, the
Pecos replied that the pueblo's patroness should remain Our
Lady of the Angels.[12] By the end of 1694, Governor Vargas had
escorted Franciscans back to a dozen Pueblo communities and
ordained their officers. In Santa Fe, meanwhile, the colonists
found fault.

Vargas had requested that Viceroy Galve authorize funding
for a hundred presidial soldiers and five hundred colonist families, without which, he implied, the restoration of New Mexico
would surely fail. Sixty such families, recruited in Puebla and
the Valley of Mexico, had reached Santa Fe in June 1694, straining available housing and food supplies. Worse, these subsidized
newcomers, many of whom boasted a trade, considered themselves *españoles mexicanos* (Spaniards from Mexico) and superior
to other New Mexicans. Vargas next sent his trusted, twenty-
six-year-old protégé Juan Páez Hurtado to sign up additional
colonists at government expense in New Spain's northern
mining districts. Although charges of fraud and faking families
of unrelated individuals (to collect the higher family rate) hung
over this effort, by May 1695 another forty-four so-called family units had been added to New Mexico's rolls.[13]

Only partially pacified, the colony agonized during 1695. A
widespread epidemic, unspecified in the documents, carried off
Pueblos and Spaniards alike. As could be expected, more of the
former died than of the latter. Vargas himself took sick from
recurring typhus; "at death's door," he dictated a hasty last will,
then recovered.[14] Food shortages persisted. Drought-stricken
crops attacked by worms were meager, and the beef and wagonloads of provisions driven north from Nueva Vizcaya were
never enough. With so many pueblos reoccupied, that earlier
source of confiscated foodstuffs had dried up.

To relieve crowding in Santa Fe, the Spanish governor
decreed that the españoles mexicanos found a new villa, or
chartered municipality, upriver at Santa Cruz de la Cañada,
twenty-some miles north of Santa Fe and barely east of today's

Española. This vicinity before 1680 had supported a considerable Hispanic farming and ranching population, Vargas's justification for again uprooting Tanos and Tewas. Taken together, such ill winds stirred a second, less general but no less passionate Pueblo revolt.[15]

———————◆◆◆———————

Rumors of rebellion were rife during the winter of 1695–96. The missionaries, alone in their pueblos, grew understandably nervous. They talked of withdrawing to Santa Fe, but in December decided against it. Governor Vargas got up from his sickbed to admonish the Tewa and Tano captains he had summoned to the capital. As a gesture of goodwill, he declared the freedom of forty-five of their women and children who had previously fled temporary servitude in Santa Fe. Christmas Eve, reportedly marked for the outbreak of an insurrection, passed without incident. Again, severe cold kept snow on the ground, making Vargas's emergency visits to various pueblos more burdensome.

Late in February, an officer awakened Vargas in the middle of Sunday night, delivering a warning from fray José Díez, the Franciscan who had agreed with him about the kiva church and who was serving now at nearby Tesuque. According to certain Tewas, even some of Vargas's trusted Pecos allies were plotting against the Spaniards. The leader of the malcontents was said to be Juan de Ye's aggrieved son, don Lorenzo, who "intended to kill the father [missionary] first and come to do the same with the Spaniards." Don Lorenzo would then retire with his faction to Piedra Blanca, an old pueblo belonging to the Pecos.[16]

The Franciscans begged Governor Vargas to station squads of soldiers in the missions, citing a growing "insolence" among their Pueblo congregations. Signs were everywhere. The Indians, swayed by itinerant agitators (*tlatoleros*), were carrying supplies to the mountains and digging horse traps. Anguishing at Tesuque, Father Díez wrote, "I do not know how, in conscience, I can say mass to apostates, which I know they already are in their knowledge of the uprising." For months, certain Indians had been meeting in Tesuque at the house of a "sorcerer," singing war songs and chanting, "Death to the Spaniards, what good are the Spaniards? We were better off before." Díez wanted a dozen soldiers—an overwrought request, given the colony's scarcely one hundred men-at-arms. He predicted that the blow would fall during the full moon in mid-March, "about eight days from now."[17]

Yet two more full moons waxed and waned. Then on Monday, June 4, 1696, during the week of the third full moon, amid seeming calm, Governor Vargas got the first garbled news of violence. As the people of Cochiti took to the hills, its missionary had barely escaped with his life. From Santa Ana, Bartolomé de Ojeda, senior Keresan war captain, reported that a gathering of Acomas was awaiting Hopis, Zunis, and Utes to launch an invasion.

A day or two later, Ojeda, writing to his old friend Father Custos Francisco de Vargas at Santa Fe, allowed that the Acomas might have dispersed. Still, he was taking no chances, since if the enemy assaulted Santa Ana, "no one but Jesus Christ Himself will be able to protect it." The Indian asked Father Vargas to inform Santa Ana's missionary, who had taken refuge in Santa Fe, that he had hidden the sacred vessels, vestments, and other items pertaining to Christian worship in a house that had been covered over with mud. Ojeda was not well. "I think I have caught typhus," he wrote to Father Vargas. "Nothing else, but may God Our Lord keep you for the many years I wish. Your lordship's servant and godson, Bartolomé de Ojeda."[18]

Alcalde mayor Roque Madrid at Santa Cruz de la Cañada heard that Tanos allied with Keres, Apaches, Hopis, and Pecos had risen. Immediately, Madrid ordered locals to catch their horses and assemble at the new villa. Governor Vargas, questioning the alleged participation of the Pecos, told Alcalde mayor Anaya to enlist a hundred Pecos warriors and, without betraying the least mistrust, escort them to Santa Fe. Two days later, led by their new governor, don Felipe Chistoe, they reported for duty, some on horseback, some afoot, eager to share in "the booty of clothing and maize."[19]

On campaign with Governor Vargas during June and July 1696, these Pecos men witnessed scenes reminiscent of 1680. Except for Tesuque, whose volatile governor decided at the last moment to side with the Spaniards, the other Tewas, along with Tanos, Tiwas of Taos and Picuris, and Jemez, had murdered outsiders and ransacked their missions. The scene at San Ildefonso sickened Vargas. Two Franciscans, huddled with members of a Spanish family inside the church as Indians set it afire, had suffocated of smoke inhalation. The bodies were decomposing. "I ordered the Pecos Indians and men-at-arms," wrote Vargas, "to cover them with adobes and a wall they tore down from the church itself; once they were buried, they could not be disturbed."[20]

One of the Franciscan victims at San Ildefonso had joined his brethren three months earlier in a debate about true martyrdom. He would gladly die, he professed, if his death would assure the salvation of some of his congregation. Believing, however, that his flock would rejoice, he questioned dying, "for two reasons: martyrdom is a crowning glory, and I do not deserve it; the other reason is that it would be rigorously an act of hatred of the faith."[21] In all, the summer outbreak of 1696 claimed the lives of five Franciscans and twenty-one Spanish colonists. A greater but unknown number of their Pueblo tormentors also died in subsequent fighting. As Vargas sought to suppress this latest insurrection, anger drove both Pueblos and Spaniards to acts of desperation and ultimately to exhaustion.

As zealous as any Spaniard, Pecos governor Felipe Chistoe suffered no opposition to his rule. He especially hated the old cacique Diego Umviro, who led a growing anti-Spanish faction within the pueblo. The revolt of 1696 suggested to

Chistoe a purge. Governor Vargas agreed to discuss it with him
and Alcalde mayor Anaya behind closed doors. Chistoe knew
Spanish and looked to be in his late thirties. Explaining that
Umviro and several other Pecos headmen openly supported
the revolt, Chistoe requested permission of the Spanish governor to execute them before they swayed more of the Pecos
people. Vargas thought out loud. If the Indian had followers
he could trust to carry out the plan, he could invite Umviro
and the others to his house at night to talk about the uprising.
"'In this way,'" Vargas then advised, "'you can surely succeed
in killing them.' That seemed good to him, and he told me he
would do it."[22]

And he did, assembling the pueblo's leaders in the sanctity
of a Pecos kiva. Umviro and his disciples spoke in favor of the
revolt "because the Spaniards were of a different blood, while
they were Indians like the others." At that moment, Chistoe,
brandishing his staff of office and professing loyalty to the king
of Spain, rose from his seat. His men quickly overpowered
Umviro and three others and hanged them. A younger man,
nicknamed Caripicado (Pockface), escaped.

The next day, two unsuspecting outside agitators arrived
at Pecos to confer with Umviro. One of them, a Jemez, carried a gilded reliquary to prove that he and his people had put
to death their missionary. Although natives of Pecos thought
the Jemez spoke queerly, and vice versa, the two communities seem to have shared the Towa language. The other visitor,
a Tewa cacique from Nambe, had spent the winter traveling
throughout the Pueblo world, even to the Hopis, urging revolt.
Now, at Pecos, Chistoe's followers seized the two emissaries
and tied them up.[23]

With his divided community left in stunned disbelief
at the murders in a Pecos kiva, Felipe Chistoe rode over
the mountain to Santa Fe with his war captains to report
to Governor Vargas and deliver the two rabble-rousers. The
Pecos governor interpreted for Vargas during interrogation of

the Jemez. Neither he nor his Tewa companion denied their
involvement in the insurrection. Vargas had them shot.

Chistoe and his warriors campaigned intermittently
throughout the summer at the Spaniards' side. Late in August,
Chistoe appeared in Santa Fe with grisly trophies: the head,
hand, and foot of young Caripicado, who had slipped out of
his trap in the kiva but unwisely returned. "When all the citizens of this villa saw them, they were surprised at this Indian's
loyalty. I thanked him," noted Vargas, "and gave him and the
others gifts."[24]

Dictating such events in his campaign journal, Diego
de Vargas rarely displayed emotion. When, however, his combined Pueblo and Spanish forces finally ran down and killed
don Lucas Naranjo, whom he considered a prime mover of
the 1696 revolt, Vargas let his hatred show. The Spanish governor had installed Naranjo as chief war captain at Santa Clara
in 1694. Variously described as mulatto or *lobo* (of Indian
and African blood), Lucas may have been a son of the Naranjo
suspected as the black representative of Poseyemu at the heart
of the Pueblo Revolt in 1680.[25]

Heading a typical mixed column of presidial soldiers,
volunteer Santa Fe militiamen, a Franciscan chaplain, and his
Pecos allies, Vargas had set out from Santa Cruz de la Cañada
before daybreak on July 23. The plan was to surprise Naranjo
and his Tewa fighters hidden among the boulders in a rugged
funnel canyon to the north. Felled trees lay across the entrance,
forcing the attackers to dismount. When the exchange began,
Naranjo evidently told his men to shoot at the chaplain, which
infuriated Vargas. Had the friar not worn high leather boots,
an arrow would have pierced his leg.

Advancing on the enemy's positions, Spaniards fired volley after volley. A shot from one of the militiamen "was lucky
enough to hit Naranjo in the Adam's apple and come out at
the nape of his neck." Another soldier shot the fallen enemy
leader in the head and decapitated him. Tewas who were able

fled, some leaving their blood on the boulders. This skirmish proved to be a turning point in suppressing the second Pueblo revolt. Not long afterward, the soldiers sent Naranjo's severed head to Vargas, who gloated: "I was very pleased to see that rebel apostate dog in that state: a pistol shot through the right temple had caused his brains to spill out, leaving the head hollow. What little remained was scooped out to take to his pueblo."[26]

As another bad winter set in, warfare trailed off. Despite recurring suspicions, it would never resume again in large scale between Pueblos and Spaniards. Both peoples had suffered severe dislocations. Some families never returned to the homes they had left, while many others came back, reclaimed their property, and laid in food and firewood. The colonists of Santa Cruz de la Cañada, who petitioned to move downriver to sites they considered safer and more easily cultivated, were forced to stick it out. Their Tewa neighbors, who had withdrawn to uncomfortable but defensible locations in rough terrain during the troubles of 1696, straggled back, reoccupying most of their pueblos. Other Tewas joined an exodus of Tiwas from Picuris who ventured eastward to live with Plains Apaches. Vargas managed to bring some of them back in November 1696, while ten years later another Spanish column retrieved an additional sixty who had not adjusted to life on the plains.[27]

Certain of the Pecos, fleeing the grim regime of don Felipe Chistoe, seem to have crossed the Rio Grande valley and moved in with the Jemez, the only other Pueblos who spoke Towa. Yet the most dislocated of all the Pueblo peoples were the Tanos. They had streamed victoriously into Santa Fe from the Galisteo Basin in 1680, been ousted from there during the winter of 1693–94, relocated north of Santa Fe, and in 1695 were told they must move again. Finally putting the Spaniards of the Rio Grande far behind them, migrant Tano families accepted invitations from the Hopis, founding on First

Mesa a pueblo they called Hano. Their descendants live there today, still speaking a dialect of the Tano language.[28]

The Hopis, who despite persistent rumors to the contrary never did join actively in the revolt of 1696, have remained since 1680 unrepentant and un-Christian. From the 1690s on, they took in a variety of Pueblo refugees from the east, newcomers who caused considerable political and social ferment among their hosts. When in 1700 Franciscan missionaries reappeared briefly at Awátovi, the Hopi pueblo nearest to the Rio Grande, Hopis from other towns, acting to purify their world as they had begun to reimagine it, annihilated that pueblo and abducted its women and children. One poignant oral tradition claims that Awátovi's own village chief called down the purge himself, appealing to the principal men of the other Hopi communities:

> You are my friends. I need your help. My people are out of control. The Castilla [Spanish] missionaries have returned and they are preparing to stay forever. The village is in chaos. The young insult the old, women are raped, the shrines are desecrated. The ceremonies are ridiculed, contempt is shown for the kachinas, and the *kwitamuh* [members of a kiva society of sorcerers] run wild. Thus the evil that followed us from the Lower World has torn us into pieces. Awatovi must be destroyed. Its people must be scattered and its houses razed to the ground.[29]

Dealing with their own internal strife, the geographically isolated Hopis had done what most subjected peoples dreamed of but few accomplished in the seventeenth century. They had successfully thrown off European colonizers.

Given time and chance, Diego de Vargas believed he could reconquer the Hopis, but he was denied both. A successor of somewhat more humble birth, don Pedro Rodríguez Cubero, presented his credentials to the town council at Santa Fe

The Hopi pueblo of Walpi, by Ben Wittick, ca. 1890. Courtesy Palace of the Governors (MNM/DCA), no. 102064.

on July 2, 1697. Through agents in Mexico City, Vargas had maneuvered to block Rodríguez's appointment, even though he had exceeded his own five-year term by more than sixteen months. The reconqueror of New Mexico desperately wanted a promotion to someplace else. Failing that, however, he supposed a grateful viceroy would continue him in office. The conde de Moctezuma y de Tula, who had succeeded his patron Galve, did not, and Rodríguez's papers were in order.

If only Vargas had accepted that fact. Instead, he set about convincing himself and anyone who would listen that he had been reappointed. Vargas's vanity, combined with the Spanish colonists' deep resentment toward him and his chosen circle of minions, explains why the former governor spent the next three years under house arrest in Santa Fe, for a time in leg irons. After conducting Vargas's uneventful, thirty-day residencia, Governor Rodríguez had presided as the cabildo of Santa Fe brought a litany of criminal charges against his famed predecessor. They ranged from misappropriation of government funds—the only charge that focused the attention of royal bureaucrats—to abuse of his authority, favoritism, and immorality. Vargas's ill-advised policies were blamed for every hardship suffered by New Mexico's returning colonists, including the loss of the twenty-two children who died in the snow outside the walls of Santa Fe in December 1693. Not until July 1700, after the viceroy had summoned Diego de Vargas to Mexico City to present his accounts, did Rodríguez release him.[30]

While the drama of the two governors played itself out in Santa Fe, life went on in Pueblo and Spanish households. With hardly a pause, Pecos carpenters were back in demand. Vargas, passing through Santa Ana in 1696 after a standoff at Acoma, had embraced not only don Bartolomé de Ojeda but also the pueblo's missionary, fray Francisco de Vargas, Ojeda's protector since the battle of Zia in 1689. Father Custos Vargas had supervised renovation of the mission convento and stockpiled adobes and timbers for the church. To square and decorate the roof beams, take measurements, and construct the doors, the friar had summoned carpenters from Pecos.

At their own pueblo, to which Father Vargas reassigned himself later in 1696, the Pecos worked to improve a temporary church. The friar must have fancied construction. "I saw," Governor Vargas had reported, "that the nave of the church had been enlarged at his order in accord with the plan he had given the Indians and with help from their alcalde mayor. They had increased its height for the clerestory and built a chancel for the high altar with two steps." The sacristy lacked only a roof, and they had built a wall around the patio with a gate to enter the convento.[31]

As Pecos carpenters, along with the pueblo's traders, farmers, and hunters, got back to their usual pursuits, and as their women dealt daily with food, the children, and replastering their houses, tension gnawed at the community. Grieving kinsmen of slain Diego Umviro and Caripicado wanted don Felipe Chistoe's head. When they failed to incite the pueblo as a whole to rise up and kill him, they began insulting him publicly, even in the presence of Alcalde mayor Anaya. To head off a violent outbreak, Anaya reported to Governor Rodríguez, who had Chistoe's principal opponents brought to Santa Fe and jailed. Even when they broke out and fled to live with Jicarilla Apaches, the rift kept festering. Five times the Pecos came to the brink of fighting each other, and each time the iron-fisted Felipe Chistoe had his way. His adversaries despaired. And in 1702, when Tewas and Taos were rumored to be plotting again, it was Chistoe who led the Pecos delegation to Santa Fe to assure Governor Rodríguez of his people's loyalty.[32]

Rodríguez, for his part, reestablished peaceful if uneasy relations with Acomas and Zunis to the west and gave formal recognition in 1699 to the breakaway pueblo of Laguna, where disillusioned Acomas and other Keres who resented Bartolomé de Ojeda had congregated. The Spanish governor's

ill-considered expedition during the summer of 1701 to punish the Hopis for their destruction of Awátovi, however, failed
ignominiously, serving only to affirm Hopi independence.

At Santa Fe, Governor Rodríguez had ordered a convento
built for the Franciscans—at his own expense, he boasted. He
also had workers tear into the defenses and alterations that
the Indian occupants had constructed, renovating the casas
reales and earning Vargas's ire for laying the capital open to
attack. Rodríguez had never liked New Mexico. When his
five-year term expired on July 2, 1702, no successor appeared
to relieve him. Suffering through another New Mexico winter, Rodríguez, whose health was failing, bolted from Santa
Fe, not waiting for anyone. But by then, he knew who was to
succeed him. Diego de Vargas, exonerated in Mexico City, had
been reappointed.

Vargas's reentry into Santa Fe in November 1703 stirred
emotions all around. Rewarded with a noble title of Castile for
his restoration of New Mexico, don Diego de Vargas, first marqués de la Nava de Barcinas, had sworn not to seek revenge.
Nevertheless, prominent New Mexicans who had previously
testified against him fell all over themselves in their efforts to
ingratiate themselves anew. Pueblo leaders sent emissaries to
welcome him. Few suspected that Vargas, just sixty years old,
had only five months to live.

The following March, he decreed a campaign against
Faraon Apaches who had been rustling scarce cattle and horses
in the middle Rio Grande valley. Through his alcaldes mayores, Vargas summoned Pueblo Indian fighters to meet him and
the soldiers at Bernalillo, just north of today's Albuquerque. A
dozen pueblos had sent warriors expecting their share of the
spoils. Don Felipe Chistoe's contingent from Pecos, numbering
almost fifty men, was easily the most conspicuous. No mention
was made of don Bartolomé de Ojeda, the most steadfast of
Pueblo allies during Diego de Vargas's first administration, who
after 1702 faded from the historical record.

Four days into their operation, Vargas's campaign journal suddenly breaks off. The governor, racked by stomach cramps and fever, could not go on. Pueblo Indians, probably carrying the agonized Spaniard between them on a litter, conveyed him back to Bernalillo to the alcalde mayor's house. Juan Páez Hurtado galloped south with medication, but this time Vargas did not respond. On April 8, 1704, at about five in the evening, the once-and-future governor of New Mexico died, seemingly of dysentery.[33]

Although ten years older than Diego de Vargas, New Mexican Francisco de Anaya Almazán lived a decade longer, into his early eighties. Anaya owned a house on the reworked Santa Fe plaza and served as mayordomo of the religious confraternity of La Conquistadora. He must have attended Vargas's funeral. As the reconqueror lay dying in Bernalillo, he dictated precise details for the honors he expected as a titled nobleman of Castile and captain general, including a pair of caparisoned riderless horses. He requested further that his body, borne in his bed draped as a funeral bier to the Santa Fe church, be buried in the main chapel "beneath the dais where the priest stands." He also provided that on that day fifty fanegas (about 125 bushels) of corn and the meat of twelve cattle be distributed in his name to the villa's poor.[34]

In 1712 Páez Hurtado and other leading citizens petitioned a succeeding governor to proclaim Santa Fe's first Fiesta commemorating Vargas's entry into Santa Fe twenty years earlier. Two years later, in 1714, a larger parish church was nearing completion. Because pertinent burial records are missing, we can only surmise that the people of Santa Fe, amid proper pomp, exhumed Vargas's remains and reburied them in the new church. Yet because of its subsequent remodeling, construction of the present cathedral on the same site, and changes to the latter in the 1960s, the earth has been badly disturbed. Hence, even though Santa Fe's Fiestas in September annually recall don Diego de Vargas, Spanish recolonizer of the

Kingdom and Provinces of New Mexico, no shrine marks his final resting place.[35]

In many ways New Mexico was much the same after the Pueblo–Spanish War. Daily dealings between Pueblos and Spaniards —for purposes of exchange, service, and social contact, both forced and consensual—resumed almost as soon as the fighting ceased. And as in the previous century, the two neighboring peoples interacted pragmatically, giving and taking articles of material culture, useful customs, words from their languages, and blood through ethnic intermarriage, all the while heeding the lines of their parallel societies. Never overwhelmed by a sudden boom in population, Pueblos and Spaniards, even as their genes mixed, strove increasingly to preserve their respective cultural identities.

Restoration during the 1690s introduced few new technologies. No innovative tool, item of horse gear, or weapon changed how jobs got done. No flood of currency altered the largely barter-and-credit economy, although manufactured goods became more readily available after the founding in 1718 of San Felipe el Real de Chihuahua, 140 miles closer than Parral. Still, people dressed and furnished their homes similarly, ate the same foods, and passed a normal day in familiar pursuits, mostly farming, tending livestock, and raising families. Just as before 1680, rangy little churro sheep, with their long-staple, greaseless wool and savory meat, fared better on New Mexico's mesas than cattle. By the mid-eighteenth century, New Mexicans were joining together every fall on long sheep drives south and running up debts to Chihuahua merchants.

Almost imperceptibly, the colony grew more egalitarian. Governor Vargas, envisioning a colony of sturdy farmers, had begun granting smaller holdings to Spaniards and guaranteeing a minimum land base to Pueblo communities. New Mexicans who had previously held large properties, or estancias, were forced to adjust. The resentful heirs of old Francisco de Anaya Almazán, dead by 1716, took their complaints to subsequent governors and asked for additional acreage. The record is silent about their success.

Encomiendas of Pueblo Indian tribute did not survive the turn of the new century; indigenous population decline throughout the Spanish Empire had convinced the crown to abandon the institution. Pueblo Indians continued to work for Spaniards, and in rare cases the reverse, most often receiving payment in produce or livestock. Salaried officers and soldiers of the Santa Fe and El Paso presidios (garrisons) took the place of encomenderos in rallying able members of New Mexico's citizen militia and the Pueblo auxiliary fighting men who routinely, as in the seventeenth century, outnumbered Spaniards on any given campaign.

New Mexico's Franciscans still dressed in blue habits. Reinstalled in Pueblo communities, the friars ministered to their mission congregations and to increasing numbers of non-Indian families who lived nearby. Most of the missionaries adopted more tolerant attitudes than their predecessors toward seeming acts of traditional Pueblo religion, so long as such practice did not interfere with daily Christian instruction, worship, and work. More than any lesson of the Pueblo–Spanish War, however, a more secular century encouraged Franciscans to reimagine Pueblo Indian kivas not as dens of diabolical worship but instead as men's clubhouses.

Most New Mexicans still had spiritual recourse only to the friars, but a few diocesan priests took up residence first in the El Paso area, then in Santa Fe, and three bishops of Durango actually carried out visitations of New Mexico in the eighteenth century. Economically, too, the friars lost ground. Before the war, they had controlled the colony's principal supply service, while the combined wealth of their mission lands, labor force, and flocks always overshadowed that of the lay community. Although one of their number still acted as agent of the Inquisition, his authority was greatly curtailed. Never again did friars rule the kingdom.

New Mexico's very reason for being had changed, from mainly missionary to mostly military. Although the government, religious life, and defense of the resource-poor colony continued to run on subsidies from the royal treasury, Spain's fundamental justification for providing them shifted. Whereas in the seventeenth century, the Spanish crown underwrote the Franciscans' City of God on the Rio Grande for the sake of Pueblo Indian souls, in the eighteenth, defense of empire eclipsed evangelism. And while the friars still looked forward to their annual stipends from the government, payrolls for the presidial soldiers at El Paso and Santa Fe cost far more.

Demographic changes, within the colony and on its borders, fostered a subtle evolution in human relations. Before the Pueblo–Spanish War, Spaniards survived as an anxious and high-handed minority. After the restoration, their numbers grew steadily, reaching parity around 1750 with a diminished but stable Pueblo population—at around ten thousand each. When there were no more of them than there were of you, tensions eased. Moreover, mounting pressures from encircling, nonsedentary peoples, particularly Comanches, compelled Pueblo and Hispanic farmers and ranchers, like it or not, to band together in mutual defense.[36]

Between the carnage at Acoma in 1599 and the siege of Santa Fe in 1680 and its aftermath, seventeenth-century Pueblos and Spaniards had worked out the basis of a dynamic coexistence. More by experience than by plan, they had learned to live together yet apart. And they continue to do so today.

A Lifetime Later, 1760

Vengeance is mine; I will repay, saith the Lord.

ROMANS 12:19 (KJV)

Was this the only way? The raft looked none too sturdy. Swollen by the late spring runoff, the Río del Norte (Rio Grande) was up, an expanse of roiling, reddish brown water between the bishop and the desert vegetation visible on the far side. Well aware of quicksand, old hands in El Paso warned that the river was always dangerous "because of its sandy and turbulent bottom."

A tourist at heart and sixty-some years old, Dr. Pedro Tamarón y Romeral, the last bishop of Durango to conduct a visitation of colonial New Mexico, prayed for a safe crossing. Tamarón recalled in his journal for May 6, 1760: "the loads, mules, horses, muleteers, one hundred live sheep for food in the uninhabited areas, and other supplies were taken across." His attendants escorted the prelate to the water's edge early the next morning. "It was very high and overflowing....When I boarded the raft, the river was covered by Indian swimmers, some pulling lines, others making them fast. I made a happy crossing to the other side."[1]

Eighty years earlier, vigorous fray Francisco de Ayeta, trying to get provisions to refugees streaming south away from the Pueblo Revolt, had driven a six-span mule team and heavily loaded freight wagon into the rushing water just above El Paso, got stuck, and had to be rescued by swimmers who carried him to shore.[2] Whether or not Tamarón knew about Ayeta's close call, the bishop gave thanks and waited on the far bank while two dismantled vehicles were brought across and reassembled. Called *quitrines* in Spain, *volantes* in the Americas, these were light, open carriages with two tall wheels, a nonfolding top, and long shafts on either side of a single horse or mule.

Four days north of El Paso, at the "dread site of Robledo," Tamarón prayed that smoke seen in the nearby sierra did not signal an Apache attack. This time, thank God, it was a forest fire. At the *paraje,* or campsite, of San Diego, he watched water barrels being filled from the river for a ninety-mile dry stretch known as the Jornada del Muerto. Once safely through it, the bishop noted "the livestock were so thirsty that they ran" to reach the river again.

Tamarón's party numbered sixty-four men in all, most of them armed. Dressed for the road in black cassock, the bishop sat side-by-side in one of the volantes with Franciscan superior Jacobo de Castro, who wore the distinctive blue habit of the Mexican province. The two men conversed amiably but with a certain restraint. For more than a century, New Mexico's Franciscans had resisted efforts by bishops of Durango to impose episcopal jurisdiction over the remote colony. As the column drew even with the deserted pueblo of Socorro on the opposite bank, the two churchmen shared a sudden, unplanned intimacy. The going was rough. Ravines had sheared off the camino. All of a sudden, in the bishop's words, "the volante in which I and the Father Custos were riding suffered a severe upset. The Father Custos fell from the side and received a blow which hurt him. I escaped injury, because I fell on him. Therefore I took a horse and continued my journey on it."[3]

Just south of Santo Domingo, the episcopal cavalcade encountered a welcoming committee led by Governor Francisco Marín del Valle, who had descended the long downhill called

La Bajada from the capital in his two-seated coach. After dinner, the governor rode a horse back to Santa Fe, leaving Tamarón his carriage. In the coming weeks, the bishop and his escort, defying the heat of mid-June, traveled to most New Mexico pueblos, likely on horseback. San Felipe, however, lay on the river's west bank. At a narrows just north of the pueblo, the bishop found himself being helped into "a good canoe" for the crossing.[4] A month later, he was back in El Paso. Another full year on the road lay ahead of him, for his diocese was immense. Preparing himself physically and spiritually for the Camino Real southward, naturally the bishop prayed.

———•◆•———

At the easternmost pueblo of Pecos, Bishop Tamarón had made a lasting impression. Solidly built, square-jawed, and solemn, yet curiously dwarfed by his own vestments, he had processed with great dignity, planting the butt end of his pastoral staff with every other step and moving so smoothly that the high-peaked miter he wore did not bob up and down but seemed instead to float on an even plane.

On Monday, May 26, 1760, a date his secretary recorded in the mission register, the resplendent bishop administered confirmation to 192 Pecos Indians, signing a cross with holy oil on the forehead of each and intoning in Latin, "I confirm thee with the chrism of salvation, in the name of the Father, and of the Son, and of the Holy Spirit." The repetition was monotonous. Unnoticed in the shadows of the cavernous, dimly lighted church—successor to fray Andrés Juárez's fallen monument—one of the pueblo's principal men, Agustín Guichí, a carpenter, studied the prelate's every move, his clothing, his attendants, his gestures.[5]

The following September, once the harvest was in, Guichí called on his memory. If sacred clowns, long a tradition with the Pecos and other Pueblo Indians, could mock even the kachinas, why not a bishop? The resourceful Pecos leader saw to every detail. He designed and cut out episcopal vestments,

Bishop Tamarón's visitation, by Betsy James, for *Pecos Ruins,* School of American Research (1981). Courtesy of the artist and School for Advanced Research.

fashioning the miter of parchment stained white. A bent reed became his staff. Mateo Cru, another Pecos, dressed up as the Franciscan superior, while a third man painted himself black to play the bishop's valet. Then, "to the accompaniment of a muffled drum and loud huzzas," a colorful, exuberant chorus led the three actors, each astride a burro, into the pueblo's main plaza, where the sham bishop with scrupulous sobriety passed between two rows of kneeling women bestowing his blessings upon them.

The burlesque lasted three days. Bishop Guichí reconfirmed his people, lining them up, marking a cross with water on the forehead of each, then cuffing them to symbolize the laying on of hands. Next day at a comic Mass, he distributed bits of tortillas as altar bread. Finally, well pleased by the festivities, Agustín Guichí withdrew to his plot of corn and sat down under a juniper tree. His program had gone well. Late

Burlesque of the Bishop's visitation, by Betsy James, for *Pecos Ruins,*
School of American Research (1981). Courtesy of the artist and School
for Advanced Research.

in the afternoon as it began to get dark, he was still sitting
there when a bear attacked him, clawing his scalp where the
miter had rested and tearing his right hand to pieces. Then,
strangely, the bear turned away and ambled back toward the
mountains. Before he died, Agustín Guichí repented, exhorting his brother and sons never to repeat his grave sin.

When the real bishop heard the story, he had it published.
To Bishop Tamarón, the message was clear. This was no coin-
cidence. God's swift punishment of Agustín Guichí served as a
warning to all the Pueblo Indians to honor "His Holy Church
and her ministers."[6]

Guichí's ill-fated parody broadcast to succeeding generations another, more enduring message. Neither oppressive
Spaniards, nor marauding nomads, nor smallpox, nor vicious
strife among them—not even the repeated decimation of their
race—had broken the spirit of the Pueblo peoples.

Postscript

> *What possible good does it do us in the year 2000, as*
> *we try to come together in community, to dredge up cruel-*
> *ties four centuries old? Can't we ever forgive? Perhaps*
> *by forgiving what our ancestors did to each other, we can*
> *begin healing and forgiving what we're doing to each other*
> *today.*
>
> JOHN L. KESSELL TO THE ALBUQUERQUE
> CITY COUNCIL, MARCH 2, 2000

The dark figures approached unseen. It was late one night
in February 1998. They had come with a mission. Belatedly
on "behalf of our brothers and sisters of Acoma Pueblo,"
these anonymous vandals proceeded to saw the right foot off
Reynaldo "Sonny" Rivera's 3½-ton, twelve-foot-high bronze
equestrian statue of Juan de Oñate in Alcalde, New Mexico,
not five miles from Ohkay Owingeh (San Juan Pueblo). There,
it was done. Whether or not Oñate had actually enforced
the dismemberment he threatened in 1599, the founder of
Spanish New Mexico stood condemned in absentia four
centuries later. An article in the *New York Times* proclaimed
that the Acoma Pueblo Indians had been nursing since 1599 a
four-hundred-year grudge over the alleged foot-chopping.[1]

In truth, the resilient people of the rock, some of whom
never left, had better things to do. By the 1620s they had

firmly reestablished their pueblo and thereafter went about the daily business of cultural survival. None of the visiting late-nineteenth- and early-twentieth-century ethnologists who studied the western pueblos sensed a festering tradition of resentment at Acoma. The documentary record of the 1599 trial, meanwhile, lay hidden in Spain's Archive of the Indies. Only in 1927, with publication of historian George P. Hammond's doctoral dissertation, *Don Juan de Oñate and the Founding of New Mexico,* did a summary of Oñate's cruel sentence reemerge. English translations of the trial documents themselves followed in 1953 in Hammond and Agapito Rey's *Don Juan de Oñate: Colonizer of New Mexico, 1595–1628.*[2]

Later, praise of Oñate leading up to, during, and after New Mexico's Cuartocentenario (four-hundredth anniversary) in 1998 (1598–1998) stuck in the craw of certain vocal Acoma Indians who vehemently opposed honoring this "murderer" of their ancestors. Another proposed Oñate monument in Albuquerque drew their ire and, after years of acrimonious controversy, finally emerged in the fall of 2005—to the credit and tenacity of both parties—as an exemplary dual commemoration of the first Spanish settlers and of the Pueblos' spiritual center place.[3]

Farther south as well, Oñate's reinvigorated foes made their voices heard in El Paso in 2003 at city council meetings where another, truly colossal statue of Hispanic New Mexico's founder had reappeared on the agenda. (Juan de Oñate had taken symbolic possession of New Mexico in 1598 just down the Rio Grande from today's El Paso.) Council members, refusing to withdraw the city's partial funding, nevertheless voted a compromise. They would drop Juan de Oñate's name and call sculptor John Sherrill Houser's gigantic bronze simply *The Equestrian.*[4] Installed in 2006, dedicated on April 21, 2007, and rearing three stories tall above the tarmac at El Paso International Airport, *The Equestrian* surely ranks today as the Southwest's most conspicuous and best-known alias.

The Equestrian, by John Sherrill Houser, is part of the XII Travelers Memorial in El Paso, Texas. Dedicated on April 21, 2007, it is currently the world's largest equestrian bronze, standing 36 feet high and weighing 16 tons. Pictured are Houser and his son Ethan Taliesan Houser, associate sculptor. Photograph by Judy Schwartz.

For nearly a generation, meanwhile, influential Pueblo Indians had quietly advocated public recognition of Po'pay—acknowledged leader among leaders of the Pueblo Revolt of 1680—in their minds the savior of Pueblo culture. He should have a monument. While on a visit to Washington, D.C., during the Bicentennial of the United States in 1976, a Pueblo delegation touring the National Statuary Hall noted that New

Mexico still lacked the second of two representatives assigned to every state. Not until 1997, however, did the New Mexico Legislature vote for Po'pay to occupy the empty niche.

Awakening belatedly—and, it would seem, as payback for Pueblo opposition to Oñate—Po'pay's critics introduced a bill in 2001 to amend the previous act and choose somebody else. It died in committee, however, and in September 2005 a seven-foot-tall Tennessee marble statue of Po'pay by Jemez Pueblo sculptor Cliff Fragua took its place alongside that of Senator Dennis Chavez in the U.S. Capitol.[5] Unbowed, those who still look upon Po'pay as the murderer of Hispanic women and children suggested an alternate name for the Pueblo Revolt (which erupted on August 10, the feast day of San Lorenzo)—the Saint Lawrence Day Massacre.[6]

Regrettably, the atrocities of Acoma and Santa Fe, 1599 and 1680, live on in bitter memory. Certain descendants of Pueblos and Spaniards today, along with their respective sympathizers, remember conflict not coexistence. Crying victim always draws attention, endowing the accusers with a false sense of having gained moral high ground. To study and deplore past brutality—yet without assigning blame in the present—can most certainly lead to cultural appreciation and understanding.

On August 9, 1980—at a gathering to commemorate the tricentennial of the Pueblo Revolt—Delfín Lovato, chairman of the All Indian Pueblo Council, reminded his audience of the Spaniards' "extreme and violent measures to again subjugate the Pueblo Indians" at the close of the seventeenth century. But, he went on to say, "the Pueblos were big enough to forgive and forget these abuses," which, in his words, has "helped us to maintain our integrity and dignity as Indian people."[7]

Four years later, in 1984, at a conference held on the site of Oñate's San Gabriel headquarters, Hispanic scholar Orlando Romero, a lifelong resident of northern New Mexico, spoke of Pueblos and Spaniards as neighbors and relatives, *vecinos* and *parientes*. This "shared reality," he urged, "must be strengthened,

Po'pay, by Cliff Fragua, represents the state of New Mexico in the United States National Statuary Hall in Washington, D.C. Installed in the Rotunda of the U.S. Capitol on September 22, 2005, it is only the seventh statue of an American Indian in the collection. Photograph by Marcia Keegan.

nurtured and continued. . . . We must bring light to the past, so we learn from it. . . . After all what are parientes for, if not to help each other?"[8]

NOTES

INTRODUCTION: CONFLICT AND COEXISTENCE

1. Elinore M. Barrett, *Conquest and Catastrophe: Changing Rio Grande Pueblo Settlement Patterns in the Sixteenth and Seventeenth Centuries* (Albuquerque: University of New Mexico Press, 2002).

2. George P. Hammond and Agapito Rey, eds., *Don Juan de Oñate, Colonizer of New Mexico, 1595–1628* (Albuquerque: University of New Mexico Press, 1953), 1:483; Stella U. Ogunwole, "We the People: American Indians and Alaska Natives in the United States," U.S. Census Special Report No. 28, February 2006.

CHAPTER 1: THE PUEBLO WORLD

1. For a fine summary of Pueblo prehistory, see Stephen Plog, *Ancient Peoples of the American Southwest* (New York: Thames and Hudson, 1997). See also Carroll L. Riley, *The Kachina and the Cross: Indians and Spaniards in the Early Southwest* (Salt Lake City: University of Utah Press, 2002).

2. Steven A. LeBlanc, *Prehistoric Warfare in the American Southwest* (Salt Lake City: University of Utah Press, 1999); Plog, *Ancient Peoples,* 150.

3. See James F. Brooks, "Violence, Exchange, and Renewal in the American Southwest," *Ethnohistory* 49 (Winter 2002): 205–18.

4. Alfonso Ortiz, ed., *New Perspectives on the Pueblos* (Albuquerque: University of New Mexico Press, 1972). The most complete book of reference about the Pueblo peoples is Alfonso Ortiz, ed., *Southwest* (Washington, D.C.: Smithsonian Institution, 1979), vol. 9 of *Handbook of the North American Indians.*

5. Robert C. Galgano, *Feast of Souls: Indians and Spaniards in the Seventeenth-Century Missions of Florida and New Mexico* (Albuquerque: University of New Mexico Press, 2005), 18–20.

6. *Surviving Columbus: The Story of the Pueblo People* (Albuquerque: KNME-TV, University of New Mexico, 1992 [PBS Video]).

7. Richard Flint, ed., *Great Cruelties Have Been Reported: The 1544 Investigation of the Coronado Expedition* (Dallas: Southern Methodist University Press, 2002), 161–88.

8. Richard Flint and Shirley Cushing Flint, eds., *Documents of the Coronado Expedition, 1539–1542* (Dallas: Southern Methodist University Press, 2005), 398, 675n203. See also Herbert E. Bolton, *Coronado, Knight of Pueblos and Plains* (Albuquerque: University of New Mexico Press, 1949), still the most readable account of the Coronado venture.

9. Flint, *Great Cruelties,* 161–88 (quotation, 170).

10. Flint and Flint, *Documents of the Coronado Expedition,* 525–32 (quotations, 526).

11. George P. Hammond and Agapito Rey, eds., *The Rediscovery of New Mexico, 1580–1594* (Albuquerque: University of New Mexico Press, 1966). See also Ralph H. Vigil, *Alonso de Zorita: Royal Judge and Christian Humanist, 1512–1585* (Norman: University of Oklahoma Press, 1987), 217–20.

12. Hammond and Rey, *Oñate,* 1:335.

13. The *Memoria* of Gaspar Castaño de Sosa quoted in John L. Kessell, *Kiva, Cross, and Crown: The Pecos Indians and New Mexico, 1540–1840* (Washington, D.C.: National Park Service, 1979), 54–55.

CHAPTER 2: SPANIARDS COME TO STAY

1. Gaspar Pérez de Villagrá, *Historia de la Nueva México, 1610,* ed. Miguel Encinias, Alfred Rodríguez, and Joseph P. Sánchez (Albuquerque: University of New Mexico Press, 1992), 205–206, 212, 242, 298; Gaspar Pérez de Villagrá, *History of New Mexico, Alcalá, 1610,* trans. Gilberto Espinosa and ed. F. W. Hodge (Los Angeles: Quivira Society, 1933).

2. Pérez de Villagrá, *History,* 269.

3. Marc Simmons, *The Last Conquistador: Juan de Oñate and the Settling of the Far Southwest* (Norman: University of Oklahoma Press, 1991), 87.

4. Pérez de Villagrá, *Historia,* 142.

5. David H. Snow, comp., *New Mexico's First Colonists: The 1597–1600 Enlistments for New Mexico under Juan de Oñate, Adelante*

[Adelantado] and Gobernador (Albuquerque: Hispanic Genealogical Research Center of New Mexico, 1998).

6. Flint and Flint, *Documents of the Coronado Expedition,* 412 (brackets in translation deleted).

7. Alfonso Ortiz, "San Juan Pueblo," in *Handbook of the North American Indians,* 9:278–95; "San Juan Pueblo Tries to Change Name," *Albuquerque Journal,* September 18, 2005, B1.

8. Hammond and Rey, *Oñate,* 1:323.

9. Ibid., 2:1116.

10. Pérez de Villagrá, *Historia,* 180–82.

11. Hammond and Rey, *Oñate,* 1:354.

12. Pérez de Villagrá, *Historia,* 205, 206, 212; Hammond and Rey, *Oñate,* 1:438. Writing a tribally approved history in the 1970s, *Ácoma: Pueblo in the Sky* (Albuquerque: University of New Mexico Press, 1976), Ward Alan Minge observed that "the reason for this attack continues to puzzle modern Ácomas" (149n5).

13. Hammond and Rey, *Oñate,* 1:457–59.

14. Pérez de Villagrá, *Historia,* 242.

15. Flint and Flint, *Documents of the Coronado Expedition,* 398.

16. Hammond and Rey, *Oñate,* 1:470.

17. Pérez de Villagrá, *History,* 268.

18. Hammond and Rey, *Oñate,* 1:478.

19. Ibid., 2:649–50.

20. Ibid., 615.

21. The author of a recent book has taken me to task for suggesting the amputations might not have taken place, an example of what he calls "not only sophistry at its feeblest, but a deep insult to the Acomans themselves." See David Roberts, *The Pueblo Revolt: The Secret Rebellion That Drove the Spaniards Out of the Southwest* (New York: Simon and Schuster, 2004), 92.

22. Hammond and Rey, *Oñate,* 1:576.

23. Pérez de Villagrá, *History,* 273–75.

24. Pérez de Villagrá, *Historia,* 298.

25. Hammond and Rey, *Oñate,* 2:1009, 1010.

26. Frederick Webb Hodge, George P. Hammond, and Agapito Rey, eds., *Fray Alonso de Benavides' Revised Memorial of 1634* (Albuquerque: University of New Mexico Press, 1945), 61, 67, 73, 77–78.

27. Hammond and Rey, *Oñate*, 2:1025, 1026.

28. Ibid., 656; *When Cultures Meet: Remembering San Gabriel del Yunge Oweenge* (Santa Fe: Sunstone Press, 1987).

29. Carla R. Van West and Henri D. Grissino-Mayer, "Dendroclimatic Reconstruction," in *Environmental Studies,* ed. E. K. Huber and C. R. Van West, *Recovery in the New Mexico Transportation Corridor and First Five-Year Permit Area, Fence Lake Coal Mine Project, Catron County, New Mexico,* vol. 3, Archaeological Data, Technical Series 84 (Tucson: Statistical Research, 2005), 33.1–33.129.

30. Hammond and Rey, *Oñate*, 1:540.

31. Ibid., 560.

32. Nancy P. Hickerson, "The *Servicios* of Vicente de Zaldívar: New Light on the Jumano War of 1601," *Ethnohistory* 44 (Winter 1996): 130.

33. Hammond and Rey, *Oñate*, 2:615.

34. Ibid., 1010.

35. Ibid., 1042–45.

Chapter 3: A Franciscan City of God on the Rio Grande, 1610s–1640s

1. Hodge, Hammond, and Rey, *Benavides' Revised Memorial;* Daniel T. Reff, "Contextualizing Missionary Discourse: The Benavides *Memorials* of 1630 and 1634," *Journal of Anthropological Research* 50 (Spring 1994): 51–67.

2. Hodge, Hammond, and Rey, *Benavides' Revised Memorial,* 99.

3. Ibid., 72–80 (quotations, 73, 77–78).

4. Hammond and Rey, *Oñate,* 2:1067.

5. Ibid., 1068.

6. France V. Scholes, *Church and State in New Mexico, 1610–1650* (Albuquerque: University of New Mexico Press, 1937).

7. Andrés Juárez showed up on the list of Alonso de Oñate's recruits published recently by Stanley M. Hordes, in *To the End of the Earth: A History of the Crypto-Jews of New Mexico* (New York: Columbia University Press, 2005), 131–32n87.

8. Kessell, *Kiva, Cross, and Crown,* 115–16.

9. Ibid., 121–29. The sequence and building of Spanish and related structures along with the development of historical archaeology at Pecos are the stuff of James E. Ivey's detailed *Spanish Colonial Architecture of Pecos Pueblo, New Mexico* (Santa Fe: National Park Service, 2005).

10. See France V. Scholes, "Civil Government and Society in New Mexico in the Seventeenth Century," *New Mexico Historical Review* 10 (April 1935): 71–111; and David H. Snow, "A Note on Encomienda Economics in Seventeenth-Century New Mexico," in *Hispanic Arts and Ethnohistory in the Southwest*, ed. Marta Weigle (Santa Fe: Ancient City Press, 1983), 347–57.

11. Fray Angélico Chávez, *Origins of New Mexico Families: A Genealogy of the Spanish Colonial Period*, rev. ed. (Santa Fe: Museum of New Mexico Press, 1992), 35–36.

12. Peter P. Forrestal and Cyprian J. Lynch, eds., *Benavides' Memorial of 1630* (Washington, D.C.: Academy of American Franciscan History, 1954), 23.

13. Hodge, Hammond, and Rey, *Benavides' Revised Memorial,* 67.

14. Alden C. Hayes, *The Four Churches of Pecos* (Albuquerque: University of New Mexico Press, 1974), xii–xiv.

15. Hodge, Hammond, and Rey, *Benavides' Revised Memorial,* 67.

16. The carpenter was Cristóbal Melgarejo. Hordes, *End of the Earth,* 131–32n87.

17. Although most scholars believe that the Pecos and Jemez spoke Towa—thus explaining the Pecos remnant's move to Jemez Pueblo in 1838—Jemez historian Joe S. Sando, in *Nee Hemish: A History of Jemez Pueblo* (Albuquerque: University of New Mexico Press, 1982), questions the assumption, citing as one bit of evidence the twentieth-century Jemez saying "Just like a Pecos, fumbling for words" (149).

18. Ivey, *Spanish Colonial Architecture,* 70–73, 83–84.

19. Rick Hendricks and Gerald Mandell, "Allegations of Extortion: New Mexico Residencias of the Mid-1600s," *New Mexico Historical Review* 80 (Winter 2005): 1–28.

20. Kessell, *Kiva, Cross, and Crown,* 156–65 (quotation, 164); Scholes, *Church and State,* 115–88. A historical novel based on the tumultuous administration of Luis de Rosas is Tim MacCurdy,

Caesar of Santa Fe: A Novel from History (Albuquerque: Amador Publishers, 1990).

21. Kessell, *Kiva, Cross, and Crown*, 158.

22. Ibid., 159.

23. Scholes, *Church and State*, 120, 137, 141, 145–46n16. Certain of the friars undoubtedly committed immoral acts. I do not believe, however, Ramón A. Gutiérrez's implication that sexual impropriety or cruelty were usual behaviors of New Mexico's seventeenth-century Franciscans. See Gutiérrez, *When Jesus Came, the Corn Mothers Went Away: Marriage, Sexuality, and Power in New Mexico, 1500–1846* (Stanford: Stanford University Press, 1991), 75–76, 114, 123, 127–28, 209.

24. Kessell, *Kiva, Cross, and Crown*, 164–65.

25. Scholes, *Church and State*, 168–90 (quotation, 189); Barrett, *Conquest and Catastrophe*, 54–62.

26. Kessell, *Kiva, Cross, and Crown*, 168.

27. For an idea of the various nonviolent ways anthropologists and ethnohistorians perceive the Pueblo peoples resisting Spanish domination, see the essays in Robert W. Preucel, ed., *Archaeologies of the Pueblo Revolt: Identity, Meaning, and Renewal in the Pueblo World* (Albuquerque: University of New Mexico Press, 2002); Heather B. Trigg, *From Household to Empire: Society and Economy in Early Colonial New Mexico* (Tucson: University of Arizona Press, 2005), 132.

CHAPTER 4: A COLONY OF COUSINS, 1630S–1660S

1. Flint and Flint, *Documents of the Coronado Expedition*, 432 (brackets deleted).

2. Jerry R. Craddock and John H. R. Polt, eds., *Zaldívar and the Cattle of Cíbola: Vicente de Zaldívar's Expedition to the Buffalo Plains in 1598* (Dallas: William P. Clements Center for Southwest Studies, Southern Methodist University, 1999), 34.

3. Chávez, *Origins*, 87.

4. France V. Scholes, *Troublous Times in New Mexico, 1659–1670* (Albuquerque: University of New Mexico Press, 1942), 14–15. See also Charles R. Cutter, *The Protector de Indios in Colonial New*

Mexico, 1659–1821 (Albuquerque: University of New Mexico Press, 1986), 31–34.

5. John L. Kessell, "Diego Romero, the Plains Apaches, and the Inquisition," *American West* 15, no. 3 (May–June 1978): 12–16 (quotations, 12, 14); Donald J. Blakeslee, "The Origin and Spread of the Calumet Ceremony," *American Antiquity* 46 (1981): 759–68. For more on Diego Romero, see José Antonio Esquibel, "The Romero Family of Seventeenth-Century New Mexico," pt. 1, *Herencia: The Quarterly Journal of the Hispanic Genealogical Research Center of New Mexico* 11 (January 2003): 1–30.

6. For López de Mendizábal's background, see Hordes, *End of the Earth,* 148–50; Scholes, *Troublous Times,* 19–33; Riley, *Kachina and Cross,* 156–85.

7. France V. Scholes, "The Supply Service of the New Mexican Missions in the Seventeenth Century," *New Mexico Historical Review* 5 (January, April, and July 1930): 93–115, 186–210, 386–404; Charles Wilson Hackett and Charmion Clair Shelby, eds., *Revolt of the Pueblo Indians of New Mexico and Otermín's Attempted Reconquest, 1680–1682* (Albuquerque: University of New Mexico Press, 1940), 2:11; Chantal Cramaussel, "Historia del Camino Real de Tierra Adentro de Zacatecas a El Paso del Norte," in *El Camino Real de Tierra Adentro, historia y cultura* (Mexico City: Prisma Impresiones, 1997), 11–33.

8. Kessell, *Kiva, Cross, and Crown,* 175.

9. Scholes, *Troublous Times,* 61; Riley, *Kachina and Cross,* 178; Chávez, *Origins,* 36.

10. Kessell, *Kiva, Cross, and Crown,* 178.

11. Scholes, *Troublous Times,* 13–14; Cutter, *Protector,* 32–33; Charles Wilson Hackett, ed., *Historical Documents Relating to New Mexico, Nueva Vizcaya, and Approaches Thereto, to 1773* (Washington, D.C.: Carnegie Institution, 1937), 3:259–60.

12. Scholes, *Troublous Times,* 98.

13. Kessell, *Kiva, Cross, and Crown,* 187.

14. Ibid., 190.

15. Hordes, *End of the Earth,* 158.

16. Kessell, "Diego Romero," 12.

17. Kessell, *Kiva, Cross, and Crown,* 193–94.

18. Kessell, "Diego Romero," 16.

19. These Inquisition trials are fully related in Scholes, *Troublous Times,* 149–97; and Hordes, *End of the Earth,* 148–65.

20. Hodge, Hammond, and Rey, *Benavides' Revised Memorial,* 170.

21. Kessell, *Kiva, Cross, and Crown,* 198.

22. Hendricks and Mandell, "Allegations of Extortion," 21.

23. Scholes, *Troublous Times,* 224–44.

24. Kessell, *Kiva, Cross, and Crown,* 209.

CHAPTER 5: TROUBLOUS TIMES, 1660S–1670S

1. John L. Kessell, "Esteban Clemente, Precursor of the Pueblo Revolt," *El Palacio* 86, no. 4 (Winter 1980–81): 16.

2. John L. Kessell, "Miracles or Mystery: María de Ágreda's Ministry to the Jumano Indians of the Southwest in the 1620s," in *Great Mysteries of the West,* ed. Ferenc Morton Szasz (Golden, Colo.: Fulcrum Publishing, 1993), 121–44. An intriguing contemporary novel featuring the nun of Ágreda is Javier Sierra's *Lady in Blue* (New York: Atria Books, 2007).

3. Hodge, Hammond, and Rey, *Benavides' Revised Memorial,* 101–102; Tomás Lozano, *Cantemos al Alba: Origins of Songs, Sounds, and Liturgical Drama in Hispanic New Mexico,* ed. Rima Montoya (Albuquerque: University of New Mexico Press, 2007), 606–19, 620–30; James E. Ivey, "Convento Kivas in the Missions of New Mexico," *New Mexico Historical Review* 73 (April 1998): 121–52.

4. Kessell, "Esteban Clemente," 16–17.

5. See James E. Ivey, *In the Midst of a Loneliness: The Architectural History of the Salinas Missions* (Santa Fe: National Park Service, 1988).

6. Kessell, *Kiva, Cross, and Crown,* 212.

7. Ibid.

8. Hackett and Shelby, *Revolt of the Pueblo,* 2:299–300.

9. Kessell, *Kiva, Cross, and Crown,* 214; Chávez, *Origins,* 58.

10. Hackett, *Historical Documents,* 271–77.

11. See James E. Ivey, "'The Greatest Misfortune of All': Famine in the Province of New Mexico, 1667–1672," *Journal of the Southwest* 36 (Spring 1994): 76–100.

12. Ibid., 96n20; Kessell, *Kiva, Cross, and Crown,* 216.

13. Hodge, Hammond, and Rey, *Benavides' Revised Memorial,* 68–69.

14. Hackett and Shelby, *Revolt of the Pueblo,* 2:300–301.

15. Ibid., 301.

16. Hackett, *Historical Documents,* 285–326.

17. Ibid., 299.

18. Ibid., 286.

19. Kessell, *Kiva, Cross, and Crown,* 231–32; Chávez, *Origins,* 113.

20. Hackett and Shelby, *Revolt of the Pueblo,* 1:3–5 (quotation, 5).

21. Ibid., 5–7.

22. Kessell, *Kiva, Cross, and Crown,* 232.

CHAPTER 6: THE PUEBLOS' HOLY WAR, 1680S

1. Hackett and Shelby, *Revolt of the Pueblo,* 1:13.

2. Ibid., 14.

3. Chávez, *Origins,* 4–5.

4. Hackett and Shelby, *Revolt of the Pueblo,* 1:15.

5. John L. Kessell, Rick Hendricks, and Meredith D. Dodge, eds., *Blood on the Boulders: The Journals of don Diego de Vargas, New Mexico, 1694–1697,* bk. 2 (Albuquerque: University of New Mexico Press, 1998), 809. For a concise review of the historical and archaeological literature on the Pueblos' holy war, see Robert W. Preucel, "Writing the Pueblo Revolt," in *Archaeologies of the Pueblo Revolt,* ed. Preucel, 3–29.

6. Hackett and Shelby, *Revolt of the Pueblo,* 2:235.

7. Hayes, *Four Churches of Pecos,* 23.

8. Ibid.

9. Hackett and Shelby, *Revolt of the Pueblo,* 2:208.

10. Ibid., 225.

11. In "Popé, Pose-yemu, and Naranjo: A New Look at Leadership in the Pueblo Revolt of 1680," *New Mexico Historical Review* 65 (October 1990): 417–35, Stefanie Beninato offers a corrective to Fray Angélico Chávez, "Pohé-yemo's Representative and the Pueblo Revolt of 1680," *New Mexico Historical Review* 42 (April 1967): 85–126.

12. Hackett and Shelby, *Revolt of the Pueblo*, 2:232, 234, 381–82.

13. J. Manuel Espinosa, *Crusaders of the Río Grande: The Story of Don Diego de Vargas and the Reconquest and Refounding of New Mexico* (Chicago: Institute of Jesuit History, 1942), 22.

14. Hackett and Shelby, *Revolt of the Pueblo*, 1:161.

15. Ibid., 137–38.

16. Chávez, *Origins*, 4; Hackett and Shelby, *Revolt of the Pueblo*, 1:151.

17. Jane C. Sánchez, "Spanish–Indian Relations during the Otermín Administration, 1677–1683," *New Mexico Historical Review* 58 (April 1983): 133–51 (quotations, 135).

18. Hackett and Shelby, *Revolt of the Pueblo*, 1:94.

19. See Daniel T. Reff, "The 'Predicament of Culture' and Spanish Missionary Accounts of the Tepehuan and Pueblo Revolts," *Ethnohistory* 41 (Winter 1995): 63–90.

20. Hackett and Shelby, *Revolt of the Pueblo*, 2:235.

21. Silvestre Vélez de Escalante, "Extracto de Noticias" (ca. 1778), trans. Eleanor B. Adams (copy in the Eleanor B. Adams Collection, Center for Southwest Research, University of New Mexico, Albuquerque), 156–61. For a biographical sketch of Ojeda, see John L. Kessell, Rick Hendricks, and Meredith D. Dodge, eds., *To the Royal Crown Restored: The Journals of don Diego de Vargas, New Mexico, 1692–1694* (Albuquerque: University of New Mexico Press, 1995), 552n61.

22. The most complete coverage of the New Mexico colony in exile is Vina Walz, "History of the El Paso Area, 1680–1692," Ph.D. diss., University of New Mexico, 1951; see also Chávez, *Origins*, 25–26.

23. Hackett and Shelby, *Revolt of the Pueblo*, 2:181–403.

24. John L. Kessell and Rick Hendricks, eds., *By Force of Arms: The Journals of don Diego de Vargas, New Mexico, 1691–1693* (Albuquerque: University of New Mexico Press, 1992), 166–70.

25. Nancy P. Hickerson, *The Jumanos: Hunters and Traders of the South Plains* (Austin: University of Texas Press, 1994), 127–45. See also Brian Imhoff, *The Diary of Juan Domínguez de Mendoza's Expedition into Texas (1683–1684): A Critical Edition of the Spanish Text*

with Facsimile Reproductions (Dallas: William P. Clements Center for Southwest Studies, Southern Methodist University, 2002).

26. Walz, "El Paso Area," 104–245. For biographical sketches of Jironza and Reneros de Posada, see Kessell and Hendricks, *By Force of Arms,* 100n3, 103n9.

27. Jack D. Forbes, in *Apache, Navajo, and Spaniard* (Norman: University of Oklahoma Press, 1960), described Jironza's 1689 battle at Zia as "one of the greatest Spanish atrocities since the days of Oñate" (217).

28. Vélez de Escalante, "Extracto de Noticias," 157.

29. Kessell and Hendricks, *By Force of Arms,* 25–27, 52–54, 76, 109n30; Walz, "El Paso Area," 246–52.

30. Quoted in Laura Bayer with Floyd Montoya and the Pueblo of Santa Ana, *Santa Ana: The People, the Pueblo, and the History of Tamaya* (Albuquerque: University of New Mexico Press, 1994), 71.

31. Vélez de Escalante, "Extracto de Noticias," 157–61.

32. Sandra K. Mathews-Lamb, "'Designing and Mischievous Individuals': The Cruzate Grants and the Office of the Surveyor General," *New Mexico Historical Review* 71 (October 1996): 341–59.

33. Kessell and Hendricks, *By Force of Arms,* 27–37; Kessell, Hendricks, and Dodge, *To the Royal Crown,* 552n61.

34. Kessell and Hendricks, *By Force of Arms,* 385.

35. Ibid., 548–51; Kessell, Hendricks, and Dodge, *To the Royal Crown,* 207–208.

36. T. J. Ferguson, "Dowa Yalanne: The Architecture of Zuni Resistance and Social Change during the Pueblo Revolt," in *Archaeologies of the Pueblo Revolt,* ed. Robert W. Preucel, 39–41; Kessell and Hendricks, *By Force of Arms,* 583–84; Hackett and Shelby, *Revolt of the Pueblo,* 1:111; Vélez de Escalante, "Extracto de Noticias," 159. Galgano, *Feast of Souls,* 64, relates the efforts by the Guale Indians of Florida to adopt fray Francisco de Avila, who was captured in their rebellion of 1597.

37. Vargas's campaign journals and his correspondence with the viceroy appear in Kessell and Hendricks, *By Force of Arms,* 341–626 (quotations, 389, 412).

38. Irving A. Leonard, ed., *The Mercurio Volante of Don Carlos de Sigüenza y Góngora: An Account of the First Expedition of Don Diego de Vargas into New Mexico in 1692* (Los Angeles: Quivira Society, 1932).

39. Kessell and Hendricks, *By Force of Arms,* 431.

CHAPTER 7: RESETTLEMENT, 1690S

1. Kessell, Hendricks, and Dodge, *To the Royal Crown,* 483, 485.

2. Kessell, Hendricks, and Dodge, *Blood on the Boulders,* 1:68–69.

3. Kessell, Hendricks, and Dodge, *To the Royal Crown,* 495–519 (quotations, 503, 506). For a one-volume narrative of the Vargas recolonization, see Espinosa, *Crusaders of the Río Grande.*

4. Kessell, Hendricks, and Dodge, *To the Royal Crown,* 469.

5. Ibid., 519–42 (quotation, 528); Kessell and Hendricks, *By Force of Arms,* 421–34, 510–12.

6. Kessell, Hendricks, and Dodge, *Blood on the Boulders,* 1:74.

7. Kessell, Hendricks, and Dodge, *To the Royal Crown,* 555–64 (quotation, 563).

8. Ibid., 538–42 (quotations, 540, 542).

9. Kessell, Hendricks, and Dodge, *Blood on the Boulders,* 1:33.

10. Kessell, *Kiva, Cross, and Crown,* 262–70; Kessell, Hendricks, and Dodge, *Blood on the Boulders,* 1:293, 315.

11. See Rick Hendricks, "Pueblo–Spanish Warfare in Seventeenth-Century New Mexico: The Battles of Black Mesa, Kotyiti, and Astialakwa," in *Archaeologies of the Pueblo Revolt,* ed. Preucel, 180–97; Sando, *Nee Hemish,* 120–21; and Kessell, Hendricks, and Dodge, *Blood on the Boulders.*

12. Kessell, *Kiva, Cross, and Crown,* 271–74; Kessell, Hendricks, and Dodge, *Blood on the Boulders,* 1:398–402.

13. See John B. Colligan, *The Juan Páez Hurtado Expedition of 1695: Fraud in Recruiting Colonists for New Mexico* (Albuquerque: University of New Mexico Press, 1995); and José Antonio Esquibel and John B. Colligan, *The Spanish Recolonization of New Mexico: An Account of the Families Recruited at Mexico City in 1693* (Albuquerque: Hispanic Genealogical Research Center of New Mexico, 1999).

14. Kessell, Hendricks, and Dodge, *Blood on the Boulders*, 2:698.

15. See J. Manuel Espinosa, ed., *The Pueblo Indian Revolt of 1696 and the Franciscan Missions in New Mexico: Letters of the Missionaries and Related Documents* (Norman: University of Oklahoma, Press, 1988).

16. Kessell, Hendricks, and Dodge, *Blood on the Boulders*, 2:678.

17. Espinosa, *Pueblo Indian Revolt of 1696*, 174–75.

18. Kessell, Hendricks, and Dodge, *Blood on the Boulders*, 2:740–41.

19. Ibid., 732.

20. Ibid., 734.

21. Espinosa, *Pueblo Indian Revolt of 1696*, 182.

22. Kessell, Hendricks, and Dodge, *Blood on the Boulders*, 2:748, 875–76.

23. Ibid., 748–62, 875–76, 911 (quotation, 749). In Kessell, *Kiva, Cross, and Crown*, 288–89, I stated mistakenly that the two emissaries had arrived at Pecos before the murders in the kiva, not the day after.

24. Kessell, Hendricks, and Dodge, *Blood on the Boulders*, 2:1008.

25. Beninato, "Popé, Pose-yemu, and Naranjo," 422–23; Espinosa, *Pueblo Indian Revolt of 1696*, 278n2.

26. Kessell, Hendricks, and Dodge, *Blood on the Boulders*, 2:888.

27. John L. Kessell, *Spain in the Southwest: A Narrative History of Colonial New Mexico, Arizona, Texas, and California* (Norman: University of Oklahoma Press, 2002), 201–203.

28. Michael B. Stanislawski, "Hopi-Tewa," in *Handbook of the North American Indians*, 9:587–602.

29. Quoted in Plog, *Ancient Peoples*, 193. My thanks to Prof. Hartman H. Lomawaima for identifying the *kwitamuh*. See also Peter Whiteley, "Re-imagining Awat'ovi," in *Archaeologies of the Pueblo Revolt*, ed. Preucel, 147–66.

30. Rick Hendricks, "Pedro Rodríguez Cubero: New Mexico's Reluctant Governor, 1697–1703," *New Mexico Historical Review* 68 (January 1993): 13–39. The struggle between Vargas and Rodríguez Cubero is detailed in John L. Kessell et al., eds., *That Disturbances Cease: The Journals of Don Diego de Vargas, New Mexico, 1697–1700* (Albuquerque: University of New Mexico Press, 2000).

31. Kessell, Hendricks, and Dodge, *Blood on the Boulders*, 2:1082.

32. Kessell, *Kiva, Cross, and Crown*, 229–30, 289–97.

33. John L. Kessell et al., eds., *A Settling of Accounts: The Journals of don Diego de Vargas, New Mexico, 1700–1704* (Albuquerque: University of New Mexico Press, 2002).

34. Ibid., 227.

35. Donna Pierce, ed., *¡Vivan las Fiestas!* (Santa Fe: Museum of New Mexico Press, 1985). The tricultural dynamics of the annual Santa Fe Fiesta are explored in a video documentary by Jeanette DeBouzek and Diane Reyna, *Gathering Up Again: Fiesta in Santa Fe* (Santa Fe: Quotidian Independent Documentary Research, 1992). See also Ronald L. Grimes, *Symbol and Conquest: Public Ritual and Drama in Santa Fe* (Albuquerque: University of New Mexico Press, 1992).

36. Kessell et al., *Settling of Accounts*, 251–66.

EPILOGUE: A LIFETIME LATER, 1760

1. Eleanor B. Adams, ed., *Bishop Tamarón's Visitation of New Mexico, 1760* (Albuquerque: Historical Society of New Mexico, 1954), 36, 40.

2. Hackett and Shelby, *Revolt of the Pueblo*, 1:cv.

3. Adams, *Tamarón's Visitation*, 41, 42.

4. Ibid., 65–66.

5. Kessell, *Kiva, Cross, and Crown*, 336, 339–41.

6. Adams, *Tamarón's Visitation*, 50–53.

POSTSCRIPT

1. James Brooke, "Conquistador Statue Stirs Hispanic Pride and Indian Rage," *New York Times*, February 9, 1998, A10. See also Tina Griego, "A Foot Note to History: Amputation of N. M. Statue Underlies 400-Year-Old-Grudge," *Rocky Mountain News* (Denver), June 21, 1998. In "Oñate's Foot: Histories, Landscapes, and Contested Memories in the Southwest," in *Across the Continent: Jefferson, Lewis and Clark, and the Making of America*, ed. Douglas Seefeldt, Jeffrey L. Hantman, and Peter S. Onuf (Charlottesville: University of Virginia Press, 2005), 169–209,

Seefeldt examines "the current memory wars between Hispanics and Pueblo peoples in the Southwest" (180).

2. George P. Hammond, *Don Juan de Oñate and the Founding of New Mexico* (Santa Fe: El Palacio Press, 1927); Hammond and Rey, *Oñate.*

3. Katy June-Friesen, "Recasting New Mexico History," *Alibi* (Albuquerque), October 20–26, 2005.

4. "Statue to Be Renamed," *Albuquerque Journal,* November 6, 2003, D3. John J. Valadez and Cristina Ibarra have produced a documentary chronicling John Houser's stunning achievement—the largest equestrian bronze in the world—and the controversy it stirred: *The Last Conquistador,* Valadez Media, 2008).

5. Joe S. Sando and Herman Agoyo, eds., *Po'pay, Leader of the First American Revolution* (Santa Fe: Clear Light Publishing, 2005).

6. Conchita Lucero, "What's in a Name?" New Mexico Hispanic Culture Preservation League (http://www.nmhcpl.org/uploads/What_s_in_a_name.pdf). Two recent articles that seek to explain the conflict are Elizabeth Archuleta, "History Carved in Stone: Memorializing Po'pay and Oñate, or Recasting Racialized Regimes of Representation?" *New Mexico Historical Review* 82 (Summer 2007): 317–42; and Yolanda Leyba, "Monuments of Conformity: Commemorating and Protesting Oñate on the Border," *New Mexico Historical Review* 82 (Summer 2007): 343–67.

7. Sando and Agoyo, *Po'pay,* 99.

8. Orlando Romero, "San Gabriel Revisited, 1598–1984," in *When Cultures Meet: Remembering San Gabriel del Yunge Oweenge* (Santa Fe: Sunstone Press, 1987), 9.

BIBLIOGRAPHY

Adams, Eleanor B., ed. *Bishop Tamarón's Visitation of New Mexico,
1760*. Albuquerque: Historical Society of New Mexico, 1954.

Archuleta, Elizabeth. "History Carved in Stone: Memorializing
Po'pay and Oñate, or Recasting Racialized Regimes of
Representation?" *New Mexico Historical Review* 82 (Summer
2007): 317–42.

Barrett, Elinore M. *Conquest and Catastrophe: Changing Rio Grande
Pueblo Settlement Patterns in the Sixteenth and Seventeenth
Centuries*. Albuquerque: University of New Mexico Press,
2002.

Bayer, Laura, with Floyd Montoya and the Pueblo of Santa Ana.
Santa Ana: The People, the Pueblo, and the History of Tamaya.
Albuquerque: University of New Mexico Press, 1994.

Beninato, Stefanie. "Popé, Pose-yemu, and Naranjo: A New Look
at Leadership in the Pueblo Revolt of 1680." *New Mexico
Historical Review* 65 (October 1990): 417–35.

Blakeslee, Donald J. "The Origin and Spread of the Calumet
Ceremony." *American Antiquity* 46 (1981): 759–68.

Bolton, Herbert E. *Coronado, Knight of Pueblos and Plains*.
Albuquerque: University of New Mexico Press, 1949.

Brooks, James F. *Captives and Cousins: Slavery, Kinship, and
Community in the Southwest Borderlands*. Chapel Hill:
University of North Carolina Press, 2002.

——. "Violence, Exchange, and Renewal in the American
Southwest." *Ethnohistory* 49 (Winter 2002): 205–18.

Calloway, Colin G. *One Vast Winter Count: The Native American West
before Lewis and Clark*. Lincoln: University of Nebraska Press,
2003.

Chávez, Fray Angélico. *Origins of New Mexico Families: A Genealogy
of the Spanish Colonial Period*. Rev. ed. Santa Fe: Museum of
New Mexico Press, 1992.

——. "Pohé-yemo's Representative and the Pueblo Revolt of 1680." *New Mexico Historical Review* 42 (April 1967): 85–126.

Colligan, John B. *The Juan Páez Hurtado Expedition of 1695: Fraud in Recruiting Colonists for New Mexico.* Albuquerque: University of New Mexico Press, 1995.

Craddock, Jerry R., and John H. R. Polt, eds. *Zaldívar and the Cattle of Cíbola: Vicente de Zaldívar's Expedition to the Buffalo Plains in 1598.* Dallas: William P. Clements Center for Southwest Studies, Southern Methodist University, 1999.

Cramaussel, Chantal. "Historia del Camino Real de Tierra Adentro de Zacatecas a El Paso del Norte." In *El Camino Real de Tierra Adentro, historia y cultura,* 21–33. Mexico City: Prisma Impresiones, 1997.

Cutter, Charles R. *The Protector de Indios in Colonial New Mexico, 1659–1821.* Albuquerque: University of New Mexico Press, 1986.

DeBouzek, Jeanette, and Diane Reyna. *Gathering Up Again: Fiesta in Santa Fe.* Video. Santa Fe: Quotidian Independent Documentary Research, 1992.

Espinosa, J. Manuel. *Crusaders of the Río Grande: The Story of Don Diego de Vargas and the Reconquest and Refounding of New Mexico.* Chicago: Institute of Jesuit History, 1942.

——, ed. *The Pueblo Indian Revolt of 1696 and the Franciscan Missions in New Mexico: Letters of the Missionaries and Related Documents.* Norman: University of Oklahoma Press, 1988.

Esquibel, José Antonio. "The Romero Family of Seventeenth-Century New Mexico," part 1. *Herencia: The Quarterly Journal of the Hispanic Genealogical Research Center of New Mexico* 11 (January 2003): 1–30.

Esquibel, José Antonio, and John B. Colligan. *The Spanish Recolonization of New Mexico: An Account of the Families Recruited at Mexico City in 1693.* Albuquerque: Hispanic Genealogical Research Center of New Mexico, 1999.

Ferguson, T. J. "Dowa Yalanne: The Architecture of Zuni Resistance and Social Change during the Pueblo Revolt." In *Archaeologies of the Pueblo Revolt: Identity, Meaning, and*

Renewal in the Pueblo World, ed. Robert W. Preucel,
32–44. Albuquerque: University of New Mexico Press, 2002.

Flint, Richard. *No Settlement, No Conquest: A History of the
Coronado Entrada.* Albuquerque: University of New Mexico
Press, 2008.

——, ed. *Great Cruelties Have Been Reported: The 1544 Investigation of
the Coronado Expedition.* Dallas: Southern Methodist
University Press, 2002.

Flint, Richard, and Shirley Cushing Flint, eds. *Documents of the
Coronado Expedition, 1539–1542.* Dallas: Southern Methodist
University Press, 2005.

Forbes, Jack D. *Apache, Navaho, and Spaniard.* Norman: University
of Oklahoma Press, 1960.

Forrestal, Peter P., and Cyprian J. Lynch, eds. *Benavides' Memorial of
1630.* Washington, D.C.: Academy of American Franciscan
History, 1954.

Galgano, Robert C. *Feast of Souls: Indians and Spaniards in the
Seventeenth-Century Missions of Florida and New Mexico.*
Albuquerque: University of New Mexico Press, 2005.

Grimes, Ronald L. *Symbol and Conquest: Public Ritual and Drama in
Santa Fe.* Albuquerque: University of New Mexico Press,
1992.

Gutiérrez, Ramón A. *When Jesus Came, the Corn Mothers
Went Away: Marriage, Sexuality, and Power in New Mexico,
1500–1846.* Stanford: Stanford University Press, 1991.

Hackett, Charles Wilson, ed. *Historical Documents Relating to New
Mexico, Nueva Vizcaya, and Approaches Thereto, to 1773.* Vol. 3.
Washington, D.C.: Carnegie Institution, 1937.

Hackett, Charles Wilson, and Charmion Clair Shelby, eds. *Revolt
of the Pueblo Indians of New Mexico and Otermín's Attempted
Reconquest, 1680–1682.* 2 vols. Albuquerque: University of
New Mexico Press, 1940.

Hammond, George P. *Don Juan de Oñate and the Founding of New
Mexico.* Santa Fe: El Palacio Press, 1927.

Hammond, George P., and Agapito Rey, eds. *Don Juan de Oñate:*

Colonizer of New Mexico, 1595–1628. 2 vols. Albuquerque: University of New Mexico Press, 1953.

——, eds. *The Rediscovery of New Mexico, 1580–1594.* Albuquerque: University of New Mexico Press, 1966.

Hayes, Alden C. *The Four Churches of Pecos.* Albuquerque: University of New Mexico Press, 1974.

Hendricks, Rick. "Pedro Rodríguez Cubero: New Mexico's Reluctant Governor, 1697–1703." *New Mexico Historical Review* 68 (January 1993): 13–39.

——. "Pueblo–Spanish Warfare in Seventeenth-Century New Mexico: The Battles of Black Mesa, Kotyiti, and Astialakwa." In *Archaeologies of the Pueblo Revolt: Identity, Meaning, and Renewal in the Pueblo World,* ed. Robert W. Preucel, 180–97. Albuquerque: University of New Mexico Press, 2002.

Hendricks, Rick, and Gerald Mandell. "Allegations of Extortion: New Mexico Residencias of the Mid-1600s." *New Mexico Historical Review* 80 (Winter 2005): 1–28.

Hickerson, Nancy P. *The Jumanos: Hunters and Traders of the South Plains.* Austin: University of Texas Press, 1994.

——. "The *Servicios* of Vicente de Zaldívar: New Light on the Jumano War of 1601." *Ethnohistory* 44 (Winter 1996): 127–44.

Hodge, Frederick Webb, George P. Hammond, and Agapito Rey, eds. *Fray Alonso de Benavides' Revised Memorial of 1634.* Albuquerque: University of New Mexico Press, 1945.

Hordes, Stanley M. *To the End of the Earth: A History of the Crypto-Jews of New Mexico.* New York: Columbia University Press, 2005.

Imhoff, Brian. *The Diary of Juan Domínguez de Mendoza's Expedition into Texas (1683–1684): A Critical Edition of the Spanish Text with Facsimile Reproductions* (Dallas: Southern Methodist University Press, 2002).

Ivey, James E. "Convento Kivas in the Missions of New Mexico." *New Mexico Historical Review* 73 (April 1998): 121–52.

——. "'The Greatest Misfortune of All': Famine in the Province of New Mexico, 1667–1672." *Journal of the Southwest* 36 (Spring 1994): 76–100.

———. *In the Midst of a Loneliness: The Architectural History of the Salinas Missions.* Santa Fe: National Park Service, 1988.

———. *The Spanish Colonial Architecture of Pecos Pueblo, New Mexico.* Santa Fe: National Park Service, 2005.

Kessell, John L. "Diego Romero, the Plains Apaches, and the Inquisition." *American West* 15, no. 3 (May–June 1978): 12–16.

———. "Esteban Clemente, Precursor of the Pueblo Revolt." *El Palacio* 86, no. 4 (Winter 1980–81): 16–17.

———. *Kiva, Cross, and Crown: The Pecos Indians and New Mexico, 1540–1840.* Washington, D.C.: National Park Service, 1979.

———. "Miracles or Mystery: María de Ágreda's Ministry to the Jumano Indians of the Southwest in the 1620s." In *Great Mysteries of the West,* ed. Ferenc Morton Szasz, 121–44. Golden, Colo.: Fulcrum Publishing, 1993.

———. *Spain in the Southwest: A Narrative History of Colonial New Mexico, Arizona, Texas, and California.* Norman: University of Oklahoma Press, 2002.

———, ed. *Remote Beyond Compare: Letters of don Diego de Vargas to His Family, 1675–1706.* Albuquerque: University of New Mexico Press, 1989.

Kessell, John L., and Rick Hendricks, eds. *By Force of Arms: The Journals of don Diego de Vargas, New Mexico, 1691–1693.* Albuquerque: University of New Mexico Press, 1992.

Kessell, John L., Rick Hendricks, and Meredith D. Dodge, eds. *Blood on the Boulders: The Journals of don Diego de Vargas, New Mexico, 1694–1697.* Albuquerque: University of New Mexico Press, 1998.

———, eds. *To the Royal Crown Restored: The Journals of don Diego de Vargas, New Mexico, 1692–1694.* Albuquerque: University of New Mexico Press, 1995.

Kessell, John L., Rick Hendricks, Meredith D. Dodge, and Larry D. Miller, eds. *A Settling of Accounts: The Journals of don Diego de Vargas, New Mexico, 1700–1704.* Albuquerque: University of New Mexico Press, 2002.

———, eds. *That Disturbances Cease: The Journals of don Diego de Vargas,*

New Mexico, 1697–1700. Albuquerque: University of New Mexico Press, 2000.

Knaut, Andrew L. *The Pueblo Revolt of 1680: Conquest and Resistance in Seventeenth-Century New Mexico.* Norman: University of Oklahoma Press, 1995.

LeBlanc, Steven A. *Prehistoric Warfare in the American Southwest.* Salt Lake City: University of Utah Press, 1999.

Leonard, Irving A., ed. *The Mercurio Volante of Don Carlos de Sigüenza y Góngora: An Account of the First Expedition of Don Diego de Vargas into New Mexico in 1692.* Los Angeles: Quivira Society, 1932.

Leyba, Yolanda. "Monuments of Conformity: Commemorating and Protesting Oñate on the Border." *New Mexico Historical Review* 82 (Summer 2007): 343–67.

Lozano, Tomás. *Cantemos al Alba: Origins of Songs, Sounds, and Liturgical Drama in Hispanic New Mexico.* Edited by Rima Montoya. Albuquerque: University of New Mexico Press, 2007.

MacCurdy, Tim. *Caesar of Santa Fe: A Novel from History.* Albuquerque: Amador Publishers, 1990.

Mathews-Lamb, Sandra K. "'Designing and Mischievous Individuals': The Cruzate Grants and the Office of the Surveyor General." *New Mexico Historical Review* 71 (October 1996): 341–59.

Minge, Ward Alan. *Ácoma: Pueblo in the Sky.* Albuquerque: University of New Mexico Press, 1976.

Ortiz, Alfonso, "San Juan Pueblo." In *Handbook of the North American Indians,* vol. 9, *Southwest,* ed. Alfonso Ortiz, 278–95. Washington, D.C.: Smithsonian Institution, 1979.

——. ed. *New Perspectives on the Pueblos.* Albuquerque: University of New Mexico Press, 1972.

——. ed. *Southwest.* Vol. 9 of *Handbook of the North American Indians.* Washington, D.C.: Smithsonian Institution, 1979.

Payne, Melissa. "Valley of Faith: Historical Archeology in the

Upper Santa Fe River Basin." Ph.D. diss., University of New Mexico, 1999.

Pérez de Villagrá, Gaspar. *Historia de la Nueva México, 1610.* Edited by Miguel Encinias, Alfred Rodríguez, and Joseph P. Sánchez. Albuquerque: University of New Mexico Press, 1992.

——. *History of New Mexico, Alcalá, 1610.* Translated by Gilberto Espinosa and edited by F. W. Hodge. Los Angeles: Quivira Society, 1933.

Pierce, Donna, ed. *¡Vivan las Fiestas!* Santa Fe: Museum of New Mexico Press, 1985.

Plog, Stephen. *Ancient Peoples of the American Southwest.* New York: Thames and Hudson, 1997.

Preucel, Robert W. "Writing the Pueblo Revolt." In *Archaeologies of the Pueblo Revolt: Identity, Meaning, and Renewal in the Pueblo World,* ed. Robert W. Preucel, 3–29. Albuquerque: University of New Mexico Press, 2002.

——, ed. *Archaeologies of the Pueblo Revolt: Identity, Meaning, and Renewal in the Pueblo World.* Albuquerque: University of New Mexico Press, 2002.

Reff, Daniel T. "Contextualizing Missionary Discourse: The Benavides *Memorials* of 1630 and 1634." *Journal of Anthropological Research* 50 (Spring 1994): 51–67.

——. "The 'Predicament of Culture' and Spanish Missionary Accounts of the Tepehuan and Pueblo Revolts." *Ethnohistory* 41 (Winter 1995): 63–90.

Riley, Carroll L. *The Kachina and the Cross: Indians and Spaniards in the Early Southwest.* Salt Lake City: University of Utah Press, 2002.

Roberts, David. *The Pueblo Revolt: The Secret Rebellion That Drove the Spaniards Out of the Southwest.* New York: Simon and Schuster, 2004.

Romero, Orlando. "San Gabriel Revisited, 1598–1984." In *When Cultures Meet: Remembering San Gabriel del Yunge Oweenge.* Santa Fe: Sunstone Press, 1987, 7–9.

Sánchez, Jane C. "Spanish–Indian Relations during the Otermín Administration, 1677–1683." *New Mexico Historical Review* 58 (April 1983): 133–51.

Sando, Joe S. *Nee Hemish: A History of Jemez Pueblo.* Albuquerque: University of New Mexico Press, 1982.

Sando, Joe S., and Herman Agoyo, eds. *Po'pay, Leader of the First American Revolution.* Santa Fe: Clear Light Publishing, 2005.

Scholes, France V. *Church and State in New Mexico, 1610–1650.* Albuquerque: University of New Mexico Press, 1937.

——. "Civil Government and Society in New Mexico in the Seventeenth Century." *New Mexico Historical Review* 10 (April 1935): 71–111.

——. "The Supply Service of the New Mexican Missions in the Seventeenth Century." *New Mexico Historical Review* 5 (January, April, and July 1930): 93–115, 186–210, 386–404.

——. *Troublous Times in New Mexico, 1659–1670.* Albuquerque: University of New Mexico Press, 1942.

Seefeldt, Douglas. "Oñate's Foot: Histories, Landscapes, and Contested Memories in the Southwest." In *Across the Continent: Jefferson, Lewis and Clark, and the Making of America,* ed. Douglas Seefeldt, Jeffrey L. Hantman, and Peter S. Onuf, 169–209. Charlottesville: University of Virginia Press, 2005.

Sierra, Javier. *The Lady in Blue.* New York: Atria Books, 2007.

Simmons, Marc. *The Last Conquistador: Juan de Oñate and the Settling of the Far Southwest.* Norman: University of Oklahoma Press, 1991.

Snow, David H. "A Note on Encomienda Economics in Seventeenth-Century New Mexico." In *Hispanic Arts and Ethnohistory in the Southwest,* ed. Marta Weigle, 347–57. Santa Fe: Ancient City Press, 1983.

——, comp. *New Mexico's First Colonists: The 1597–1600 Enlistments for New Mexico under Juan de Oñate, Adelante [Adelantado] and Gobernador.* Albuquerque: Hispanic Genealogical Research Center of New Mexico, 1998.

——. Stanislawski, Michael B. "Hopi-Tewa." In *Handbook of the North American Indians,* vol. 9, *Southwest,* ed. Alfonso Ortiz, 587–602. Washington, D.C.: Smithsonian Institution, 1979.

Surviving Columbus: The Story of the Pueblo People. PBS Video. Albuquerque: KNME-TV, University of New Mexico, 1992.

Trigg, Heather B. *From Household to Empire: Society and Economy in Early Colonial New Mexico.* Tucson: University of Arizona Press, 2005.

Valadez, John J., and Cristina Ibarra. *The Last Conquistador.* Video. Valadez Media, 2008.

Van West, Carla R., and Henri D. Grissino-Mayer. "Dendroclimatic Reconstruction." In *Fence Lake Project: Archaeological Data Recovery in the New Mexico Transportation Corridor and First Five-Year Permit Area, Fence Lake Coal Mine Project, Catron County, New Mexico,* ed. E. K. Huber and C. R. Van West. Vol. 3 of *Environmental Studies.* Technical Series 84. Tucson: Statistical Research, 2005.

Vélez de Escalante, Silvestre. "Extracto de Noticias" (ca. 1778). Translated by Eleanor B. Adams. Copy in the Eleanor B. Adams Collection, Center for Southwest Research, University of New Mexico, Albuquerque.

Vigil, Ralph H. *Alonso de Zorita: Royal Judge and Christian Humanist, 1512–1585.* Norman: University of Oklahoma Press, 1987.

Walz, Vina. "History of the El Paso Area, 1680–1692." Ph.D. diss., University of New Mexico, 1951.

Weber, David J. *The Spanish Frontier in North America.* New Haven: Yale University Press, 1992.

——, ed. *What Caused the Pueblo Revolt of 1680?* Boston: Bedford/St. Martin's, 1999.

When Cultures Meet: Remembering San Gabriel del Yunge Oweenge. Santa Fe: Sunstone Press, 1987.

Whiteley, Peter. "Re-imagining Awat'ovi." In *Archaeologies of the Pueblo Revolt: Identity, Meaning, and Renewal in the Pueblo World,* ed. Robert W. Preucel, 147–66. Albuquerque: University of New Mexico Press, 2002.

INDEX

All references to illustrations are in italic type.

Abo Pueblo (Tompiro), 92, 99, 103, 105

Acoma Pueblo (Keresan), 30, *39,* 92, 110, 125, 146, 162, 169–70; Apache assault of, 104; battle at (1599), 25–26, 37–40, 43, 123, 137; factionalism at, 139, 170; Franciscans at, 55; resistance of (1598), 33–36, 191n12; slaves from, 41–42, 45; trial of prisoners from, 40–42, 183–84

Ágreda, María de Jesús de, 98–99, *100,* 196n2; biographical sketch of, 51–52

Aguilar, Nicolás de, 101–102

Aguilera, Teresa de (wife of Governor López), 81, 91

Alameda Pueblo (Tiwa), 129, 134

Alcaldes mayores, 84, 101–102

Alemán, 108

Amputation, as punishment, 40–42, 44, 183, 191n21

Analco, barrio of Santa Fe, 120

Anaya Almazán, Cristóbal de, 122

Anaya Almazán, Francisco de, 121–22, 128, 158–59, 162, 164, 170, 172–74; as the enduring colonist, 152

Anián, Strait of, 5

Apache Indians, 20–21, 104, 133, 139, 142; allied with Pueblos, 71–72, 105–106, 108–109, 146; "depredations" of, 97, 104, 108–109, 113. *See also* specific Apache groups

Architecture, European, 32, 45, 59–61, *62,* 63. *See also* Pueblo Indians, architecture of

Arms and armor: of Pueblo Indians, 11, 35, 153; Pueblo use of Spanish, 77–78, 120, 158; of Spaniards, 112, 137. *See also* Firearms

Awátovi Pueblo (Hopi), 54, 77, 86; destruction of, 167, 171

Ayeta, fray Francisco de, 97, 112–14, 130, 133, 135, 177–78

Baca, Antonio, 70

Bal, fray Juan de, 146

Benavides, fray Alonso de, 57, 98–99, 103, 152; quoted, 44, 54–55, 63, 92–93, 99–100, 109; writings of, 53–55

Bernal, fray Juan, 95, 107–108, 113, 116–17; quoted, 103–104

Bernalillo (New Mexico), 171–72

Bigotes (Pecos leader), 19–20

Black Mesa. *See* San Ildefonso Mesa

Bolsas, Antonio, 153–54

Bua, Nicolás, 127

Buffalo, 74–75, *75*

Caciques. *See* Pueblo Indians, caciques and governors of
California, Gulf of, 44
Camino Real de Tierra Adentro, 81–82, 107–108, 136, 150, 178–79
Cannibalism, 11
Capital punishment. *See* Executions
Caripicado (Pecos leader), 164–65, 170
Carlos II (king of Spain), Pueblo babies named after, 134, 148
Carpentry. *See* Pecos Pueblo, carpenters of
Carpintero, El (Pecos leader), 64, 78–79
Casas reales. *See* Santa Fe, governor's palace at
Castañeda, Pedro de, 31, 40, 74
Castro, fray Jacobo de, 178
Catití, Alonso, 127–29, 134, 139
Catua, Nicolás, 116–17
Cervantes, Miguel de. *See Don Quijote*
Chato, El (Pueblo leader), 123, 127
Chihuahua, San Felipe de (Nueva Vizcaya), 173
Children, Hispanic, 17; death of, 151, 169; ransomed captive, 146
Children, non-Pueblo Indians as household servants, 77
Children, Pueblo, 17; as prisoners, 41, 138–39
Chistoe, Felipe, 163–66, 170–71
Cicuique. *See* Pecos Pueblo
Clemente, Esteban, 96–102,
104–105; condemns kachinas, 98; failed Pueblo revolt of, 105–107, 118
Cochiti Mesa, as Keresan refuge, 158–59
Cochiti Pueblo (Keresan), 77, 134, 141–42, 162
Colonists of New Mexico. *See* Spanish colonists of New Mexico
Comanche Indians, 175
Confraternities, religious: of La Conquistadora, 172; of Nuestra Señora del Rosario, 85
Conquest culture, Spanish, 16–17, 28, 41. *See also* Possession, Spanish rituals of
Conquistadora, La (Our Lady of the Assumption), 62, 152; confraternity of, 172
Coronado, Francisco Vázquez de, 18–22, 30–31. *See also* Castañeda, Pedro de
Cortés, Hernán, 18
Council of the Indies, 114
Cruzate. *See* Jironza Petrís de Cruzate, Domingo
Cruzate grants, 139–40
Crypto-Jews, 30, 63, 67, 87–89, 91
Cueloce Pueblo (Tompiro), 47
Cuyamungue Pueblo (Tewa), 77

Díaz de Betansos, Luisa, 84
Díez, fray José, 149, 161–62
Diseases, 4, 92; dysentery, 172; smallpox, 108; typhus, 160, 162. *See also* Epidemics

Dogs, 9; of war, 20, *21*, 33–34
Domínguez, Francisca (wife of Francisco de Anaya Alamazán), 128
Domínguez de Mendoza, Juan, 133–35
Dominicans, 56
Don Pedro, ranchería de, 78
Don Quijote, 43–44, 49, 81
Dowa Yalanne (Corn Mountain), 109, 145–46. *See also* Zuni Pueblos
Drought, 45, 102–104, 126, 160
Durán y Chavéz clan, 133
Durango (Nueva Vizcaya), 112; bishops of, 174, 177–81

Education: lack of teachers in New Mexico, 85; mission boys' schools, 99–100
El Paso (New Mexico), 112, 130, 152, 155, 177–78; colony in exile at, 128, 132–33, 135, 140; Nuestra Señora de Guadalupe at, 114; Oñate statue at, 184–85; presidio of, 135–36, 141, 174–75
Encomiendas, 61–62, 77, 92–93; end of, 173; value of tribute from, 84, 92
Enríquez de Rivera, fray Payo, 112, 114
Epidemics, 68, 97, 160. *See also* Diseases
Escobar, fray Francisco de, 44
Españoles mexicanos, 160–61. *See also* Santa Cruz de la Cañada
Ethnicity. *See* Lobos; Mulattos; Racial Mixing

Eufemia, doña. *See* Sosa, Eufemia de
Executions: of alleged Pueblo rebels, 36, 71–72, 105–106, 111, 122, 136, 138, 154; of Spaniards, 33, 70

Famine, 97, 102–104
Faraon Apaches, 171
Felipe II (king of Spain), 22, 26, 34
Felipe III (king of Spain), 43, 49
Felipe IV (king of Spain), 51
Firearms: cannons, 137, 141; harquebuses, 38, 112; swivel guns, 38
Fonte, fray Francisco, 99
Fragua, Cliff, statue of Po'pay by, 186
Franciscans in New Mexico, 12, 16–17, 39, 52–65, *55*, 72, 92, 130; alleged immorality of, 53, 68, 86, 194n23; color of habits of, 98, 178; Convento Grande of (Mexico City), 58; desertion of, 48, 81; martyrdom of, 54–55, 117, 120, 128, 130, 131, 146, 163–64; mission supply service of, 62, 66, 82, 88; with Oñate, 32, 36–37, 52; and Pueblo languages, 54, 59, 64; after restoration, 174–75; succor colony, 108. *See also* Education, mission boys' schools; Kachina religion; Spanish governors of New Mexico, curse Franciscans

Galinda, Francisca, 46
Galisteo Pueblo (Tano), 83, 109, 113, 116–17
Galve, conde de, 141, 169; and reoccupation of New Mexico, 160
García, Joe, 31
Gasco de Velasco, Luis, 42, 47
Gender roles, Pueblo, 32, 53–54, 60–61, 102. *See also* Women, Hispanic; Women, Pueblo
Godparenthood, 133–34, 145, 148, 153
Gómez, Francisco, 61–63, 67, 69, 85, 89
Gómez Robledo, Francisco, 85, 91–93, 115–17; household of, 128; as Inquisition prisoner, 87–89
Governors of New Mexico. *See* Spanish governors of New Mexico
Gran Quivira. *See* Cueloce Pueblo; Las Humanas Pueblo
Grayrobe, fray Juan, 145–46
Gruber, Bernardo, 107–108
Guanajuato (New Spain), 91
Guichí, Agustín, 179–81, *181*

Halona Pueblo (Zuni), 146
Hano Pueblo (Hopi Tewa), 166–67
Hawikuh Pueblo (Zuni), 18, 34, 54; overrun by Apaches, 108–109
Herrera Horta, Ginés de, 41–42
Hidalgo, as title, 31, 43
Hidalgo, Pedro, 116–17

Historia de la Nueva México (1610), 26–28, 34, 37–38, 43, 137. *See also* Pérez de Villagrá, Gaspar
Hopi pueblos, 35, 40, 54, 88, 139, 145, 162, 164; factionalism in, 167; invite Pueblo refugees, 166–67. *See also* specific Hopi pueblos
Horses, 112; acquired by Apaches and Navajos, 78; games of skill with, 32, 136; ridden by Pueblos, 77–78, 111; traps for, 33, 37–38
Houser, John Sherill, Oñate statue by, 184, *185,* 203n4
Humanas. *See* Las Humanas Pueblo

Indian laborers, 130, 174; levies of, 32; in missions, 83; salaried, 83–84, 85
Indios ladinos, 98, 106–107, 120, 123, 128, 131, 139, 153
Inquisition, Holy Office of the. *See* Mexican Inquisition
Interpreters of Pueblo Indian languages, 127, 142, 146, 150, 156, 164. *See also* Clemente, Esteban; Franciscans in New Mexico, and Pueblo languages; Ojeda, Bartolomé de; Tomás
Isleta Pueblo (Tiwa), 88, 125, 128–29, 133–34, 135. *See also* Ysleta del Sur Pueblo

Javier, Francisco, 110, 113–17, 123, 126, 142–43
Jemez Pueblos (Towa), 111, 129,

139, 166; resisting Spaniards, 68, 71, 115, 134, 156–57, 159; and revolt of (1696), 163–64

Jesuits, 56, 83
Jews, expulsion from Spain, 63. *See also* Crypto-Jews
Jicarilla Apaches, 170
Jironza Petrís de Cruzate, Domingo, 135–40; attacks Zia Pueblo, 137–39, 141, 148, 197n27
José (Pueblo leader), 145, 153
Juan (Pueblo leader), 120
Juan of Tesuque (Pueblo witness), 127, 131, 140, 149
Juárez, fray Andrés, 57–65, 67–68, 71, 76; and Pecos church, 59–61
Juego de gallo, 136
Jumano Indians (Plains), 51, 98–99, 135
Jumano Pueblos (Tompiro), resistance of, 47. *See also* Cueloce Pueblo; Las Humanas Pueblo

Kachina religion, 11–17, *13*, 29, 124, *147*, 167; destruction of artifacts of, 86–87, 106, 125, 134; Franciscan opposition to, 15, 53, 59, 71–72, 110–11, 130; Spanish governors' support of, 67, 85–86, 98, 102; taken underground, 72, 95–96, 106–107. *See also* Poseyemu
Keresan Pueblos (Keres), 21, 127, 129, *132*, 139, 141–42; factionalism of, 148, 156–57;

resist Spaniards, 71–72, 134, 136–38, 158–59. *See also* specific Keresan pueblos
Kessell, John L., 183
Kivas, 13, *14*, 15, 29, 34, 72, *151*, 174; in Christian context, 60, 101, 149–50; murders in, 164

Lady in Blue. *See* Ágreda, María de Jesús de
Laguna Pueblo (Keresan), 139, 170
Land grants, 31, 84, 173–74; to Pueblo Indians, 139–40, 173
Languages. *See* Interpreters of Pueblo Indian Languages
Las Humanas Pueblo (Tompiro), 98, 101–103, 105; abandonment of, 109
Lobos (ethnicity), 165
López de Mendizábal, Bernardo, 77, 81–89, 101–103, 110; as Inquisition prisoner, 88, 91, 103; memory of, 127
López Zambrano, Diego, 105–106, 110, 111–13, 142–43
Lovato, Delfín, 186
Luján, Miguel, 150, 153

Madrid (Spain), 141
Madrid, Roque, 156, 162
Malacate, Antonio, 148, 156–57, 159
Manso Indians, 129, 133
Marín del Valle, Francisco, 178–79
Márquez, Gerónimo, 33
Martínez, fray Alonso, 41–42

Meco, Cristóbal el, 77
Melgarejo, Cristóbal, 193n16
Mercurio volante, 146
Mestas, Juan de, 77
Mexican Indians, 120; with
    Coronado, 18, 35; with
    Oñate, 30
Mexican Inquisition, 63, 72, 87;
    agents of in New Mexico,
    57, 86–88, 91, 93–95, 107–
    108, 174–75; seal of, *90;* trial
    of New Mexicans by, 88–91
Mexico City, 18–19, 21, 112–14,
    135–36, 141, 146, 169;
    Franciscan Convento
    Grande in, 58
Mines and mining, 21, 31,
    43, 56
Missionaries. *See* Franciscans in
    New Mexico
Moctezuma y de Tula, conde
    de, 169
Montesclaros, marqués de,
    43–44, 49
Moros y Cristianos, 32
Mosoyo (Pecos leader), 59, 64
Muerto, Jornada del, 108, 178
Mulattos, 35, 46, 126–27, 165
Mules, 82; price of, 77
Music: mission, 99; of Plains
    Apaches, 79
Muza, Lorenzo, 129–30

Nambe Pueblo (Tewa), 65, 111,
    164
Naranjo, Domingo, 126, 165
Naranjo, Lucas, 165–66
Nava de Barcinas, marqués de
    la. *See* Vargas, Diego de

Navajo Indians, 20–21, 104, 129,
    133; as allies of Pueblos, 71,
    146, 156
New Mexico: isolation of, 5;
    naming of, 21–22; poverty
    of, 5, 18, 33, 50, 52, 56; relief
    of, 112–14. *See also*
    Franciscans in New Mexico;
    Pueblo Indians; Spanish col-
    onists of New Mexico
Nueva Vizcaya, 33, 136–37; sup-
    plies and reinforcements
    from, 141, 160

Ohkay Owingeh. *See* San Juan
    Pueblo, Ohkay Owingeh
Ojeda, Bartolomé de, 96,
    106–107, 131, 136–40; and
    Cruzate grants, 139–40; as
    Governor Vargas's ally, 141–
    42, 148, 156–57, 169–71; let-
    ters by, 157, 162
Ollita, Francisco el, 127, 134
Olvera, Isabel de, 46
Omtua, Pedro, 116–17
Oñate, Alonso de (Juan de
    Oñate's brother), 57, 62
Oñate, Cristóbal (Juan de
    Oñate's son), 34
Oñate, Juan de, 22, 49–50, 56,
    74–75; charges against, 48;
    as don Quijote, 43–44, 49;
    memory of, 126, 152; settle-
    ment of New Mexico by,
    26–50; statues of, 183–86,
    185.
Oraibi Pueblo (Hopi), 9
Order of Friars Minor. *See*
    Franciscans in New Mexico

Ortiz, Alfonso, 3, 19
Otermín, Antonio de, 113–17, 120–23, 126–28, 130; reentry of, 125, 133–35

Pacheco, Francisco, 158
Pacheco de Heredia, Alonso, 70
Páez Hurtado, Juan, 160, 172
Parral (Nueva Vizcaya), 67, 115, 173
Pecos Pueblo (Towa), 9, 19–20, 40, 58–59, 93, 139, 142; architecture of, 22–24; auxiliary fighters from, 78, 154, 161–63, 165, 171; carpenters of, 63–64, 84, 125, 159, 169–70; encomienda of, 61–62, 92; factionalism of, 64–65, 115, 148, 163–65, 170; Juárez church at, 59–61, 62, 63, 93, 122–24, 179; mission reestablished in, 159–60; parody of a bishop's visit to, 179–81; Towa language of, 164, 166, 192n17; and trade with Plains Apaches, 58–59, 67, 75, 76, 78, 157–58
Pecos River, 58
Pedrosa, fray Juan de, 117, 123
Peñalosa, Diego de, 88, 93–94
Peralta, Pedro de, 56, 75
Pérez, Gaspar, 76–77
Pérez de Villagrá, Gaspar, 25–43, 27, 121. See also Historia de la Nueva México
Pests: locusts, 103; worms, 160
Picuris Pueblo (Tiwa), 54, 125, 131, 139; exodus to the plains from, 166

Pinkley, Jean M., 63
Pío, fray Juan, 117
Piro Pueblos, 105, 128–29; as auxiliary fighters, 136
Plains Apaches, 64, 74, 76, 80, 115, 166; calumet ceremony of, 78–81, 89; music of, 79. See also Pecos Pueblo, and trade with Plains Apaches; Siete Ríos Apaches
Popé (Po'pay) (Pueblo leader), 96, 106, 115, 119, 122–23, 126–30, 131–32, 134; statue of, 111, 185–86, 187
Posada, fray Alonso de, 86–88, 91, 93–94
Poseyemu (Pueblo deity), 12, 16, 116, 122, 126, 165
Possession, Spanish rituals of, 34, 44, 143–45
Presidios. See El Paso; Santa Fe
Puaray Pueblo (Tiwa), 134
Pueblo Indians: architecture of, 12–13, 22–24, 23, 28–30, 58, 76; as auxiliary fighters, 4, 78, 101, 107–109, 110, 117, 133–34, 136, 141–43, 154, 159, 161–63, 171–72, 174; caciques and governors of, 70–71, 102; clowning and parody by, 13–14, 16, 86, 127–28, 179–81; destruction of Christian artifacts by, 130, 133, 145–46; dress of, 12, 24, 143; factionalism of, 64–65, 95, 108–109, 115, 131, 142, 148, 163–65; geography of, 9, 10; languages of, 9, 17, 21, 98–99, 193n17; mobility of,

4, 15; population of, 4, 5–6,
53, 56, 71, 92, 95, 114, 175;
pottery of, 24, 31, 72; prehistory of, 9–15, 58; social
organization of, 11; warfare
of, 11. *See also* Kachina religion; Kivas; specific Pueblo
groups; Women, Pueblos
Pueblo-Plains trade, 58–59, 67,
101
Pueblo Revolt: of 1680, 4–5,
115–31 , 137, 141, 152, 165,
186; of 1696, 161–66. *See also*
Clemente, Esteban
Pueblo-Spanish War (1680–96),
130, 141, 148, 155, 173–75
Punishment. *See* Amputation,
as punishment; Executions;
Whipping
Pupiste, El (Keresan leader), 134

Quintana, Luis de, 110, 113,
141–42
Quivira, 20, 48

Racial mixing, 30, 89–90, 92,
127, 131
Raleigh, Walter, 25
Ramírez, fray Juan, 55
Reconquista of Iberian
Peninsula, 16
Reneros de Posada, Pedro,
135–38
Robledo, Ana (wife of
Francisco Gómez), 62
Robledo, 141, 178
Rodríguez, Sebastían, 141
Rodríguez Cubero, Pedro,
167–71
Rodríguez de Medrano y
Mesía, Juan, 104

Rodríguez de San Antonio,
fray Salvador, 150, 152
Romero, Diego, 76–81, 87–91
Romero, Juana, 89–90, 92
Romero, María (wife of Gaspar
Pérez), 76
Romero, Orlando, 186–87
Rosas, Luis de, 66–70; memory
of, 133; murder of, 69–70

Saca (Jaca), El (Pueblo leader),
123, 127
Salazar, Isabel de, 84
Salinas Pueblo Missions
National Monument, 47
Salinas Pueblos, 46–47, 64,
97–104; abandonment of,
109; salt from local lakes of,
101; water reclamation in,
103
San Bartolomé, valley of
(Nueva Vizcaya), 42
San Diego (Calif.), 178
San Felipe Pueblo (Keresan),
111, 123, 141–42, 174; aligned
with Vargas, 156–57
San Gabriel, 45–50, 76, 186
San Ildefonso Mesa, 157–59
San Ildefonso Pueblo (Tewa),
110; revolt at (1696), 163
San Juan Bautista, church of, 32
San Juan Pueblo, Ohkay
Owingeh (Tewa), 28–30,
106, 127; called San Juan
de los Caballeros, 31; as
Oñate's headquarters,
31–33, 36–38, 45
San Miguel, church of, 120–21,
149
Sandia Pueblo (Tiwa), 68, 88,
92, 125, 134

Sando, Joe S., 119

Santa Ana Pueblo, Tamaya
    (Keresan), 106, 127, 131, 134,
    138–39, 162, 169; assaulted
    (1687), 136–37; contact nar-
    ration of, 73; aligned with
    Vargas, 156–57

Santa Bárbara (Nueva Vizcaya),
    33, 48

Santa Clara Pueblo (Tewa), 121,
    126

Santa Cruz de la Cañada,
    160–62, 166

Santa Fe (N.Mex.): annual fies-
    tas in, 143, 172–73; battle for
    (1693), 153–55; besieged,
    120–22; cabildo of, 68–69,
    95, 112–13, 152, 155, 167–69;
    founding of, 56–57; gover-
    nor's palace at, 57, 81, 121–
    22, 142, 149, 155; occupied
    by Tanos and Tewas, 142–45,
    149–55; presidio at, 114,
    174–75; urban renewal in,
    171

Santander, fray Diego de, 98,
    101–103

Santiago, 43; as battle cry, 154

Santo Domingo Pueblo
    (Keresan), 127, 129, 139,
    141–42; as Franciscan head-
    quarters, 68–70, 87–88; trial
    of Acomas at, 40–41

Senecú Pueblo (Piro), 9; del
    Sur, 138

Sheep: churros, 173; Franciscan
    flocks of, 65; driven off by
    Apaches, 104

Shimitihua, Alonso, peace mis-
    sion of, 128–29

Shongopavi Pueblo (Hopi), 93

Siete Ríos Apaches, 101, 109

Sinaloa, 114

Slavery of Indians: of Apaches,
    66–68, 115; of Navajos,
    66–68; of Plains Indians, 77,
    101; price for, 77; of Pueblos,
    41–42, 45, 136, 138

Smallpox. See Diseases

Socorro del Sur Pueblo (Piro),
    138

Sosa, Eufemia de, 38

Spanish colonialism, 3–5, 34;
    Pueblo Indian response to,
    3–4; Hopis throw off, 167

Spanish colonists of New
    Mexico, 30–31, 46, 107, 131,
    152; desertion of, 33, 48–49;
    incentives of, 30–31; popula-
    tion of, 95, 128, 175; recruit-
    ing of, 160

Spanish governors of New
    Mexico, 46; curse
    Franciscans, 69, 82–83,
    93–94, 101; as entrepreneurs,
    66–67, 77, 81–84, 104; pur-
    chase of office by, 66, 141;
    terms of, 141, 169; visitations
    of, 82, 88, 92

Spanish public ritual, 32, 57,
    172–73. See also Possession,
    Spanish rituals of

Tamarón y Romeral, Pedro de,
    177–81, 180

Tamaya. See Santa Ana Pueblo,
    Tamaya

Tano Pueblos, 115–16, 121–22,
    157–69, 161; occupy Santa
    Fe, 142–45, 149–55. See also
    Galisteo Pueblo

Taos Pueblo (Tiwa), 9, 68, 92,

110, 115, 125, 126, 130, 139, 158
Tesuque Pueblo (Tewa), 85, 92, 116–17, 130; and revolt (1696), 161–63
Tewa Pueblos, 109–13, 115, 121–25, 139, 157–59, 161, 163; creation story of, 7–8; occupy Santa Fe, 142–45, 149–55; and revolt (1696), 161–63, 166. *See also* specific Tewa pueblos
Tipton, William M., 140
Tiwa Pueblos, 21, 128–29; as auxiliary fighters, 136; occupy Santa Fe, 142–45; resist Spaniards, 71–72; and revolt (1696), 163. *See also* specific Tiwa pueblos
Tomás (Pueblo interpreter), 34, 41
Trent, Council of, 16–17
Treviño, Juan Francisco de, 109–13
Troyano, Juan, 18–20
Tupatú, Luis, 131, 134, 139, 143, 146

Umviro, Diego, 163–64, 170
U.S. Court of Private Land Claims, 140
U.S. Surveyor General, 140
Ute Indians, 139, 162

Vargas, Diego de, 140–41, *144;* character of, 148, 169; death of, 172; relieved of office, 167–69; reoccupation by,

147–61; ritual reconquest by, 141–48; second term of, 171–72; and suppressing revolt (1696), 161–66
Vargas, fray Francisco de, 123, 138–40, 162, 169–70
Vázquez de Coronado. *See* Coronado, Francisco Vázquez de
Velasco, fray Fernando, 115, 117, 123
Velasco, Luis de, 56
Veracruz (New Spain), 91
Villagrá. *See* Pérez de Villagrá, Gaspar

Walpi Pueblo (Hopi), *168*
War, doctrine of just, 36
Weather: cold, 45–46, 68, 161; extremes of temperature, 45; snow storms, 33–34, 134–35, 151–52, 155. *See also* Drought; Famine; Pests
Whipping, 77, 111
Wichita Indians, 76; captive children of, 77
Woman in Blue. *See* Ágreda, María de Jesús de
Women, Hispanic, 17, 62; defend San Juan, 38; dress of, 46; of property, 84; as prostitutes, 89–90
Women, Pueblo, 17, 20, 53–54, 60–61; dress of, 12, 24. *See also* Gender roles, Pueblo

Ye, Juan de, 115, 148, 154, 156–59
Ye, Lorenzo de, 158–59, 161

Ysleta del Sur Pueblo (Tiwa), 138. *See also* Isleta Pueblo

Yunque Pueblo. *See* San Gabriel

Zacatecas, 21, 26, 82; colonists from, 152, 160

Zaldívar, Juan de, death of, 35, 40

Zaldívar, Vicente de, 36–41, 47–48, 74–75, 103

Zeinos, fray Diego, 159

Zepe, El, 159

Zia Pueblo (Keresan), 77, 131, 134, 136; assaulted (1689); 137–41, 148, 199n27; aligned with Vargas, 156–57

Zuni, Juan, 77

Zuni Pueblos, 110, 139, *147,* 162, 170; resist Spaniards, 18. *See also* specific Zuni pueblos